FROM THE *erotic* TO THE

FROM THE *erotic* TO THE *demonic*

ON CRITICAL MUSICOLOGY

DEREK B. SCOTT

OXFORD
UNIVERSITY PRESS

2003

OXFORD
UNIVERSITY PRESS

Oxford   New York

Auckland   Bangkok   Bogotá   Buenos Aires   Cape Town   Chennai
Dar es Salaam   Delhi   Hong Kong   Istanbul   Karachi   Kolkata
Kuala Lumpur   Madrid   Melbourne   Mexico City   Mumbai   Nairobi
São Paulo   Shanghai   Taipei   Tokyo   Toronto

Published by Oxford University Press, Inc.
198 Madison Avenue, New York, New York, 10016

www.oup.com

Oxford is a registered trademark of Oxford University Press

Library of Congress Cataloging-in-Publication Data
Scott, Derek B.
   From the erotic to the demonic : on critical musicology / Derek B. Scott.
      p.   cm.
   Includes bibliographical references (p.) and index.
   ISBN 0-19-515195-X; 0-19-515196-8 (pbk.)
      1. Music—Philosophy and aesthetics. 2. Style, Musical.
      3. Musical criticism. I. Title.
   ML3800 .S272 2002
   780—dc21   2002002844
                     Rev.

9   8   7   6   5   4   3   2   1

Printed in the United States of America
on acid-free paper

$\mathcal{A}$CKNOWLEDGMENTS

I WISH TO THANK the Arts and Humanities Research Board (UK) for granting me a research leave award in 2000 that enabled me to complete this book. Earlier versions of some of the material presented here were published originally as follows: "Sexuality and Musical Style from Monteverdi to Mae West," in S. Miller, ed., *The Last Post: Music after Modernism* (Manchester: Manchester University Press, 1993), 132–49; "The Sexual Politics of Victorian Musical Aesthetics," *Journal* of the Royal Musical Association 119, no. 1 (1994), 91–114; "Incongruity and Predictability in British Dance-Band Music of the 1920s and 1930s," *Musical Quarterly* 78, no. 2 (1994), 290–315; "The Jazz Age," chapter 4 of the *Blackwell History of Music in Britain*, vol. 6, ed. S. Banfield (Oxford: Blackwell, 1995), 57–78; "Bruckner and the Dialectic of Darkness and Light," *Bruckner Journal* 2, no. 1 (1998), 12–14, no. 2, 12–14, no. 3, 13–15, no. 1 (1999), 24–27; "Orientalism and Musical Style," short version in *Critical Musicology Journal* (1997) (http://www.leeds.ac.uk/music/Info/CMJ/cmj. html), full-length version in *Musical Quarterly* 82, no. 2 (1998), 309–35.

CONTENTS

INTRODUCTION   3

PART ONE   SEXUALITY, GENDER, AND MUSICAL STYLE

1   Erotic Representation from Monteverdi
to Mae West   17

2   The Sexual Politics of Victorian Musical Aesthetics   33

PART TWO   IDEOLOGY AND THE POPULAR

3   The Native American in Popular Music   61

4   Incongruity and Predictability in British Dance Band
Music of the 1920s and 1930s   80

PART THREE   THE SACRED AND THE PROFANE

5   *Lux in Tenebris:* Bruckner and the Dialectic of Darkness
and Light   103

6   *Diabolus in Musica:* Liszt and the Demonic   128

PART FOUR   IDEOLOGY AND CULTURAL OTHERNESS

7   Orientalism and Musical Style   155

8   The Impact of African-American Music Making on the
European Classical Tradition in the 1920s   179

NOTES   203

INDEX   245

FROM THE *erotic* TO THE *demonic*

INTRODUCTION

FOR OVER TEN YEARS now, I have found myself confronted again and again with questions of ideology and musical style in my musicological research. I can say at the outset, then, that my broad intention in this book is to present a review of where my quest for answers has taken me and to outline my current epistemological position. Several of the chapters are revised and updated versions of essays that originally appeared elsewhere, essays in which I have been concerned, especially, to develop a critique of musical styles as discursive codes. My critical perspective, therefore, has not surprisingly been shaped by semiotics and poststructuralist theory. The concept of ideology I put forward is much broader than, for example, that of political propaganda or Marxist "false consciousness." Perhaps my approach is best epitomized by V. N. Volosinov's neat remark: "Wherever a sign is present, ideology is present, too."[1] For me, ideology exists in all forms of representation and the sound images of pieces of music are as ripe for ideological inquiry as any other cultural artifact. The blunt acceptance of either the humanist notion of an inner expressive essence in music or the antihumanist position epitomized by Stravinsky's declaration that any apparent expression is "simply an additional attribute" thrust upon the music's "essential being"[2] seems to me to yield a cruder framework for the interpretation of musical meaning than the rich cultural theorizing that has developed over the past twenty years.

Before moving on, it is important to consider why cultural theory was to have an increasing impact upon musicology in the last two decades of the twentieth century[3] and to account for the paradigmatic shift that occurred in musicological thought. I would argue that it came about for three major reasons. First, the idea that a mass audience did no more than passively consume the products of a culture industry had become discredited, making it necessary for musicologists to contest the binary divide between "classical" and "popular," since both may be perceived as intimately related to the same social formation. Second, postmodernism had arrived, ousting notions of universalism, internationalism, and "art for art's sake" and replacing them with concerns for the values of specific cultures and their differences. The neglect of the social significance of music had become more apparent, especially the way changing social factors alter our response to existing works[4] and cultural context often determines the legitimacy of styles of playing and singing. Not least, the impact of technology had been insufficiently considered. Thus, what became necessary was a concern with social and cultural processes, informed by arguments that musical practices, values, and meanings related to particular historical, political, and cultural contexts. Third, the musical genealogical tree had needed surgery too often: lines that connected composers and charted musical developments and influences had been redrawn too many times and music had occasionally been conjured up from nowhere (for example, New Orleans jazz). The related issue of the evolution of musical style was now questioned: if atonality was presented as an inevitable stylistic evolution, then clearly Duke Ellington was a musical dinosaur. Causal narration in musical historiography had been found problematic,[5] and the teleological assumptions of historical narrative (for instance, the "inevitability" of atonality) now needed to be avoided. Other factors that bear upon the current situation were the rise of "authentic" performances that made old music seem new (and arguably a replacement for the new) and crossovers between classical and popular idioms by increasing numbers of performers and composers.

The rise in the 1990s of feminist musicology, critical musicology, and gay and lesbian musicology prompts the question: Are we living in an age of alternative musicologies, or are we witnessing the disintegration of musicology as a discipline? Is the unitary concept of a discipline part of a now discredited paradigm for musicological thought? The fences around disciplines are certainly in a bad state of repair these days, as Saul Bellow recognized by declaring that a series he edits, *Critical Voices in Art, Theory and Culture*, "acknowledges the deterritorialized nature of our present intellectual environment."[6] In embracing postdisciplinarity, therefore, musicology joins a growing intellectual movement. This alternative view is one in which musicology is no longer perceived as an autonomous field of academic inquiry but as, to employ Julia Kristeva's terminology, "a field of transpositions of various signifying systems."[7] Critical musicology has revealed what it means to regard musicology as an *intertextual field* and why this, rather than the notion of a *discipline*, offers a more productive epistemological framework for research.[8] It may often entail a necessity to examine a broad range of discourses in order to explain music, its contexts, and the way it functions within them. For example, questions of music and sexuality cannot be considered in isolation from political, biological, psychological, psychoanalytical, and aesthetic discourses. There may be no intention or need, however, to document each area comprehensively.

A Critical Musicology Forum was established in the United Kingdom in 1993 to discuss the character and purpose of critical musicology and whether its purpose was to extend or challenge other forms of musicological inquiry. The term was chosen to indicate a concern with critique, including the critique of musicology itself. The growth in numbers attending meetings over the next two years led to a major conference in Salford, Greater Manchester, in 1995, which, by attracting some seventy delegates who represented thirty different universities in Europe and North America, demonstrated the relevance and topicality of the new theorizing. The group came to consist of not only those working in more recent fields, such as film music, music semiotics, and constructions of gender and sexuality in music, but also researchers in ethnomusicology and the psychology of music who had long felt themselves to be out of the musicological mainstream.

Critical Musicologists in the United Kingdom were united in agreement that one of the biggest problems that faced musicology was the collapse of the binary divide between pop and classical. It was the importance accorded to this perception that set them apart from the New Musicologists of the United States, who tended (with few exceptions) to concentrate on canonic works. The disintegration of high and low as aesthetic values had, of course, been theorized for some time by anthropologists, poststructuralists, and sociologists of culture. Yet what was urgently needed was a new theoretical model capable of embracing the values and meanings of all musical practices and musical texts. A model ready to engage with, rather than marginalize, issues of class, generation, gender, and ethnicity in music and to address matters such as production, reception, and subject position, while questioning notions of genius, canons, universality, aesthetic autonomy, and textual immanence. Different cultures need to be studied in terms of their own specific cultural values, so that a cultural arbitrary is not misrecognized as an objective truth, though musicologists also have to recognize the necessity of extending the terms of such study beyond explicit cultural self-evaluation itself. Above all, we need to be ready to respond to the multiplicity of music's contemporary functions and meanings (for example, the drama/art/music/film/video/digital software fusions variously described as time-based arts and multimedia arts). This may be achieved by adopting the epistemological position and methodology outlined earlier (one that requires intertextual study). Again, I stress that this contrasts with a narrow discipline-based study of music as performance art or as composition (typically represented by the printed score).

As an illustration of my method of engaging critically with music practice and music historiography, I have listed here ten questions that I consider to be important in helping to tease out the ideological dimension in judgments about music. It should be noted that I have used terms here that are by no means innocent—"expression," "aesthetics," "intention," etc.—yet I have made no attempt to problematize them. That I leave to the reader. It is not my wish to become overly prescriptive (or even proscriptive). Depending on the music under discussion, however, I should point out that some of the questions here might link together to produce similar answers, while others may not be at all relevant.

1. *Why does it sound the way it does?* Does the way it sounds indicate that it is intended as, for example, music for a salon, a concert hall, or a park? Has this affected it in terms of form and instrumentation, or has the composer been guided only by imagination in choice of timbre?

2. *What does it mean or express?* Accounting for meaning is the concern of semantics and hermeneutics. It is important to look for conventions, upon which all meanings eventually rely. Intended and perceived meanings should be distinguished where these are known to differ. Why is the *tune* of "Land of Hope and Glory" considered nationalistic? Is it solely because of association with the words? Why is "Born in the USA" often seen as nationalistic *despite* Springsteen's critical words?

3. *What is its instrumentation, and does this affect its status?* Certain ensembles carry greater status. For example, a string quartet would be regarded in some circles as more refined and "elevated" than a saxophone quartet no matter what music each played.

4. *Under what circumstances was it produced?* Is there, for example, evidence that historical, social, or psychological factors have influenced its musical character? Does it matter knowing that Mahler turns his faltering heartbeat into a rhythmic idea in the first movement of his Ninth Symphony? What are the revolutionary connotations of brass in Beethoven's music? Do representations of the East in nineteenth-century Western music link with colonialist ideas and ambitions?

5. *To whom is it addressed?* What is the implied audience for this music (its subject position)? How can you tell? Why did Haydn make folk-song arrangements for piano and voice rather than guitar and voice? Whom do Nanci Griffith, Shirley Bassey, and Kiri Te Kanawa think they are singing to?

6. *In what environment is it experienced, and does this affect its status?* Music has more status in a concert hall than in a public house or saloon; because of this, the status of jazz was negatively affected for many years. Almost automatically, a concert hall accords the status of art to any music played there. The extreme case is when there is no music actually played: does Cage's 4' 33" exist as a work of art under anything other than concert hall conditions?

7. *How is the music disseminated, and how does this affect its status?* Certain publishers carry high status. Publication in a "popular" periodical would carry less artistic status than separate publication. Music type

and music lithography did not carry the elevated status of engraving. How far does all this become a question of economics rather than artistic value?

8. *What have past and present critics said and what have past and present audiences done?* Sometimes current critics contradict past critics (for example, regarding the artistic merit of Berlioz's *Les Troyens*). Sometimes audiences respond with enthusiasm to music condemned by certain critics (for example, the music of Andrew Lloyd Webber). Is there evidence of a critic working to a particular agenda—for example, a dislike of a particular musical style or a contempt for music that suggests entertainment rather than art?

9. *Has this musical style, or this particular piece of music, been used to illustrate an artistic movement?* Is it seen as an example of Romanticism, Impressionism, or whatever? Is it regarded as an example of an artistic coup? Are canons being created? Or is it seen in terms of social function (for example, dance music) or social history (for example, labor songs)?

10. *Who is marketing it and why?* Usually the answer to the "why" is "for money," but not always. Sometimes, for example, it may be a concern for a national heritage; at other times, it may be for political or religious reasons. When money is not a prime object, less consideration has to be given to who may or may not like the music in question. This may affect its status positively if, for instance, the music is linked to an affluent and dominant social group (such as the English court of Charles II) or negatively if, say, it is linked to those involved in a failed political struggle (such as the Levellers).

Defining ideology

It is now time to explain in more detail my usage of the term "ideology." I employ it in the broad sense it began to acquire in the 1970s. Roland Barthes in his earliest work used the term "mythology" for what he and others would later describe as "ideology."[9] Just about every major French cultural theorist of the past thirty years uses "ideology" in the same way, and a very large number of North American theorists do so, too. Moreover, cultural thinkers not associated with poststructuralism or deconstruction have also widened its meaning. For example, it has been more than a decade now since the English literary theorist Terry Eagleton published a book titled *The Ideology of the Aesthetic*.[10]

Let me make reference to Rose Rosengard Subotnik's insightful book *Developing Variations: Style and Ideology in Western Music* (1991). In this work, she defines ideology "not narrowly, as a specific and explicitly political doctrine, but broadly, as a network of assumptions and values shaped by experience and culture."[11] She also asserts that "ideological values contribute inevitably and fundamentally to the structural definition of human utterance, even musical utterance, as well as to the understanding and judgment of utterance, even aesthetic judgment."[12] My own working definition of ideology would be as follows: *the study of how meanings are constructed within signifying practices and how that impacts upon our understanding of the world we live in.*[13] I am particularly interested in how "truths" are constructed and the role played by historical and cultural determinants of human consciousness. In this book, my major preoccupation is examining the ideology encoded in a diversity of Western musical styles. At the risk of oversimplifying, I am trying to explain how metaphysical ideas are communicated through music. This is not to make the absurd claim that in this book I am attempting to exhaust all there is to say about metaphysical philosophy and music. Indeed, what I am offering here is a collection of essays that should be regarded more as speculative experiments than as explications of fully worked out theoretical positions. Furthermore, my focus is on musical representation, and some metaphysical concepts (for example, that of justice) do not lend themselves readily to sound images.

If the preceding issues are understood as my central concerns, then the various chapters that make up this book can be seen as taking off in different directions like roots from the stem of a rhizome. The chapters share a kinship in that each attempts to decode the communication of meaning in musical style structures, but they do not link together in the shape of a linear, let alone teleological, narrative. My contention, then, is that the coherence of my work is to be found in its focus on ideology and musical style.

Music and representation

Readers familiar with Peter Kivy's stimulating book *Sound and Semblance: Reflections on Musical Representation* (1984) will want to know how my ideas about representation relate to his. There is no room for a detailed comparison here, but I will list half a dozen ways in which we differ:

1. I insist upon the role of the conventional in *all* musical meaning; he is unwilling to go this far.
2. My understanding of musical representation is informed by semiotic theory (attempting to *account for* perceived meanings), whereas his thinking is guided by classical logic (attempting to *validate* meanings).
3. Intention is a necessary condition for representation for him, but I make room for unconscious and even "accidental" representation (for example, I would maintain that representations of the East are not always consciously constructed and often unintentionally reveal Western attitudes; see my chapter 7).
4. I am concerned with the socially constituted values of musical *styles;* Kivy says little about style.

5. He is not shy of making an appeal "at the level of common sense" or to "anyone of musical taste,"[14] whereas for me common sense and taste are not ideology-free zones and often embody ideology at its most powerful.

6. Kivy is prone to an unproblematized use of adjectives, being prepared to speak of a "sunny cadence" or "languid, drooping chromaticism" or to describe music as having a "somber, chilly character" without explaining *why* it sounds that way.[15] He thus implies that such moods are *not* represented, that they exist in the music as an inner essence. For me, not only are atmospheric moods and emotions *represented,* but also the manner in which they are represented differs according to particular musical style codes (see, for example, my chapter 1).

A similarity I do share with Kivy, however, is that of following an argument where it leads without making an attempt to ensure its completeness.[16] I have also tried to emulate his admirable clarity and to keep the argument as free from unnecessary jargon as possible. Finally, for me, reception overrides intention. Certain associations can become attached to music. Kivy insists that a person is musically misguided who hears rustling leaves in Bach's C-minor Prelude (from *The Well-Tempered Clavier,* book 1);[17] yet what if this music was used to accompany a prolonged shot of rustling leaves during the opening credits of a popular television series? Could "anyone of musical taste" who watched that series detach the music successfully from the image next time he or she heard it, just as, in the words of an old gag, a "real musician" was someone who could listen to the *William Tell* Overture without thinking of the Lone Ranger?[18] Surely not: music does not reside in some isolated domain of its own; no cultural artifacts do. That is the lesson of intertextuality. It is also a lesson we learn, not from the dyadic relations of Saussurean semiology but from the triadic relations theorized by Ferdinand de Saussure's contemporary Charles Peirce. In Peirce's semiotics, a sign stands for something for *someone:* Peirce's *interpretant* mediates between a sign and its relation to another thing. As Eero Tarasti puts it, "One could say that, in music, signs in relation to their interpretants concern those sign processes that take place in the mind of the listener, whereby he or she interprets the musical experience."[19] A common error is to insist upon the arbitrary nature of the musical sign while failing to recognize the equally arbitrary nature of the linguistic sign. To remain with the Bach example, there is certainly nothing actually "leafy" in any part of that C-minor prelude, but *there is nothing actually "leafy" in the word "leaf."* In saying this, my intention is not to argue that music is a language but, rather, to claim that music and language are both signifying practices and both make use of arbitrary signifiers. Language philosopher Donald Davidson has detailed the problems encountered by those who have tried to build a theory of communication based on meanings; he concludes, "it seems clear that the semantic features of words cannot be explained directly on the basis of non-linguistic phenomena."[20]

In recent years, topical analysis has appealed to many musicians whose toleration of musical semiotics does not extend beyond the self-referential or, in other words, beyond music qua music (Eero Tarasti is a notable exception). There may be token remarks about the socially constituted character of *topoi,* but social content is quickly dissolved into form for the analysis to proceed. Kofi Agawu has recently provided a topical analysis of the British national anthem that ignores the topic of the galliard, though this dance rhythm is one of the anthem's striking features.[21] It is a telling omission, since this is a sign with a referent outside of the "music itself" a sign that requires us to consider social meaning. In the book before you, my commitment is to social semiotics, not to semiotics as a means of demonstrating musical-theoretical positions divorced from social meaning. In pursuing this critical aim, I willingly acknowledge my indebtedness to the work of Richard Leppert, Susan McClary, and Lawrence Kramer. The reader will no doubt find that my concerns differ here and there from those of the preceding authors, that I make different emphases, and that I have taken up either more extreme or less extreme theoretical positions. For example, I would distance myself from some (though not all) of Kramer's arguments that are based on Freudian theory. As might be imagined, given some of the statements I have made earlier, it is the ahistoricism of Freudian psychoanalysis that I resist most strongly (thus, I am obviously more drawn to the work of Gilles Deleuze and Félix Guattari).

An overview

To conclude this introduction, I will allude briefly to the chapters that follow and try to underline what is new or distinct about some of the positions I am adopting. Each successive chapter considers the workings of a particular relationship between ideology and musical style. My intention is to illustrate my current understanding of how musical styles construct ideas of class, sexuality, and ethnic identity. In doing so, I am concerned to demonstrate how such constructions relate to particular stylistic codes in particular historical contexts. This, of course, necessitates a consideration of the subject position offered by the music in question and of the way "truths" inscribed within contemporaneous discourses (political, aesthetic, medical, biological, etc.) impact upon the music. The book is divided into four parts that present the chapters in related pairs.

Part I concerns sexuality, gender, and musical style, and my first chapter, "Erotic Representation from Monteverdi to Mae West," explores the mutability of constructions of the erotic in various styles of music from the seventeenth to twentieth centuries. My argument, here, is that music does not act as a simple channel through which ideology is mediated and can therefore be renegotiated. For example, it is not a straightforward matter to negotiate different *expressions* of sexuality in music; a representation of sexuality in music must relate to the pregiven code of the particular musical style within which it is articulated. As Gino Stefani has pointed out, style codes are not only rooted in social practices but also "a blend of technical features, a way of forming objects or events."[22] If that were not the case, then two of the pieces discussed in this chapter, David Rose's "The Stripper" and Richard Strauss's "Dance of the Seven Veils," would surely resemble each other a little more than they do.

The past ten years have witnessed a wide-ranging debate about the feminine and masculine in music, particularly as it relates to social issues such as public and private performance and to compositional matters such as gendered themes or gendered conflict in sonata form movements. Chapter 2, "The Sexual Politics of Victorian Musical Aesthetics," moves from considering how metaphors of masculinity and femininity solidified into biological truths to teasing out the ideological dimension of the supposedly disinterested and universally applicable aesthetic theories of the beautiful, ornamental, and sublime in music. I would add that, like Susan McClary, it is not my intention or wish to see any composer's music reduced solely to issues of sexuality.[23] However, I do wish to challenge the idea of "absolute music" or "pure music" whenever and wherever it appears. An important reason for choosing Bruckner as a case study in chapter 5 is because his symphonies have usually been interpreted as pure music—however murky the ideological reception of them has been at times (the extreme being reached with the appropriation of Bruckner as German nationalist by the Nazis).

Part II explores the workings of ideology in relation to popular music and, in so doing, underlines the resistance of postmodern theory to the metaphysical spell of a universal aesthetic. In chapter 3, "The Native American in Popular Music," I examine representations of the American Indian in popular styles of Western music from the eighteenth century to the present. Having tackled issues of gender and sexuality and the relationship between them and musical style, I now consider ethnicity for the first time. Here my intention is to show how cultural difference is represented when little is known or understood about the culture of those being represented and to consider how shifting perceptions of the Native American can be related to changes in attitude to the "civilized" and the natural world. The emphasis on the popular sharpens the argument, because this kind of representation needs to be widely understood and easily assimilated in order for it to be popular. The ideology embedded in the way the American Indian is represented tells us, predictably, about the attitudes of the person who stands outside Native American culture.

My concern in chapter 4, "Incongruity and Predictability in British Dance Band Music of the 1920s and 1930s," is the ideology of "high" and "low" art and how this impacts upon both musical style and reception. Defenses of the popular that relate its value to its historical context often provoke the question: How is it to be valued once its historic moment has passed? The purpose of this chapter is to show how a "popular musicology" might tackle the problem of discussing music once loved but now regarded by many as valueless. To this end, it explores qualitative issues in British dance band music. A critique of musical style needs to take account of incongruity between styles. In chapter 1, I argued that modes of representation needed to be related to different styles; here I argue that the same goes for qualitative values. For instance, what is admired as good singing in one style may not be so perceived in another. Part II is the popular counterpart to part IV. The Self versus Other binarism introduced in chapter 3 is revisited in a more complex manner in chapter 7, which largely concerns the representation of different cultures in concert music and opera. British dance bands and their music can be seen, in some measure, as a response, in the popular arena, to the impact of African-American music making, the impact of which on European composers working in the classical tradition is explored in chapter 8.

Part III presents two case studies to explore the ideology embedded in representations of two concepts that are themselves conjoined in a binary opposition, the sacred and profane. In chapter 5, "*Lux in Tenebris:* Bruckner and the Dialectic of Darkness and Light," the construction of the sacred in music is discussed by way of a study of a particular composer. Bruckner is chosen because he is widely seen as a "pure" musician, impervious to ideological assault. It becomes clear, however, that he often makes musical choices with reference to Christian religious discourse and thus for ideological rather than structural reasons. This chapter examines the usefulness of a "darkness and light" trope for understanding the compositional process in his music. It affords an opportunity to import ideas from Gilles Deleuze and Félix Guattari, as well as to apply Jacques Derrida's antidialectical arguments through use of the deconstructive strategies that were referred to so cursorily at the end of chapter 1.

One purpose of chapter 6 is to present a typology of the demonic in the music of Liszt, but I am also seeking to answer a number of related questions: What impact did his representations of the demonic have on his stylistic development as a composer? Do demonic elements appear even where Liszt has not chosen to indicate their presence by title? Do we find them in nondemonic programmatic works, like "Mazeppa" and even in a work like the Sonata in B minor, for which Liszt offers no program? In the eighteenth century, the demonic topos is found, most famously, in the music of Mozart. In the music of Liszt, demonic *topoi* abound and a typology of the demonic becomes necessary. Moreover, I argue that building on the work of others (Mozart, Beethoven, Schubert, Mendelssohn, Berlioz), Liszt plays an important part in establishing particular demonic genres, such as the *danse macabre,* the demonic scherzo, the demonic ride, and the more abstract study like *Unstern* (a dark counterpart to the *méditation religieuse* genre). In so doing, he was to bequeath a fertile legacy to the likes of Saint-Saëns, Dvořák, Mussorgsky, Balakirev, and others less known. I contend that the primary demonic technique for Liszt is that of *negation:* negation of the beautiful, the noble, the graceful, and so forth. The secondary technique is parody, though qualities are often negated and parodied (or mocked) at the same time. There is a sense that the demonic is not just evil but gleefully evil. I discuss Liszt's strategies in the context of ideas of the demonic in the work of Goethe and Kierkegaard.

The fourth and final part of the book tackles the issue of ideology and cultural otherness. In chapter 7, "Orientalism and Musical Style," I discuss constructions of the East in Western music and the development of Orientalist styles independently of the objective conditions of non-Western musical practices. This chapter explores a variety of questions that concern the impact of Orientalist ideology on Western music. Is there any consistency to be found in the way non-Western cultures have been represented? Is it often only the exotic, or the cultural Other, that is signified rather than a particular ethnic musical practice? Are there reductive sets of musical conventions that signify something vaguely Asian, Spanish, or Chinese/Japanese and little else? When did these styles become recognizable? Once established, did they perpetuate themselves as musical discursive codes in which a musical text of the East replaced the actual East? Is there a change in representations of non-Western cultures that can be related to the growth of Western nationalism and imperialism?

Chapter 8, "The Impact of African-American Music Making on the European Classical Tradition in the 1920s," offers another exploration of cultural otherness in music. Black Africans, before the time of Columbus and knowledge of the "New World" were thought of as the third race and often depicted as such in art (for example, in paintings of the three Magi). Of course, that in itself would not prevent the black African from being "Orientalized"—witness what happened in the case of the Spanish Moors. However, the lack of identification of the black African with an Orientalist style is explained by the association of black people with African-American music making. This had become familiar, from the mid–nineteenth century on, as "folk art" such as spirituals and plantation songs, as well as being misrecognized in much of the repertoire of blackface minstrel troupes. In the early decades of the twentieth century, the African becomes represented in and by jazz. In the late 1920s the Cotton Club's jungle exoticism can be interpreted as one more variety of Orientalism. To a certain extent, much of the Caribbean and South America became "Orientalized" in this manner (the bossa nova, "Tiki" music, and so forth). Moreover, from the 1960s on, debates about "authentic" blues, gospel, and soul have often had lurking in the background the idea of a black Other.

This final chapter is concerned with the early impact of ragtime, blues, and jazz on music of the European classical tradition and concentrates on the same period as chapter 4. Consideration is given to the social and ethnic connotations of references to African-American styles in these pieces. The broader European social context—modernity, the alienated creative artist, and cosmopolitanism—is also found to be important. The chapter discusses the relation of jazz to modernism and confronts the question: How far are African-American elements seized upon by composers as mere tricks of the trade to give a new lease on life to a tradition in crisis? It goes on to explore the use of jazz-influenced styles as satiric weapons and, finally, discusses the misconceptions of African-American music making that were widespread among European composers of this period.

It will be obvious from this overview of my chapters that the kinds of broad arguments I am making rely for their persuasiveness on a considerable amount of supporting evidence. They do not permit me to concentrate on a small number of examples, since I would immediately be open to the charge of either having relied on too tiny a "control group" or having cunningly selected those few examples that reinforce my exaggerated claims. On top of this, I am aware how easily a detailed analysis (or close reading) tends to become fixated on musical structure rather than on historicizing musical discourse.[24] For this reason, the close reading has become problematic for poststructuralists, and it is compounded by the challenge poststructuralism poses to the very idea of deep structure. To the reader who bemoans the plethora of examples, I will simply say that where I have felt that they merely lend additional weight to rather than deepen my argument I have consigned them to the notes. There they may be savored or ignored at will.

part one

SEXUALITY, GENDER,
AND MUSICAL STYLE

1

EROTIC REPRESENTATION FROM

MONTEVERDI TO MAE WEST

THIS CHAPTER EXAMINES some of the conventions involved in representing the erotic in music and reveals the ideological character of these conventions. The disparity and mutability uncovered by a comparison of representations of sexual desire in three differing musical styles (Baroque opera, the Victorian drawing-room ballad, and Tin Pan Alley in the 1920s and 1930s) show that a genealogy of sexuality in music needs to address disjunctions rather than developments, historical contingencies rather than evolutionary questions.

Representations of sexuality in music are not restricted to eroticism; it would be possible to devote an essay to a discussion of how musical representations of masculine and feminine laughter differ or to a comparison of masculine and feminine grief. However, I have chosen eroticism—if that is not too strong a word to describe my Victorian examples—because it offers such clear examples of how gender difference is constructed in music. What we find, here, are disjunctions in representation rather than any kind of universals or constants that can be traced through the changes brought about by an autonomous evolution or progress of a Western musical language. There is certainly no progress to be discovered in the way eroticism has been depicted in music: representations of eroticism in contemporary music are not more real now than they were in the seventeenth century. The fact that the latter can seem cool or alien to us today points to the way sexuality has been constructed in relation to particular stylistic codes in particular historical contexts and is therefore cultural rather than natural.

It may be accepted already that everyday notions of sexuality are socially constructed rather than a reflection of the natural world. Indeed, we may follow Julia Kristeva in regarding the categories of masculine and feminine as metaphysical; but, in the light of the foregoing remarks, it does not follow from this acceptance that music acts as a simple channel through which ideologies of gender are mediated and may be renegotiated. In other words, *sexual ideology cannot be straightforwardly renegotiated in music, because a representation of sexuality in music has to relate to the pregiven code of the particular musical style within which it is articulated.*

Certain popular musical styles, however, have sometimes been treated as if they had arisen from attempts to negotiate differing *expressions* of sexuality in music. In their early, pioneering study "Rock and Sexuality" of 1978,[1] Simon Frith and Angela McRobbie have a tendency to see the bifurcation of rock into what they call cock rock and soft rock in this way. John Shepherd, too, argues that "notions of gender and "sexuality" can be renegotiated by "popular" musicians," adding: "Negotiation is the key concept in understanding how the politically personal is articulated from within the internal process of music."[2] Roland Barthes's essay "The Grain of the Voice,"[3] a frequent departure point for considerations of the radical possibilities of timbre (though Barthes's "grain" is not synonymous with timbre), encourages Shepherd to theorize about the potentialities of female timbres within a male musical hegemony. Leaving aside that the biological terms "male" and "female" are often used when the cultural terms "masculine" and "feminine" would be more appropriate, the contention is problematic in that timbre is considered to be an arena for hegemonic negotiation in "popular" music, while vocal timbre is apparently regarded as a fixed, ideologically encoded parameter in "classical" music. This does not bear scrutiny: not only have classical timbres changed remarkably even in the past hundred years (compare a recording of Dame Clara Butt with one of a contralto of even fifty years later), but also particular timbres have, by way of contrast, been long-established features of certain popular styles (for example, the high, "lonesome" tenor of Appalachian music, still to be heard in contemporary bluegrass).

With this in mind, it is clear that a much-discussed song like Tammy Wynette's "Stand by Your Man" (Wynette-Sherill) cannot be fully understood solely in terms of its being an *expression* in music (negotiated or otherwise) of the ideology of supportive and submissive femininity but must also be considered in relation to the stylistic expectations and constraints of 1960s Nashville country music. Think of how different Billie Holiday sounds (arguably more submissive than Tammy) when "standing by *her* man" in songs like "Don't Explain" (Holiday-Herzog). What should be recognized, however, is that one singer is not offering a more "real" submission than the other but a different musical discourse of submission. In the words of Jenny Taylor and Dave Laing, the issue is "the radically different codes and conventions of representation involved in different genres."[4]

Given that representations of sexuality are constructed within particular musical styles and that musical styles are signifying practices, it is evident, as deconstructionists have shown, that what is being signified is "up for grabs" (something the lesbian appropriation of country music[5] in the 1980s demonstrated). You may feel convinced that something is a reflection of reality if, in Althusserian terms, its ideological character interpellates you as a subject (that is, calls out to you in a manner that makes whatever it is appear obvious to you),[6] but history has a way of slowly revealing the ideological character of representations. Readers of an appropriate age may like to weigh up how campy Mick Jagger appears today in film shot in the 1960s and how wild and sexy he seemed at the time. My intention here, however, is to consider how differing musical idioms represent eroticism—from Poppea's "O mio ben, o mio cor, o mio tesoro" to Mae West's more economical "Oh, oh, oh." Along the way, we have three things to ponder:

1. How does a composer represent sexuality?
2. How does a performer convey sexuality?
3. How does a listener interpret sexuality (for example, interpret a performance as erotic or interpret a composition as erotic)?

Taking the case of eroticism and music, we can see how the possibilities and complexities of this relationship increase as we move from one to another of the preceding questions.

There are two possibilities to bear in mind in relation to 1: either the composer has encoded eroticism or *not* (as musical text). There are three possibilities to consider in relation to 2: the performer may convey eroticism by decoding the eroticism in the composition, *or* the performer may add eroticism, encoding it, for example, in a particular vocal timbre, *or* there is no eroticism represented by the performer. When we turn to 3, there are four possibilities: the listener may decode eroticism in the composition but may find the performer nonerotic, *or* may find the performance erotic but the composition not, *or* may find both erotic (decoding at two levels), *or* interprets eroticism where no such representation was intended (perhaps because of expectation). In the instance of the listener who finds the performer's voice erotic but the composition not, then, taking up Barthes's terminology, the *jouissance* of the nonsignifying "genosong" may be said to have obliterated the communicative structure of the "phenosong"; in other words, the signified is ignored in favor of the sensually produced meaning Barthes calls *signifiance.* The terms "genotext" and "phenotext" were coined by Kristeva[7] but applied adroitly to music by Barthes as "genosong" and "phenosong."[8] The member of the audience who finds the performer physically erotic, while finding neither the composition nor the performer's voice erotic, may still be displaying a cultural response, but this response can be eliminated on the grounds that it has nothing to do with the subject of *musical style* under discussion here.

The performer, it must be emphasized, is a complex communicative channel. Susan Cusick has demonstrated how the ideas of Josephine Butler, that in our everyday life we engage in performances of sex and gender, may be applied to the performance of music.[9] Cusick explains, for example, that even if the intention is to sing a piece in a manner suited to its historic context, this is still likely to be in a dialogic relationship with a performance of the singer's gendered body as it exists in the here and now.[10] It is not just a contrast between past and present that brings the performer's body to the fore; it can be in the way a performer subverts a musical style. Sheila White-ley, also indebted to Butler, has described k. d. lang's performance of coun-try, in part stylized and in part subverted through self-dramatization, as pre-senting "a problematic sexuality which suggested an identity that was gendered and only ambiguously sexed."[11] A final word on performance is that the visual element should not be underrated. Richard Leppert has shown conclusively that music's effects and its meanings "are produced both aurally *and* visually" in *The Sight of Sound* (1993), a study that examines the work of artists who paint the visual only.[12]

SEXUAL DISCOURSE IN THE BAROQUE ERA

The present study of representations of eroticism begins in the seventeenth century. This was a time, according to Michel Foucault, when the transfor-mation of sexuality into discourse that began in the previous century was completed:

> First the Reformation, then tridentine Catholicism, mark an impor-tant mutation and a schism in what might be called the "traditional technology of the flesh." A division whose depth should not be under-estimated; but this did not rule out a certain parallelism in the Catho-lic and Protestant methods of examination of conscience and pastoral direction: procedures for analysing "concupiscence" and transform-ing it into discourse were established in both instances.[13]

Although the sixteenth century was not lacking in ability to represent affec-tive states, as the Netherlands motet shows,[14] it was in seventeenth-century music that a *stile rappresentativo* was consciously established. This develop-ment in representational techniques has been described by Susan McClary as a "tangle of gender, rhetoric and power."[15] Unlike Jacques Attali, who identifies the period of representation in music history as beginning in the eighteenth century with the rise of the musical commodity as spectacle,[16] McClary proposes that it was "ushered in with great fanfare with the inven-tion of opera, monody, and sonata in the first decade of the seventeenth century."[17]

In Baroque opera, the problem that faces today's audience may be a lack of recognition of a representation of eroticism by the composer. Such has been the case, for example, where the composer's style is thought to be "petrified": for instance, the only aesthetic titillation the eminent musicolo-gist Carl Dahlhaus was willing to concede might be found in Monteverdi's music was related exclusively to its remoteness in history.[18] This problem may be solved by an editor, an arranger, or a performer. For example, in the

1960s, when it was considered dramatically unacceptable for a woman to sing the castrato role of Nero in *L'incoronazione di Poppea* (1642), it was the practice for the part to be sung one octave lower by a man. That was done, in spite of its impact on the sound of the music (sometimes inverting dissonances, for example), in order to conform to audience expectations of male operatic sexuality. Worries about Poppea's music not being found sexy enough were solved by "tarting up" the instrumentation and ensuring Poppea's personal wardrobe (or the lack of it) absorbed the masculine gaze. Producers of this opera found themselves in a very different position from that of those working with Wagnerian music drama, where it was accepted that eroticism would be recognized in the music, if not in the performer.

We will now consider the Nero and Poppea duet "Pur ti miro" as a representation in music of the mutual arousal thought necessary for sexual reproduction in the seventeenth century. The idea that both men and women needed to ejaculate seed lies behind the following advice given by the surgeon Ambroise Paré:

> When the husband commeth into his wives chamber hee must entertaine her with all kinde of dalliance, wanton behaviour, and allurements to venery: but if he perceive her to be slow, and more cold, he must cherish, embrace, and tickle her, and shall not abruptly, the nerves being suddenly distended, break into the field of nature, but rather shall creepe in by little and little intermixing more wanton kisses with wanton words and speeches, handling her secret parts and dugs, that she may take fire and bee enflamed to venery, for so at length the wombe will strive and waxe fervent with a desire of casting forth its owne seed, and receiving the mans seed to bee mixed together therewith.[19]

Since this duet is now thought not to be by Monteverdi, though it was once readily accepted as such, it serves all the better to illustrate musical conventions (which are in themselves ideological constructs), since there is less likelihood of our being sidetracked into questions of individual artistic genius. Moreover, as Margaret Murata has argued, there was something of an oral character to Western seventeenth-century music, evidenced by its common pool of musical materials.[20] Susan McClary has discussed how the seventeenth-century concern for mutual arousal may be perceived in music, and here we certainly have an example of her two equal voices rubbing up against each other, "pressing into dissonances that achingly resolve only into yet other knots, reaching satiety only at conclusions" (see Ex. 1.1).[21]

The rapid exchanges of the middle section of the duet form a neat example, too, of the stimulating "friction to heat" that Stephen Greenblatt has suggested lies behind the erotic repartee in Shakespearean comedy.[22] We are more used to hearing the original pitch of Nero's part now, thanks to the familiarity of high male voices in early music performances (and the high falsetto in pop music), but can we recapture the significance of that male

EXAMPLE 1.1. Duet: Nero and Poppea

pitch for a seventeenth-century audience? Was it *intended* to sound unnatural, in the sense of befitting a god or someone more than ordinarily human?

The next example to consider is Cleopatra's aria "V'adoro pupille," from Handel's opera *Giulio Cesare in Egitto* of 1724. It contains short phrases suggestive of breathlessness as in the Nero and Poppea duet, but note Cleopatra's rhetorical skill: she is able to extend a phrase unexpectedly and to wind Caesar into her musical embrace (see Ex. 1.2). At every point where we anticipate closure, the line continues; it is as if she is clinging on to Caesar and allowing him no opportunity to escape. She takes the lead in their relationship, while to Caesar "her bold courtship [is] taken as passive yearning."[23]Rising sequences are also used in this aria to suggest erotic stimulus, as in the duet. The instrumentation is unusual: it includes a harp, which may be regarded as a substitute for the lyre, the instrument of the erotic muse, Erato. Poppea has the rhetorical skills of the courtesan, Cleopatra the rhetorical skill of the sovereign. In Monteverdi's *Orfeo* (1607), Euridice has none, the sign of an "innocent" young woman, as McClary has argued and demonstrated.[24]

Scientia sexualis AND THE NINETEENTH CENTURY

The second and "especially productive moment" in the proliferation of sexual discourse is located by Foucault in the nineteenth century, with the "advent of medical technologies of sex."[25] The nineteenth century witnessed the development of a "completely new technology of sex":

> Through pedagogy, medicine, and economics, it made sex not only a secular concern but a concern of the state as well; to be more exact, sex became a matter that required the social body as a whole, and virtually all of its individuals, to place themselves under surveillance.[26]

"Won't You Tell Me Why, Robin?" by Claribel (1861) (Ex. 1.3) is as close as we get to a seduction song from female to male in a Victorian drawing-

EXAMPLE 1.2. Handel, "V'adoro pupille" (Cleopatra)

le vos - tre fa - vil - le son___ gra-te nel sen_____ le vos–

room ballad, the content being full of delicately phrased hints, pleas, and ac-cusations: "I thought you'd see me home, Robin" and "I thought you'd surely come, Robin If but to dance with me." Moreover, Robin no longer does his chivalric duty at the wicket gate, even though "it's very hard to open." The use of a diminished seventh chord exchanging with the tonic (a nonfunc-tional coloristic effect) is a seductive harmonic resource drawn upon by Venus in Wagner's *Tannhäuser*,[27] and it is still around to provide a romantic frisson in Cole Porter's "True Love."

There are short phrases again; here they do not suggest breathlessness but rather decorous restraint, a sign, perhaps, that the singer has placed her-self "under surveillance." The $\frac{6}{8}$ rhythm is a pastoral convention inherited from the eighteenth century that suits the rural setting, but the song is for an urban market, so there is an element of fantasy present. As advised ear-lier, however, we need to take performance into consideration. This ballad offers itself as a possible vehicle for drawing-room flirtation behind a mask of Arcadian otherness, just as at Vauxhall the songs of nymphs and shep-herds subtly underlined from a respectful distance the use of the pleasure gardens for courtship. The question we have to leave in abeyance, though it is one that Lawrence Kramer has attempted to answer, is how far male same-sex desire in the nineteenth century might have encouraged an identifica-tion with the position of the female singing to the beloved male.[28]

The choice of the name Robin is an odd one for a love song destined for performance in the respectable middle-class home. Robin had long been a name with sexual connotations, and these were sometimes explicitly phal-lic, as in "Poor Robin," published in *The Man of War's Garland* of 1796.[29] The first verse is as follows:

> One night as I came from the play
> I met a fair maid by the way
> She had rosy cheeks and a dimpled chin
> And a hole to put poor Robin in.

"Colin and Susan," published as "A Famous New Smutty Song" in an erotic songbook of the 1830s, shows that the association between the name Robin and the phallus continued into the nineteenth century.[30] So why did the possible scatalogical connotations of Claribel's song and its possible use for flirting cause no Victorian eyebrows to be raised? The answer is that her song can also be interpreted as being about two children, which makes the raising of objections embarrassing.

EXAMPLE 1.3. Claribel, "Won't You Tell Me Why, Robin?"

It is obvious from the style of "Only" by Virginia Gabriel (1871) that a man is admiring a woman, even though the words of the first verse make no reference to either sex (however, "angel" in the last line, which would have automatically had feminine connotations for most Victorian listeners, begins to give the game away). Here a woman composer is adopting a "thrust-

ing" style to represent male ardor (see Ex. 1.4). A vigorous rhythm on alternating tonics and dominants would have associations with such things as
timpani parts in martial music; it would connote power and boldness, activity rather than passivity, in other words masculinity rather than femininity. Yet was it appropriate for a Victorian woman composer to write this kind
of music?

As more and more women took to composition, nineteenth-century
criticism moved away from the metaphorical use of "masculine" and "feminine" in describing music and, instead, began to use these terms as an aesthetic confirmation of sexual difference. It is surely significant that this development in aesthetics coincides with the emergence of a *scientia sexualis*.[31]
From the figurative use of these terms, a practice that in characterizing some
music by men as feminine offered the possibility of masculine music by
women, "the language of Romantic music criticism," as Judith Tick remarks,
"degenerated into a language of sexual aesthetics, in which the potentialities of the individual female composer were defined through the application
of sexual stereotypes."[32] It came to be interpreted as a failing for a woman
to seek to write masculine music, and, in the words of a sympathetic nineteenth-century male critic, she "received much advice to cultivate art from
the feminine stand-point."[33] The sexual politics involved in this aesthetic
theorizing form the subject of the next chapter. Suffice it to say, here, that the
feminine in music was charming, sweet, delicate, and sensitive and that
women songwriters were expected to produce work that was pretty, charming, and either simple or, if not, decorative rather than complex or learned.
Women's composition was to be of a character that could be labeled or
thought of in ways distinct from male composition. The drawing-room ballad came to be thought an ideal outlet for female compositional creativity in
the 1860s because even its performance associations were feminine. A writer
in *Macmillan's Magazine* at the beginning of that decade explains:

> The preference for the English ballad is easily accounted for: the mel-
> ody is not uncommonly very pretty, the words are understood, and
> every repetition of it in any form recalls the touching voice and the
> pretty face of the singer from whom we first heard it.[34]

The reception of Virginia Gabriel's "Only," however, would have been
problematic. It is composed by a woman, but its gendered musical style is
masculine: it characterizes the male in love, not the female in love. It would
have been seen not as an example of a woman successfully challenging a
male composer on his own ground (as we may be tempted to view it today)
but as an example of "a striking reproduction of masculine art," as one critic
described Alice Smith's *The Passions* in 1882.[35] A similar argument could not
be used in the case of men, since they were deemed able to be original. The
ability to reproduce only, rather than originate, was held to be a peculiarity
of the female mind. If a woman's temperament was at the same time generally esteemed as "naturally artistic," the Reverend Hugh Haweis advises us in

EXAMPLE 1.4. Virginia Gabriel, "Only"

his *Music and Morals,* those words are to be understood "not in a creative, but in a receptive sense."[36] Sexual aesthetics were part of "separate spheres" ideology: John Ruskin, for example, had proclaimed in 1864 in his lecture "Of Queen's Gardens" that a woman's intellect was "not for invention or creation, but for sweet ordering, arrangement, and decision."[37] It is important to recognize that there was nothing conspiratorial in such statements; once formulated, these ideas were understood as truths always and already present.

The musical style that represents a jilted male or a male pleading with the female object of his desire is similarly gendered. "Come into the Garden, Maud" (Tennyson-Balfe, 1857) pleads with a beloved, like "Won't You Tell Me Why, Robin?" There is a well-known anecdote about how the risqué music hall artist Marie Lloyd made this song sound indecent when she sang it during a court case to prove that "filthy thoughts" were in the mind. A remarkable deconstructive strategy and, if it did not actually happen, there is still a lesson to be learned. It is difficult today to understand how easy it would have been for a woman to make this song sound indecent, something that would have been accomplished effortlessly then. The crucial point is that its musical style conforms to a Victorian representation of virile *masculine* sexuality. That passionate conclusion is utterly unseemly for the ideal, submissive "perfect lady" of the times. And yet the song amuses now, especially the conclusion, thus providing another example of disjunction in representational codes and the all-important specificity of the sociocultural contexts within which their meanings are construed. So much, then, for an expression of "real" eroticism.

PSYCHOANALYSIS AND THE TWENTIETH CENTURY

Finally, we turn to the early twentieth century, which, for Foucault, was marked by a deployment of sexuality "spread through the entire social body," the birth of the "theory of repression,"[38] and the emergence of psychoanalysis in response.[39] Lawrence Kramer has used Freudian theory to offer new insight into representations of desire in nineteenth-century music[40] and Robert Fink has applied the theory of repression to a study of Brahms,[41] but here we will look at music contemporaneous with the widespread acceptance of psychoanalytic theory. Three female stereotypes dominate American erotic songs of the 1920s and 1930s: one is the "predator" (she'll get her man), a second is the "innocent" (she's available to men, but doesn't know what she's doing), and a third is the "prim and proper." The last is more difficult to describe: she may be a schoolteacher, or a secretary in tweeds wearing severe glasses that, once removed, cause the astonished male to gulp out, "But . . . you're beautiful!" Her potentially seething passion is kept in check by her sense of duty or her strict moral code; hence, uniforms are popular, particularly of a military or religious kind. However, we are given to understand that her concern for ethics, duty, morals, and so forth is nothing but a symptom of her "repressed desire." She is a woman whose sexual feelings need to be "awakened" by a strong man who will reassure her and calm her fear of letting those passionate "repressed" feelings rip. Needless to say, this is popular culture's take on what is needed to combat repression, not that of Freudian psychoanalytic practice.

These three are not the only possible erotic stereotypes of female sexuality, of course, but they were the ones favored in the United States at this time. By way of contrast, in Germany there was the "indolent" stereotype, best known from the languid sensuality of Marlene Dietrich, and in England there was the "saucy local girl" stereotype in the tradition of Marie Lloyd. A stereotype is a representation that is repeated as if it were natural, or a known constant. It is an imitation that Barthes maintains is "no longer sensed as an imitation."[42] The danger of a stereotype, therefore, is that it may come to be misrecognized as "truth": "Nietzsche has observed that 'truth' is only the solidification of old metaphors. So in this regard the stereotype is the present path of 'truth,' the palpable feature which shifts the invented ornament to the canonical, constraining form of the signified."[43] We have, indeed, already seen how metaphors of masculinity and femininity solidified into truth in the nineteenth century.

In "I Like a Guy What Takes His Time" (Rainger), recorded in New York early in 1933, Mae West fits firmly in the dominatrix or predatory category.[44] She was, incidentally, cast as a lion tamer in the film *I'm No Angel* later that same year. Prominence is given in the recording to West's erotic moaning, though other erotic devices of the time, for example, the Sophie Tucker or Bessie Smith growl or the heavy breathing of Ethel Waters (as in her 1930 recording of the Fain-Norman song "You Brought a New Kind of Love to Me"), play no part. In this context, West's Brooklyn accent and nasal delivery would have carried suggestions of low life and loose morality. Moreover, a change to double time, which elsewhere would have been simply a characteristic jazz technique, operates in this song as a humorous reference to the amateur lover who does not "take his time."

In "Come Up and See Me Sometime" (Swanstrom-Alter), recorded in New York in 1933, Cliff Edwards's voice sounds campy, and intentionally so, for there is no other way a man can handle this kind of Mae West material (West did not record this song, but it is clearly indebted to her performances in style, title, and content). Marybeth Hamilton suggests that West's style would have resonated with a 1930s gay sensibility and observes that exaggerated speech and mannerisms had already begun to be labeled "camp" in the 1920s and that "West had learned both the word and the concept from her friends in New York's gay underground."[45] The dominant culture did not permit a "real man" to indulge in techniques associated with the supposed seductive skills of women. Cliff Edwards, in fact, is faced with the same problem (how to exhibit eroticism as a man) that Susan McClary sees as hampering the eponymous character in Monteverdi's *Orfeo*.[46]

In "Is There Anything Wrong in That?" (Magidson-Cleary), recorded in New York in 1928, Helen Kane plays the "innocent abroad" or "dumb blonde" stereotype. The trumpet on this recording, played with a wa-wa mute, is intended to be both sexy and comic, just like Kane's voice, which it resembles. We cannot be sure which is imitating which—an ambiguity of considerable importance to the development of an instrumental erotic code in dance band music of this period.

In "Pu-leeze! Mister Hemingway" (Drake-Kent-Silver), recorded in London in 1932, Ann Suter portrays the "prim and proper but pliable" stereotype, the woman who needs to be conquered by the male. There are elements of sadomasochism present: the record concludes with a resounding slap as she fights off the libidinous Mr. Hemingway (while throughout the song we hear clear signs of her excitement at his presence).

Mae West and others who played the predatory stereotype appropriated the smears, bent notes, and growling plunger-mute effects of the Cotton Club in Harlem. There Duke Ellington, aided by trumpeter Bubber Miley and trombonist Joe "Tricky Sam" Nanton, satisfied the expectations of their white patrons by serving up such effects as "jungle music" (Ellington's orchestra sometimes recorded under the name The Jungle Band). Hence, associations of the wild and the primitive pass over to the singer who utilizes these devices. Then, becoming associated with representations of wild, predatory female sexuality, these effects (which are now heard as female cries, purrs, moans, groans, and breathless gasps) can return as a highly charged yet nonvocal musical eroticism. In a well-known later piece, David Rose's "The Stripper" of 1962, eroticism is enhanced by quasi-vocal slides on trombone and a wailing *tremolando* on a blue seventh followed by "jungle" drums.[47]

It is instructive to compare it with another musical discursive code, Richard Strauss's *Salome* (1905), which Ernst Krause claims "established the modern musical formula for the portrayal of ecstatic sensual desire and brought it to perfection."[48] The eroticism of the "Dance of the Seven Veils" is encoded in the sensual richness (timbral and textual) of a huge orchestra, the quasi-Oriental embellishment of melody (intimations of "exotic" sensuality), and the devices of *crescendo* and quickening pace (suggestive of growing excitement). However, it is no coincidence that, despite the anachronism, the Viennese waltz with its connotations of fin-de-siècle decadence lies just below the surface of the Strauss (see Ex. 1.5) as the fox-trot lies below that of the Rose.

EXAMPLE 1.5. Richard Strauss, "Salomes Tanz"

There is no sense, of course, in which one is really sexier than the other; each encodes eroticism in a different way and for a different function. It would be just as ludicrous to imagine Strauss's "Dance of the Seven Veils" in a seedy strip club as to imagine Rose's "The Stripper" incorporated into *Salome*. There *is* no perfect musical portrayal of "ecstatic sensual desire" independent of sociocultural context. Strauss is drawn to the waltz as the sexiest of music, a reputation it continued to hold in Vienna for some years after the production of *Salome*.[49]

Rose's piece sounds like camp eroticism now and seems to confirm the idea that a new erotic era began the following year. As Philip Larkin put it memorably in his poem "Annus Mirabilis":

Sexual intercourse began
In nineteen sixty-three
(Which was rather late for me)—
Between the end of the *Chatterley* ban
And the Beatles' first LP.[50]

Is this partly why Mae West sounds campy now—because the timbres used in her vocal delivery and the instrumental accompaniment have become part of a historical museum of clichés? It is perhaps difficult for some to accept that sexy music is not sexy in itself but only in relation to its cultural and historical context, but the examples in this chapter indicate that this is so. It is surely significant that Larkin mentions the Beatles in the poem cited earlier. New ways of encoding eroticism in music were developed in the rock style of the 1960s, and this code differs markedly from what came before: consider, for example, the recording of "Wild Thing" (Chip Taylor) by the Troggs in 1966. The rock critic Lester Bangs described this song as "the supreme manifestation of Rock and Roll as Global Worldmind Orgasm." Admittedly, he has his tongue a little in his cheek, but not when he asks us to accept this song as "just a simple expression of something."[51] As is obvious by now, I am arguing that we can never accept anything as "a simple expression."

In the early 1930s, West did represent a sexuality that many felt reflected a "real," if threatening, female sexuality. Indeed, she was arrested and charged in 1927 with staging an obscene and morally corrupting production. At issue was her play *SEX*,[52] in which she played a prostitute so convincingly that, in Hamilton's words, "most critics could not see it as a performance."[53] The *New York Daily Mirror* accused her of using her performance as a means of giving herself sexual pleasure: "She undresses before the public, and appears to enjoy doing so."[54] Even when West began to mediate her sexuality through a historical setting (to avoid charges of literally transporting New York's sexual underworld to the Broadway stage), her representation of late-nineteenth-century "low life" was thought authentic. Consideration, of course, needs to be given to the question of how far West began to introduce self-parody into her performances of the 1930s. These performances were certainly ambiguous, allowing her ironic detachment to be read as parody. Hamilton, however, claims that in the early 1930s West understood her irony as simply a suggestive inflection, a means of hinting that more was going on than lay on the surface, "suggesting some private joke that she seemed to be savoring but never revealed."[55] The Legion of Decency, campaigning for movie reform in 1933–34, failed to recognize irony, parody, or comedy of any kind in West's performances and considered her a moral threat to young women. It was after 1934, to appease the Production Code Administration, that West was obliged to provide an unambiguous mediation of her sexuality, one that would be perceived as nonthreatening because recognized as unreal. As we noted earlier, however, Cliff Edwards in imitating her only ever had the option, as a man, of sounding unreal. It seems that representations of male and female sexuality can occupy the same territory only when one or the other of them is the camp version. Furthermore, camp is not something that is produced only when a man behaves like a woman; a woman may turn a representation of femininity into camp. This is what began to happen in the gay and lesbian appropriation of country in the later 1980s, and it was so successful because, as Martha Mockus observes, "the strict gender definition presented in country music provides excellent material for queer drag and butch-femme role-playing among lesbians and gay men."[56] In trying to make sense of all this, it is helpful to draw upon Lacanian psychoanalytical theory. Relevant here, for example, is Ellie Ragland-Sullivan's carefully worded elucidation of Jacques Lacan's phallic signifier:

> Feminine sexuality—not necessarily correlated with gender—is a masquerade not only because s/he can disguise her desire, can fake it, can cover her body with cosmetics and jewels and make of *it* a phallus, but also because her masquerade hides a fact—that masculine sexuality is a tenuous matter. Things do not work so easily between man and woman, or between any sexual partners for that matter. If *only* this point were understood, Lacan's phallic signifier would not be read imaginarily—i.e., essentialized—as a privileging of the masculine. It would be seen, rather, as a dividing effect created by learning difference as gender difference.[57]

When Mick Jagger was thought to reflect an unbridled male sexuality, there were no female imitators of his unambiguous, up-front "Let's Spend the Night Together" style.[58] By the late 1980s, when those old Rolling Stones records were beginning to take on camp airs, Annie Lennox was able to appropriate the style in a song such as "I Need a Man" (Lennox-Stewart, 1987). The difference between this and the case of Mae West and Cliff Edwards is that performances by the last two were contemporaneous, whereas Lennox was quoting a style of representation that had become historic. It is the historic character of her quotation that makes it an example of the playing with signs that is a feature of postmodernism. The "dominatrix" as well as the "innocent" stereotypes of Hollywood femininity discussed earlier are deliberately quoted in songs by Madonna, which is partly what makes her a post-modern artist. The other typical feature of the postmodern (which Lennox and Madonna both seem aware of) is that it is double-coded: on the one hand, the quotation serves to inscribe, but on the other hand, the sense of parody or self-consciousness about the quotation serves to subvert. Linda Hutcheon has explained the latter as follows:

> Parody in postmodern art is more than just a sign of the attention artists pay to each other's work and to the art of the past. It may indeed be complicitous with the values it inscribes as well as subverts, but the subversion is still there.[59]

I would argue, however, that authorial intention is not essential for post-modern subversion to work; the subversion can take place in reception and interpretation—no postmodernist would accept a servile position toward a text (that is, being confined to struggling toward an understanding of the artist's intentions). A single example must suffice by way of illustration, since this is not the place to suddenly launch into a fresh debate about the self-present subject, poststructuralist arguments that concern the incompleteness of all texts, or the concept of *différance* that Jacques Derrida has used to designate "the production of differing/deferring."[60] When Kate Bush quotes the innocent girlish voice in her song "Wuthering Heights," our reception may be colored by a knowledge of the novel, where the little girl's plea to be let in at the window is met with misogynistic violence. Such a response does not rely upon Bush's intended meaning, whatever that may have been.

THE SEXUAL POLITICS OF VICTORIAN

MUSICAL AESTHETICS

A SEXUAL DIVISION of musical composition emerged in nineteenth-century Britain: during that period, metaphors of masculinity and femininity solidified into truths about musical style. Contemporary social theory, domestic sphere ideology, the new *scientia sexualis,* and aesthetics of the sublime and the beautiful ensured that certain musical styles were considered unsuitable or even unnatural for women composers. Female creativity was also denied or inhibited by educational and socioeconomic pressures born of ideological assumptions. In consequence, many women found themselves marginalized as composers, restricted to "acceptable" genres such as the drawing-room ballad. Men, too, were affected by the sexual politics of the age, because the supposed revelation of biological truths in music meant that the presence of feminine qualities in their compositions could lead to invidious comparison with the less elevated output of women.

Questions about the nature of music, its purpose, and whether it had a predominantly masculine or feminine character occupied the thoughts of many Victorians. Darwin was convinced that music had developed from the need to attract a mate and, noting that most creatures become more vocal during the breeding season, observed: "Women are generally thought to possess sweeter voices than men, and as far as this serves as any guide we may infer that they first acquired musical powers in order to attract the other sex."[1] However, most Victorian theories of music can be related to the tendency since the Enlightenment to identify men with reason and women with nature.[2] The use of a gendered vocabulary that consisted of words such as "mastered" and "grasped" to describe human understanding illustrates that tendency.

The emotional world was woman's;[3] hence, so was the moral world that was associated with feelings and susceptibilities: "Let men enjoy in peace and triumph the intellectual kingdom which is theirs," advised Sarah Lewis in *Woman's Mission*. "The moral world is ours."[4] This not to claim that all aspects of music belonged to the emotional realm and were therefore identified with woman. In fact, man's less emotional nature gave him superiority in certain musical areas: "Because of the fact that the emotional nature in man is less active than in woman," wrote T. L. Krebs in 1893, "he is superior to her in his ability to penetrate the mysteries of musical theory."[5] In this connection, it is interesting to note Susan McClary's argument that the "daunting structuralist graphs used to distance and objectify the passionate music of nineteenth-century opera" may be seen as an example, in our own times, of the fear that "to admit that music moves one affectively means that one may not be a proper masculine subject."[6]

The idea that "difficult thoughts" were man's sphere received support from nineteenth-century psychiatrists. Around midcentury, explanations were being sought for the large number of women among the institutionalized insane. These efforts led to what Elaine Showalter has called the "feminization of insanity."[7] Building upon a biological explanation that women's brains functioned differently from men's because "intimately connected with the uterine system,"[8] Henry Maudsley argued, in "Sex in Mind and in Education" (1874), that intellectual training in adolescence could damage both a woman's brain and her reproductive system. He supported his argument by reference to Dr Edward Clarke of Boston, Massachusetts, who had supposedly discovered that a young woman's energy was needed to establish "the periodical tides of her organization" (her menstrual cycle) and her body could not endure a simultaneous draining of mental energy.[9] This is reminiscent of Schopenhauer's idea concerning the difficulty he supposed people to have walking and talking at the same time: "For as soon as their brain has to link a few ideas together, it no longer has as much force left over as is required to keep the legs in motion through the motor nerves."[10] Psychiatrist Daniel Hack Tuke thought he had detected cases of "prostration of the brain" in girls who had overtaxed themselves in studying for exams.[11] Despite the counterarguments of women such as Elizabeth Garrett and Emily Davies,[12] these ideas were to result in the received wisdom summed up in Samuel Smiles's words: "Women have not the physical health to stand heavy work, still less heavy brain-work, which is more exhausting than muscle-work."[13] All the same, hard evidence of the unsuitability of the theoretical side of music for the female brain was difficult to come by. In fact, sometimes the opposite was found; a writer in the *Monthly Musical Record* in 1895 remarks on the number of women in classes at the Royal College of Music, the Royal Academy of Music, and the London Academy, adding:

> As far as I am informed, they do not lag behind the young men. I have known some young women, and know of many more, who were quicker and surer in the study of harmony and counterpoint than most men. If it be objected that there are few women composers, I

reply that that is true chiefly because there has been little encouragement held out to women composers hitherto.[14]

Women composers lacked the encouragement of both concert opportunity and academic recognition. Indeed, back in 1856 Elizabeth Stirling[15]
had passed the compositional exercise for the Mus.Bac. at the University of
Oxford but was refused the degree; Oxford first conferred degrees in music
on women in 1921, and that was six years before Cambridge saw fit to do so.

WOMEN AS MUSICIANS

For women, musical performance was regarded as an accomplishment not
an art requiring mental effort. In the late eighteenth century, Thomas Gisbourne had explained the "end and use of all such attainments" in *The Purposes of Ornamental Education* (1797): they are "occupations which may prevent the languor and snares of idleness, render home attractive, refresh the
wearied faculties, and contribute to preserve the mind in a state of placid
cheerfulness;" in addition, they enable the woman "to communicate a kin-
dred pleasure, with all its beneficial effects, to her family and friends."[16] It
will be noted that idleness, perceived as a threat to a woman's virtue, is mentioned as the first benefit, closely followed by an emphasis on domestic duty.
John Stuart Mill, in *The Subjection of Women* (1869), attacked the notion of
music as an accomplishment, making the point that "women in the educated classes are almost universally taught more or less of some branch or
other of the fine arts, but not that they may gain their living or their social
consequence by it."[17] It is important to stress the lack of social consequence
to be gained from musical skill, since this accounts for the low standard of
amateur performance complained about by many Victorian critics:

> Clever young ladies have been told, "My dear, you don't want to play
> or sing like professionals; you only require to know enough to amuse
> your own domestic circle."[18]

The female singer alone had a tradition to relate to (documented by
Ellen Clayton in *Queens of Song,* 1863), one that came about, perhaps, because she aroused the erotic interest of men.[19] The female composer appeared to be nowhere, an absence Mill explained as follows: "Women are
taught music, but not for the purpose of composing, only of executing it:
and accordingly it is only as composers, that men, in music, are superior to
women."[20]

The piano, which from the 1850s became the preeminent woman's instrument, ousting the guitar and harp, was an object to be looked at as well
as played and heard and had connotations that need to be considered:
Richard Leppert has called it "the visual-sonoric simulacrum of both family, wife and mother."[21] In the early nineteenth century, before the upright

"cottage piano" began to corner the market, some square pianos were designed so that they could also be used as sewing tables. Leppert notes that in postbellum America sewing machines and pianos were often bought from the same retailer. It was a state of affairs that must have persisted for some time, since the British Library catalog lists a periodical published in Philadelphia in 1880 titled *The Musical and Sewing Machine Courier*.

None of this was calculated to have women taken seriously as pianists, yet some, notably Clara Schumann (1819–96) and Arabella Goddard (1836–1922), did achieve warm recognition. A critic in the *Musical Gazette* (25 April 1857) writes enthusiastically of the latter's performance of Beethoven's Piano Sonata in E, op. 109, mentioning the "boldness" needed to "attack" such "difficult" music by the "mighty" Beethoven and, continuing to use a masculine vocabulary, claims: "Only those who have seen this sonata or have attempted to play it can thoroughly appreciate the triumph achieved by an artist who conquers it."[22] However, Goddard's performances took place not in a public concert room but during soirées at her own residence, 47 Welbeck Street, Cavendish Square, London, from which address she sold tickets at half a guinea each. Marcia Citron has stressed the importance of the salon for women, but as professionalism increased, there was an attendant decline in the salon music making, and professionalism, as Citron has shown, created a whole range of problems for women.[23]

In public concerts, women pianists were addressees of the masculine gaze; Susan Godard performing at the Hanover Square Rooms three months later elicited the following review from the same periodical:

> The extreme youth, pretty countenance, and small and sylph-like form of the fair performer, should not be omitted in the list of her good parts. True, one who sits aloft in the critical chair, has nothing to do with such sublunary matters, but if folks *will* raise their lorgnettes at such little gear, we must needs report the truth, and so there is an end of the matter.[24]

Arabella Goddard, too, "went public" in 1858, and it was not long before the tone of the reviews changed. A critic at a matinée concert she gave with three male musicians (who included violinist Joseph Joachim) writes:

> Looking on her sylph-like form, and her handsome and intelligent face (with the marks of early youth still upon it) hyper-criticism itself, while she goes through her arduous task with a confidence at once modest and firm, might willingly be silent on what she has *not* done, in reflecting on what she *has*.[25]

Needless to say, the three men were not subjected to any such commentary. This sort of leering interest is not confined to the concert hall but even extends to "lady organists": a correspondent to the *Musical Gazette* in 1857 remarks of Madame Vonholf, the recently appointed organist of Marylebone

Rectory Church: "This fair minister of religion is very young and (Heaven forgive us) very pretty."[26]

Women began to take to string instruments (which, like wind instruments, were long thought unfeminine) later in the century, influenced by a handful of female violin virtuosi such as Wilhelmine Néruda (1839–1911), and some were even learning wind instruments. However, they tended to end up in the novelty of the all-women orchestra or women's quartet (the most famous of the latter was Emily Shinner's quartet, 1887–97), just as the women who took up wind and brass to play jazz in the 1940s found themselves in outfits such as Ivy Benson's All-Girls Band. A critic in the *Musical Times* in 1880, after advancing some "progressive" thoughts on the matter, soon lapses into a familiar pattern of reception for the "Orchestra of Ladies" that performed at the Newbury Musical Festival (Berkshire) in October of that year:

> Twenty years ago the idea of an "Orchestra of Ladies" would have been received with derision; but we have now begun to acknowledge the absurdity of limiting the utterance of so beautiful a language as music to the male sex. Presuming, however, that they intend to challenge a public verdict upon their performance, it is a question whether, with a band of such powerful attraction, we can hope to secure perfectly independent critics.[27]

Not every member of this orchestra was a woman, but the majority were (twenty out of twenty-five), though the leader was male (Mr. T. S. Liddle). Women's orchestras had grown in size a decade later—the "eighty ladies or so who play in Mr. Moberly's string band" are mentioned in the *Monthly Musical Record* in 1895[28]—and they were also a familiar part of musical life in the United States, where it was commented in 1893: "We have numerous orchestras in which women occupy prominent positions, and even some composed entirely of women."[29] Yet the same writer reflects: "Twenty years ago it was an odd sight, and one that rarely failed to elicit visible and audible comment, not always charitable, when a girl or young woman carried a violin case through the streets of a city."[30] This, too, accords with the British experience, as expressed by a critic in 1885 who, while observing that "few feminine violinists have as yet made great mark," stated:

> Nobody is astonished now to see a lady playing the violin. There is the organ also. At one time it was considered unlady-like to play it. But there must surely be less to remark upon in a lady playing the organ than in turning the levers of a tricycle, as we may see them doing constantly in the streets.[31]

The reference to to a tricycle here anticipates the anticycling propaganda of the 1890s, when the attraction cycling held for women caused anguish in the music trades, since it was taking them away from their pianos.[32]

MUSIC AND FEMININITY

Worries about the effeminacy of music were already present in the eighteenth century, as Richard Leppert has shown.[33] The nineteenth century was
no different. Charles Hallé remarked that when he came to London in the
late 1840s if he "asked any gentleman belonging to society, 'Do you play any
instrument?' it was considered an insult."[34] Hallé was later (in 1864) to be
outraged by John Ruskin's musical taste, when the latter confessed to having
enjoyed his performance of Sigismond Thalberg's variations on "Home,
Sweet Home" better than his performances of Beethoven.[35] Realizing Hallé
had taken offense, Ruskin wrote to him stating: "It is quite true that I don't
understand Beethoven, and I fear I never shall have time to learn to do
so."[36] The inference to be drawn from these words coming from such an indefatigable aesthete is that there were more important matters to occupy his
study hours.[37] In contrast, it was no shame for a woman to be moved by
"Home, Sweet Home": Queen Victoria listening to Adelina Patti sing this
song in the Red Drawing Room of Windsor Castle noted in her journal that
the performance "was touching beyond measure, and quite brought tears to
one's eyes."[38]

Further fears about the effeminacy of music come unwittingly to light
when the Reverend Stephen Hawtrey, mathematical assistant master at Eton,
was examined by the Public Schools Commission on 15 July 1862. He was
asked questions about his largely unsuccessful attempts to encourage the
study of music at his school (where it was not an official subject). The min-
utes of evidence record the following exchange:

> 6657.   . . . do the boys take the same view of it that you do, and think
> it manly to learn music?—I think that many boys would be very glad
> to learn.
> 6658.   And there would be no laughing at them by the rest of the
> boys?—Not the least.[39]

William Johnson, another assistant master at Eton, had conveyed a
rather different impression, five days before, about the enthusiasm of the
boys for music:

> 4562.   Do you think there are many boys who care (as volunteers)
> about learning music in the school?—No, there are not many who
> learn it.[40]

A little later, H. Halford Vaughan, of the commission, wanted to know (min-
ute 4573) if Johnson considered it desirable that more boys should study
music "bearing in mind the class of boys who receive their education at
Eton, and their position in society."[41] Given the importance of a classical education at Eton, Vaughan may have had in mind Aristotle's opinion that
"learning music must not be allowed to have any adverse effect on later ac-
tivities" and that it was necessary to consider "to what extent boys, who are

being educated to discharge the highest functions in the state, ought to take part in music."[42] In fact, improvements in musical provision at public schools were a long time coming, though matters began to get a little better in the 1870s, particularly at Uppingham, Sherbourne, and Harrow. The situation at Harrow in midcentury was summed up in the comment: "A Harrow boy who went in for the study of music in those days would have been looked upon as a veritable milksop."[43]

The issue of class, raised by Vaughan, is an interesting one, since music was thought beneficial (refining and humanizing) to males of the "lower orders." The brass band springs immediately to mind, but working-class boys were also trained for military careers as bandsmen and bandmasters. Many of the bandsmen who trained at the Military School of Music at Kneller Hall, Twickenham (founded in 1857, after the Crimean War, and taken over by the War Office in 1875), were drawn, at the age of 15, from the Chelsea Hospital, the Royal Hibernian Military School (Dublin), and the Metropolitan Poor Law schools.[44] However, worries about the effeminacy of music persisted throughout the century both in Britain and the United States, where, Krebs pointed out, "many young men, and old ones too, who live in a more or less circumscribed sphere, seem to be afraid that they might jeopardize their manly dignity were they to study thoroughly the art of music."[45]

The male fear of being feminized by music is often, as Lawrence Kramer has commented in the case of a later composer, Charles Ives, "a dread of being feminized in relation, not to women, but to other men."[46] It thus encourages the development of a misogynistic outlook and demeanor in order to rebut charges of effeminacy or emasculation. There is, in fact, a painting titled *Music* by Frederick Leighton (c. 1865)[47] that depicts a male figure whose groin-hugging tights might be used to give new meaning to Derrida's concept of the presence of an absence. Yet the terms "masculine" and "feminine" were first used as metaphors in musical criticism, not as biological truths. It is clear that this is the case in Schumann's well-known remarks about Schubert:

> To one who has some degree of education and feeling Beethoven and Schubert may be recognized and distinguished, from the very first. Schubert is a more feminine character compared to the other; far more loquacious, softer, broader; compared to Beethoven he is a child, sporting happily among the giants.[48]

Whatever the gender ideology here, it is evident that Schumann is speaking metaphorically—note that he also uses a childhood metaphor—and this is made clear when he modifies his pronouncements:

> To be sure, he brings in his powerful passages, and works in masses; and still he is more feminine than masculine, for he pleads and persuades where the man commands. But all this merely in comparison with Beethoven; compared to others, he is masculine.[49]

In the second half of the nineteenth century, however, such metaphors were solidifying into biological "truths" as they became enmeshed with psychological and physiological theories about women's minds and bodies. The following thoughts, by Frederick Niecks (later to become Reid Professor of Music at the University of Edinburgh), appeared in the *Monthly Musical Record* in 1877:

> Women are not without energy and aspiration; what they lack, if history teaches us aright, is sustained strength and wide-reaching comprehensive thought. . . . Now what Schubert is wanting in is just this sustained strength and comprehensive thought.[50]

However, Niecks concludes, Schubert "has enough of the man to distinguish him from the woman," because "sex can never be quite disguised."

Although a gay and lesbian musical criticism has only recently emerged,[51] some tentative observations may be made that relate Schubert's music to his sexual orientation.[52] If a reading of his music as feminine is accepted too readily as evidence of his homosexuality, it not only sidesteps the thorny issue of the historical specificity of Schubert's experience but also can lead to the error of equating homosexuality with femininity. A reminder that gay identities in the last century involved a variety of negotiations with codes of masculinity ("butchness") and femininity should correct this misconception: one need only consider the parodic appropriations labeled "camp."[53] The gender ideology that essentialized masculinity and femininity and found its way into sonata form analysis (masculine first subject, feminine second subject) has to be historicized. Today, when we recognize masculinities and femininities as culturally constructed pluralities, we could perhaps interpret sonata form conflict, particularly of the nineteenth-century variety, in terms of a dominant masculine code and a sexual otherness. This remains problematic, since feminine connotations of certain musical material undoubtedly existed; yet a gay composer might feel inclined to identify with such material in its struggle against another kind of material that was assured of dominance, especially when a self-association with the latter necessitated an identification with hegemonic normalcy. A reading along these lines would be possible, for example, in the first movement of Schubert's "Unfinished Symphony," where the "feminine" second subject initially resists absorption by the tonic in the recapitulation, rejecting the norms of tonic minor and tonic major; moreover, as Susan McClary has observed, this is the tune "with which we are encouraged to identify."[54] The opinion of the critic in the *Monthly Musical Record,* quoted earlier, that "sex can never be quite disguised," accords with contemporary psychological theory, as expressed in Henry Maudsley's statement: "There is sex in mind as distinctly as there is sex in body."[55] This idea convinces Niecks that "woman has work to do in art, as well as in life, which can only be done by her,"[56] although the absence of a woman composer to place alongside a writer like George Eliot is then simply offered to the reader as a puzzling fact.

WOMEN AND COMPOSITION

The question "Why has there been no female Beethoven?" was returned to often. A correspondent to the *Monthly Musical Record* in 1877 writes, under the non-gender-specific pseudonym "Artiste," on the subject of the "want of creative power in women" and is clearly influenced by the notion that women's brains cannot cope with too much concentrated and disciplined thought:

> A woman endowed with a lively, excitable imagination, rarely possesses the enormous perseverance and energy necessary for a composer . . . It is an established maxim that "a woman can never be a great composer," and I do not mean to dispute its truth; certainly no female Beethoven has appeared as yet, nor do I think that such will ever be the case; setting aside everything else, no woman has the *physical* strength without which such a genius could not exist.[57]

Having put together these by now familiar thoughts that mark the interrelatedness of mental and physical energy, the correspondent concluded by advising the woman composer to "aspire humbly but earnestly," conjecturing that, in so doing, "she might work out a path of distinction for herself." This path was to be gender-specific, so that

> in music, as in literature and painting, a man's work might be easily distinguished from that of a woman, but withal each should possess merits to be gratefully recognised, and mutual profit be gathered therefrom.[58]

Also in 1877, an American writer, Fanny Raymond Ritter, considers the subject of women and composition and argues that a feminine side of music already exists:

> It would be unnatural to think that the beautiful lullabies and cradle-songs, of which hundreds exist, in different languages, were composed by martial barons, rough serving-men, and rougher peasants, and not by their wives and daughters. . . . We can scarcely doubt but that many of those simple, touching, heart-breaking melodies and poems that have descended to us, were created by women.[59]

A version of this article[60] was skittishly reviewed by Niecks, whose views on Schubert have already been referred to. The preceding sentiments elicited the following response:

> This is very probable, and yet how strange again that in the song-literature one meets with no touching and heart-breaking melodies composed by women—at least not heart-breaking in the sense of the authoress. Surely no one will wonder at my denying these epithets to the melodies of the female composers who have made themselves a name as song-writers![61]

The joke here is intended to be doubly wounding: first, because "touching and heart-breaking melodies" were acceptably feminine and, therefore, what many women composers aspired to; and second, because women had so far only managed to acquire any reputation as composers by writing the very music Niecks ridicules.

The idea that if female creativity existed at all, it existed in a separate feminine sphere had become commonplace in the next decade.[62] Stephen S. Stratton remarked to the Musical Association in 1883, "Women have received much advice to cultivate art from the feminine stand-point."[63] The ideology of separate creative spheres could, however, be used to undermine the achievement of a woman composer, since it made possible the accusation that she was not being true to her nature and, instead, was merely imitating what men have created. Stratton cites a reviewer whose description of Alice Mary Smith's *The Passions* as "a striking reproduction of masculine art"[64] we have already encountered in chapter 1. A speaker in the discussion that followed the presentation of Stratton's paper remarks scornfully of the composition classes at "academies or colleges where young ladies are taught to do only what men have done."[65] But where could women receive training in the feminine side of composition? Moreover, we have seen that what constituted masculinity and femininity in music originated in metaphors; and so, when women composers were being told to express their femininity in music, they were really being asked to offer evidence that these metaphorical and therefore ideological representations of femininity were, in fact, biological truths. Hence, once the presence of "feminine" qualities in music was accepted as evidence of a feminine nature, it must inevitably have affected the reception of male composers. Eustace J. Breakspear, for example, laments the neglect in the mid-1870s of Chopin, a composer he praises for "ethereal beauty," "fascinating charm," and music that attains "the acme of the graceful and the refined in expression."[66] This is certainly a description to evoke the feminine. Indeed, Jeffrey Kallberg came across the following statement while researching nineteenth-century critical associations of femininity with the nocturne: "The poetic side of men of genius is feminine, and in Chopin the feminine note was overemphasized—at times it was almost hysterical—particularly in these nocturnes."[67] The full impact of this description relies on the knowledge that hysteria, along with neurasthenia (nervous exhaustion) and anorexia, was an illness particularly associated with women in the later nineteenth century.[68] Nevertheless, if Carlyle could consider heroism possible for the poet, while maintaining poetry was "musical thought" and that "all passionate language does of itself become musical,"[69] then surely there was a place for the hero as composer. Richard Leppert suggests that

> the pronounced "masculinity" evident in the aggressiveness, assertiveness and insistence in so much nineteenth-century instrumental music—from piano sonatas to symphonies—in part consti-

tutes an impassioned outburst by male artists entreating not only for the centrality of their artistic exercise as protest over their own marginalization but also as the sonoric denial of the cultural effeminization which accompanies them as artists.[70]

THE SUBLIME AND THE BEAUTIFUL

Nineteenth-century aesthetics tended to bifurcate into theories of the sublime (which was typified by qualities such as the awesome, solemn, pathetic, colossal, lofty, and majestic) and the beautiful (typified by qualities of the graceful, charming, delicate, playful, and pretty). The thesis I want to advance is that the ideology of the sublime and the beautiful worked to exclude women from particular compositional choices (unless they were to be untrue to their "nature") and also effectively fenced off the category of "greatness" in music as a male domain. To posit an ideology of the aesthetic is not new: Terry Eagleton has produced a searching critique of the ideology of aesthetic theory from a Marxist perspective,[71] relating it to a ruling class's need to confront, explain, and defuse the class conflict that arises from the capitalist mode of production; there is less emphasis in his work, however, on how aesthetics, as a discourse of the body, encodes ideologies of gender and sexuality. That it does so is not surprising, given the original concern of aesthetics with perception by the senses (αἰσθησις).

On the Sublime (Περι ὑψους), by the first-century Greek writer Longinus, was rediscovered in the seventeenth century. Longinus was concerned with the power of rhetoric to express grand ideas that create an intense, emotional response. For a more general philosophical inquiry, it is instructive to turn to Edmund Burke's thoughts on the sublime and beautiful, written in 1757, when aesthetic theory was in its infancy:

> Sublime objects are vast in their dimensions, beautiful ones comparatively small: beauty should be smooth and polished; the great, rugged and negligent; beauty should shun the right line yet deviate from it insensibly; the great in many cases loves the right line; and when it deviates it often makes a strong deviation: beauty should not be obscure; the great ought to be dark and gloomy: beauty should be light and delicate; the great ought to be solid and even massive.[72]

Though the beautiful and sublime may be found united, they are distinct qualities. Burke illustrates this with an analogy: "Black and white may soften, may blend; but they are not therefore the same."[73] However, by replacing sublime and beautiful not with black and white but with masculine and feminine we can see how the two pairs of binary oppositions are related and, accordingly, how in a gendered discourse such as this the sublime is ruled out as an aesthetic category for women. It then becomes significant to note how readily the sublime becomes the "great"; admittedly that word is first chosen to communicate vastness, but it is soon being used of line, light, and mood. So, even at this date, it is obvious that the sublime is not going to be an option for women, although the beautiful clearly has possibilities.

When Niecks was discussing Schubert and femininity, he went on to outline features "known to be characteristic of the literary works of female writers" that may readily be discovered in Schubert's compositions. Some of the features Niecks picks out are

> fine sensitiveness, delicacy of feeling, ready sympathy, acute observa-tion—especially of little things that are nearest and dearest—occa-sional outbursts of power, short glimpses of far-reaching vision, and, along with this, a languid dreaming[74]

There are some obvious parallels here with Burke's concept of the beautiful: "delicacy of feeling" accords with Burke's statement "beauty should be light and delicate," and the "acute observation—especially of little things that are nearest and dearest—" would fit in well with Burke's idea that, compared to the sublime, beautiful objects are small and "beauty should not be obscure."

William Crotch, professor of music at Oxford from 1797 and, later, prin-cipal of the Royal Academy of Music, suggested a tripartite division of music into the sublime, the beautiful, and the ornamental, though he pointed out that these qualities could and did mix.[75] From some of the devices he cites as means of achieving the sublime in music it is evident that women were going to face obstacles of gender ideology as well as a lack of compositional training should they try to emulate these devices. Here is part of his de-scription of sublimity in music: "a great compass of notes employed in a full orchestra . . . the deep science of the organ fugue . . . a passage performed by many voices or instruments in unisons or octaves, and one in full and florid counterpoint."[76]

Where beauty is concerned, however, the way seems clearer. This is how Crotch describes the beautiful in music:

> The melody is vocal and flowing, the measure symmetrical, the har-mony simple and intelligible, and the style of the whole soft, delicate, and sweet.[77]

The ornamental, on its own, seems ruled out; it is typified by "eccentric and difficult melody, rapid, broken and varied rhythm, wild and unexpected modulation."[78] Nevertheless, when the ornamental is combined with the beautiful, which Crotch states it frequently is, he sees it (quoting Uvedale Price) as "the coquetry of nature" that makes beauty "more amusing, more varied, more playful" and gives as an example of this union the "flowing and elegant melody with playful and ingenious accompaniment."[79] The use of the term "coquetry" with its connotations of trifling, and especially of a woman trifling with a man, would appear to show that this combination of qualities was already being considered feminine in character, and we can perhaps take Crotch's remark that "it forms the leading characteristic of modern music" as the wry observation of an academic composer on the music of his rivals. There is no question but that an issue of artistic status is involved in these divisions, and this is evident when Crotch ponders: "If with Burke we separate the sublime and beautiful into two styles, which shall we prefer? Surely the sublime, as requiring most mind in the person gratified and in the author of the gratification."[80]

Consider, too, these words from later in the century: "Beethoven, in most that he composed, rises higher than either Mozart or Haydn. His ideas are larger, the thought is deeper, the outlines are grander, and the mind with which they are imbued is loftier."[81] Thus are women excluded from achieving "greatness" in music.

Now we may move to consider the typicalities and particularities of "feminine" as distinct from "masculine" musical style. In order to set male and female on as equal a terrain as possible, the genre of the drawing-room ballad has been chosen since, after 1860, it offered a more equal opportunity to composers of either sex than any other genre. It allowed women composers to avoid some of the constraints created by the rise, during 1800–1870, of an integrated, international musical canon that William Weber identifies as establishing "a much stronger authority in aesthetic and critical terms."[82] Marcia Citron has summed up the constraints of the canon as "negative stereotypes for women and creativity . . . , problematic notions of professionalism and of what public and private mean . . . , and the widely held assumption that music and the experiencing of music are gender-neutral."[83]

Surveying the output of the most successful women ballad composers,[84] we find a propensity for diatonic melody and concords and a clear preference for major keys[85]—interesting, in the light of Crotch's remark that a minor key "of itself confers an expression of seriousness and dignity, and is frequently on that account adopted by second-rate composers."[86] Since women were perceived to be, if anything, second-rate composers, then perhaps one reason for the avoidance of minor keys by women was that they wished to avoid being accused of affecting unfeminine seriousness and dignity. However, women composers of this time do not generally use vigorous rhythms or fast tempi, which suggests that they would not like to err on the side of lacking *any* seriousness or dignity by using parameters whose connotations might invite the descriptions "strong-minded" (pejorative when used of women) and "giddy." It would, of course, be unfeminine to be loud, yet loudness is mentioned by Burke as a factor in the sublime.[87] And since he also mentions the "shouting of multitudes,"[88] we may take it that thickness of texture is a factor as well.

Let us look at five women's ballads, which cover a range of musical styles and literary content that were acceptably feminine. "Children's Voices" by Claribel (Charlotte Alington Barnard)[89] is an example of the hymn like ballad, though the harmonic rhythm is slow, with chords changing once or twice a bar. It consists of a regularly phrased 24-bar tune for a soloist, the last 8 bars then being repeated for a chorus in four-part harmony. It would seem to fit perfectly Crotch's description of the beautiful in music quoted earlier. The words, written by Claribel herself, concern children praying, a suitably feminine subject, since the moral education of the young was a womanly duty (see Ex. 2.1).

Miss M. Lindsay's "Sacred Song" "Queen Mary's Prayer" makes use of arioso techniques from oratorio. Miss Lindsay[90] was the first woman to make a success of composing sacred songs of this type, songs that adapted

EXAMPLE 2.1. Claribel, "Children's Voices"

the oratorio manner to the requirements of the "home circle." Sandwiched between refrains is a section that relies upon word-painting devices common in oratorio, such as melodic notes and harmonies chosen for their "expressive" effects. Note the change to tonic minor on the word "pain," the German sixth coupled with a *rallentando* on the word "only," and the conventional representation of a sigh, the falling minor second on the word "feeble" (see Ex. 2.2). This was about as serious as a woman composer could be without being thought disloyal to her femininity.

Dolores (real name Ellen Dickson)[91] provides an example of the "playful intricacy" of the union of the beautiful with the ornamental in the lyrical melody and rippling accompaniment of "Clear and Cool." Even when, in the third verse, the words call for loudness, the pitch of the accompaniment ensures that this is not excessive (see Ex. 2.3). The morally uplifting words of the song, taken from Charles Kingsley's *The Water Babies,* are addressed throughout to a mother and child and thus entirely becoming for a woman composer.

Caroline Norton[92] wrote "Juanita" in the early 1850s before the interest in Spanish "Peninsular Melodies" was exhausted.[93] At that time the guitar was still common in drawing rooms, and it looks as though the song was written with that instrument in mind: note the spacing of the chords and the

EXAMPLE 2.2. Miss M. Lindsay, "Queen Mary's Prayer"

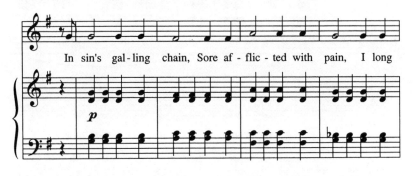

EXAMPLE 2.3. Dolores, "Clear and Cool"

unusual downward motion of the arpeggios, which seems designed to allow the melody to be more easily reinforced from time to time on the guitar's highest string (see Ex. 2.4).

Writing imitation foreign airs allowed a woman composer to act a role—it was a way of saying, "This is not really me." Nevertheless, only a restricted number of roles were available; and when Norton borrowed an Arab air for one of her songs, she wisely avoided connotations of "Oriental" sensuality by writing a religious text for it (this same tune was to become a famous "belly dance" later in the century[94]). The enormous success of "Juanita" created its own problems, though, and highlighted an unexpected handicap that could face a commercially successful woman composer. Norton's husband, from whom she was separated, chose the year of "Juanita" to claim his legal entitlement to all the money she was able to earn through her songs and poems.

"The Charming Woman" by Caroline Norton's sister Helen Blackwood (Lady Dufferin)[95] is of the humorous variety; such pieces were not intended to prompt raucous laughter but rather to be listened to with a knowing smile. The present example adopts the rum-ti-tum $\frac{6}{8}$ meter and repeated-note style of melody of a bucolic patter song in comic opera (see Ex. 2.5).

EXAMPLE 2.4. Caroline Norton, "Juanita"

EXAMPLE 2.5. Helen Blackwood, "The Charming Woman"

The subject matter of a comic song composed by a woman was usually restricted to the peculiar customs and utterances of the "lower orders," but in this particular example the butt of the humor is the strong-minded middle-class woman. Here is verse 5:

> She sings like a Bullfinch or Linnet
> And she talks like an Arch-bishop too

She can play you a rubber and *win* it,—
   If she's got nothing better to do!
She can chatter of Poor-laws and Tithes
   And the value of Labour and Land,—
'Tis a pity when *charming* women
   Talk of things which they don't understand!

Blackwood wrote the words as well as the music, and it may seem remark-able that, as an intelligent woman, probably the recipient of similar barbed comments herself, she could not resist such ideology. Yet we have to consider how long it was before a woman was able to find a way of being funny in public on the subject of women other than at her own expense. Humor in drawing-room ballads reinforced ideologies of both class and gender.

None of these five ballads transgress codes of femininity. The kinds of ballads inappropriate and hence unavailable to women composers can be suggested by a list of titles alone: "Sons of the Sea," "A Bandit's Life Is the Life for Me," and "Yes! Let Me like a Soldier Fall."[96] These embrace the masculine world of imperial adventure, rebellion, and heroism. We must also include the boisterous sailor ballads such as "Nancy Lee."[97] So, did women avoid the masculine ballad? Most of them did, but as we saw in chapter 1, some very definitely did not. In the midcentury we find Caroline Norton imitating the "Call for the Cavalry" from Franz Kotzwara's piano fantasia *The Battle of Prague* in her song "The Officer's Funeral," and at the end of the century we have Frances Allitsen adopting the conventions of the fervent patriotic style in her setting of William Henley's "England, My England." We will now look at two ballads in more detail to see women confidently applying the mascu-line style:[98] Virginia Gabriel's[99] setting of Jean Ingelow's poem "When Spar-rows Build," and Maud Valérie White's[100] setting of Browning's cavalier song "King Charles."

The reiterations in the accompaniment of "When Sparrows Build" have a percussive, thus, by implication, masculine character—compare "To Anthea" (Herrick-Hatton), "If Doughty Deeds My Lady Please" (Graham-Sullivan), and "Ich grolle nicht" (Schumann-Heine). Gabriel's ballad is in sonata form in the key of G major and contains some daring modulations: the second subject, for example, begins in the unusual key of E major and four bars later abruptly modulates to $G\sharp$ major followed by $C\sharp$ minor, one of the remotest keys possible from the tonic (see Ex. 2.6). One of the devices the Kantian musical critic Christian Friedrich Michaelis cited in 1805 for producing "astonishment and awe" and stimulating "sublime ideas" was the sudden veering of the established tonality "in an unexpected direction."[101] It would seem that that is very much Gabriel's masculine intention in this song. However, I would contend that the use of sonata form for a song tends to feminize that form by giving emphasis to the second subject. This hap-pens if verse and refrain form is suggested, with the second subject cast in the important role of refrain tune (even where the poem does not itself fall

EXAMPLE 2.6. Virginia Gabriel, "When Sparrows Build"

EXAMPLE 2.6. *Continued*

low?   Nay,   I   spoke once, and   I   griev'd thee sore, I re–

into such a pattern). A song in sonata form has a tendency to create this impression, because lyricism is as much an established characteristic of a second subject as it is of a refrain melody. In fact, if Gabriel's setting of Ingelow's poem is compared with a setting of the same poem by Miss Lindsay,
it will be found that the two appearances of Gabriel's second subject (in the
exposition and recapitulation) coincide exactly with words chosen for Lindsay's two melodic refrains. Furthermore, in another sonata-form unortho-
doxy, it is Gabriel's second subject that is triumphantly affirmed at the end.
If, for comparison, we turn to the masculine Beethoven, whom Wagner
praised for raising music "far above the realm of the aesthetically beautiful
into the sphere of the sublime,"[102] and consider the treatment of the second
subject in the first movement of the Fifth Symphony (the symphony Hoff-
man thought the composer's most characteristic work[103]), we find that there
is no clearer example of a second subject being dominated and finally
crushed by a first subject (even the horn call that announced it is gradually
worn down and reshaped into the first subject's falling thirds).

Maud Valérie White's "King Charles" was composed in the late 1890s,
nearly thirty years after Gabriel's ballad, and after the "new woman" of the
1880s and 1890s had excited much attention and debate.[104] Aesthetic theory
had been changing, too, with the growth of British interest in Schopenhauer
encouraged by the Wagner cult. According to Schopenhauer, the artistic intellect needed to be freed from blind obeisance to what he called the Will,
the boundless and unquenchable desire that constitutes life's ultimate reality. Freed from service to the Will, the composer could write music that was
an objectification of the Will, fit for aesthetic contemplation. However,
Schopenhauer's ideas did little for women, since he considered them too
subjective to possess the objectivity or genius necessary to free themselves
from the Will.[105] The American critic George Upton complained, in his

book *Woman in Music* (1880), that women could not objectify emotion by transforming it into art.[106] In Upton's opinion, "Man controls his emotions, and can give an outward expression of them. In woman they are the dominating element, and so long as they are dominant she absorbs music."[107] In other words, being emotional by nature, she cannot "project herself outwardly."[108] It leads to a familiar conclusion, that woman "will always be the recipient and interpreter, but there is little hope she will be the creator."[109]

The ideas of the Austrian music critic Eduard Hanslick were also gaining ground, particularly among "anti-Wagnerites." Hanslick opposed the notion that music acted directly upon the feelings, arguing: "Beauty in music appeals primarily to the imagination and only secondarily to the feelings."[110] This was the kind of idea that could be used to "defeminize" music; it allowed music to be moved from the emotional feminine sphere to the intellectual masculine sphere. However, it also meant that women's music had to be taken more seriously, since Hanslick claimed that *all* beauty in music appealed primarily to the imagination, a faculty that, according to Kant, harmonized "with the *cognitive capacity* of the intellect or of reason."[111] Indeed, Hanslick restored the description "feminine" to metaphorical usage, by asserting: "Music must . . . be grasped simply as music and can only be understood in its own terms and only enjoyed in its own way."[112] In making the case for music's autonomy Hanslick brought new status to music, so that later in the century many accepted the truth of Walter Pater's famous remark about all art aspiring to the condition of music.

Another important intervention in aesthetic theory was made by Nietzsche, who, having become disenchanted with Wagner, started attacking "the *lie* of the great style" and expressing a preference for music that "approaches lightly, supplely, politely" and "does not *sweat*."[113] Eventually this kind of polemic began to destroy the mystique of the sublime. Indeed, it is a moot point whether White is appropriating the "masculine sublime" for her song or parodying it. Certainly the song can be interpreted either way, depending on the degree of exaggeration or restraint the singer and accompanist adopt toward the "sublime" devices found therein. I shall describe some of these, finding relevant quotations to support my labeling them as "sublime." I place the term in "scare quotes" to underline that I am using "sublime" in the sense of sublimely *butch* (though I fear that some will accuse me of moving from the sublime to the ridiculous). These are the features that delineate an aesthetic domain of potent, monumental masculinity. I am not concerned here with moments of Kantian epistemological transcendence where these masculine features have been transformed into a desexualized sublime. We should remember that it is not without significance that Freud uses the term "sublimation" to describe the desexualization of the libido.[114]

If we look at the introduction, we see that a *tempo di marcia* is called for. Taken together with the tonic-dominant "oompah" bass, the military connotations are immediate. Yet no sooner have we begun to register the tempo and make the necessary masculine associations than we are held in suspense with a pause on a dominant seventh in preparation for the first "sublime" device. What follows is thrice unexpected: first, because we cannot anticipate its arrival (because of the pause); second, because it is not the tonic chord that we anticipate after hearing the dominant seventh; and third, because the dynamic level is *fortissimo* in sudden contrast to the previous *piano* (see Ex. 2.7).

Burke, although speaking of *sounds,* not music, mentions, in connection with the sublime, "a sudden beginning or sudden cessation of sound of any considerable force," and he goes on to observe that "a single sound of some strength, though but of short duration, if repeated after intervals, has a grand effect."[115] Now, while admitting that the chords of bars 3–6 are not strictly equivalent to Burke's "single sound," the introduction of this song does seem to offer a striking musical parallel to his comments.

As the singer begins, the accompaniment is low-pitched, loud, and thick in texture, and the singer's melody is reinforced at masculine pitch in the bass clef. The bass clef was thought of as a uniquely masculine domain, for whereas men were taught both treble and bass clefs in training colleges, women were taught only the treble.[116] At bar 15, the dynamic falls to *piano,* the pace quickens, and a *crescendo* begins with the singer being asked to increase dynamic level during sustained notes. This last effect occurs again at

EXAMPLE 2.7. Maud Valérie White, "King Charles"

the end of the refrain, where the singer has a *crescendo* over five bars on a single note. Let us now consider what aesthetic theorists from the British tradition have to say about effects like these. We may recollect Burke's remarks on "the shouting of multitudes," which, it has been previously suggested, might be related to thickness of texture; moreover, here there is reinforcement of the melody, too. Concerning the use of *crescendi,* we might consider Alison's recipe for the "most sublime" of sounds (in his *Essays on the Nature and Principles of Taste* published in 1790), which was a "loud, grave [i.e., low-pitched], lengthened and increasing sound."[117] We could also consider Daniel Webb's opinion that "a growth or climax in sounds exalts and dilates the spirits and is therefore a constant source of the sublime."[118]

Perhaps, given that it would be very familiar in piano arrangement at this time, we can once more choose the first movement of Beethoven's Fifth Symphony for a comparison. Here we find a similar use of a pause to ensure and enhance the unexpected. Note how the second pause in the opening bars arrives after the note has already been held for the duration of a minim and, therefore, since this note is held longer than the previous pause note, the listener is prevented from predicting the beginning of the next bar. We also find an unexpected change of dynamic in this bar. Furthermore, in this movement there are many *crescendi,* some unusually long for the date of its composition, and there is a general thickness of texture: indeed, the function of the wind and brass instruments is, for the most part, to thicken the orchestral texture. Of course, no one is going to claim that White is seeking to recreate the "awesome sublime" in her song, but she uses techniques that are strongly coded as masculine and does so within such a short time span that they take her song into the realm of parody or, to repeat my earlier phrase, the sublimely butch.

At the end of the nineteenth century there was a return in some critical quarters to the metaphorical usage of the terms "masculine" and "feminine." Bernard Shaw, for example, wrote to Ethel Smyth[119] to say:

> It was your music that cured me for ever of the old delusion that women could not do men's work in art and other things (it was years ago, when I knew nothing about you, and heard an overture—*The Wreckers* or something—in which you kicked a big orchestra round the platform). But for you I might not have been able to tackle *Saint Joan,* who has floored every previous playwright. Your music is more masculine than Handel.[120]

Here we should perhaps advance a caution similar to that given concerning Schubert's femininity. If a simple correlation is made between Smyth's lesbian preferences[121] and her masculine music, we fail to account for the variety of negotiations with feminine and masculine codes involved in lesbian identities. At the same time, just as it was posited that for Schubert a disinclination to identify with normative masculinity might have urged him toward musical devices that had feminine connotations, it could now be suggested that Smyth's musical masculinity might well have been prompted by a disinclination to identify with normative femininity.

That the power relations embedded in nineteenth-century sexual discourse gave rise to gendered discursive codes in music is evidence that music should not be considered in isolation from the political arena. The biological arguments about masculinity and femininity in music did not disappear in the twentieth century. In a paper given to the Royal Musical Association in 1920, women were once again placed in a double bind, being told on the one hand that the woman's mind is receptive, not productive,[122] and on the other hand that by imitating men (which, it would follow, is the only possibility available) a woman "insults her own sex."[123] There is no room here to discuss how and why the sexual politics of Victorian musical aesthetics proved so enduring. The opinions just cited, for example, need to be considered alongside a discussion of the impact of women having taken over male roles when they did the work of those who had been sent to the front during the First World War. Biological determinism returned in the 1990s with a vengeance in the writings of Camille Paglia. Raising the subject of serial killing, she states that though it is a "perversion of male intelligence" it is nevertheless "masculine in its deranged egotism and orderliness" and claims: "There is no female Mozart because there is no female Jack the Ripper."[124] Paglia's confidence in the absence of female serial killers must have been shaken the year after this book was published, when Aileen Wuornos confessed to the murders of seven men in Florida.

part two

IDEOLOGY AND

THE POPULAR

THE NATIVE AMERICAN

IN POPULAR MUSIC

FIRST A WORD ON TERMINOLOGY: the description "Native American" is not universally admired or accepted (since it performs an assimilating function), but it has gained wide currency and so I use it here, as Jacques Derrida might say, "under erasure." Indians had no legal status as American citizens until 1924.[1] The term "Indian" presents difficulties, too; these have been explained by Robert F. Berkhofer:

> That the idea of the Indian originated and continues up to the present as a White image poses major dilemmas for modern Whites as well as for Native Americans. Through continued use of the term *Indian*, does the present-day White still subscribe to past stereotype?[2]

In addition to these words of caution, I should warn the reader that my title is ambiguous, since my focus for most of this chapter is not on Native American performers of popular music. A title such as "The Pretend Indian in Popular Music" would not completely solve the problem, however, since it may suggest a certain *intentional* artificiality in the representation or even deliberate misrepresentation. That is often not the case. The American Indian in song and film was, for the larger part of the twentieth century, as much a simulacrum, in Jean Baudrillard's use of the term,[3] as the American cowboy: there was rarely any attempt to relate the representations of either of them to the actualities of their lives.[4] In the main, we simply witness the reproduction of copies of what had never existed in the first place. Moreover, these copies of a nonreality, it must be emphasized, *became* reality. Native American actor Chief Thundercloud had to be transformed by makeup artists into what a chief was expected to look like in *Geronimo* (1939)—the disconcerted movie men "didn't think he looked real enough."[5]

EARLY REPRESENTATIONS

No obvious musical signs of difference accompany the earliest appearances of Native Americans in Western music.[6] Rameau's harpsichord piece *Les Sauvages,* for example, was inspired by seeing two North American Indians perform in Paris in 1725, yet we are, in Miriam K. Whaples's words, "bemused to read" Rameau's claim that he had captured the character of their song and dance.[7] In Stephen Storace's opera *The Cherokee* of 1794,[8] the "Cherokee March" and the "British March" could be interchanged without noticeable effect (see Exx. 3.1 and 3.2). Interestingly, these examples show a reverse of later Orientalist representational convention, since it is the Self that is feminized here rather than the ethnic Other. The "British March" can easily be heard in the position of a feminine second subject to the masculine first subject gestures of the "Cherokee March." Perhaps the intention was to contrast the latter with British refinement and grace. A feature in this opera that was to prove significant later, however, is the emphasis given to the Indians' "war whoop." Storace does offer a musical representation of this by setting the word to longer note values, but its otherness is dissipated by his weaving it into imitative part writing so as to suggest agitation in the conventional eighteenth-century manner.[9] Nevertheless, the "War-Whoop Chorus," as it came to be known, was a big success and, in recognition of that, was moved to the end of act 1 to provide an exciting close.[10]

The accolade of "first Indian play by an American"[11] was given to *The Indian Princess* of 1808, a tale revisited many times, most recently in the Walt Disney animated film musical *Pocahontas* (1995).[12] The importance of music is such that, despite the nonsinging roles, *The Indian Princess* could be described as an opera, and its composer, John Bray, again happened to be English. He makes some attempt to match the ethnic origins of certain characters to suitable music. The Indians as an undistinguished group, such as those who drag in Captain Smith for execution,[13] are treated in much the same manner as are Turks by eighteenth-century European composers (see chapter 7): a drone bass supports a tune made up of repetitions of a rhythmic cell, a tune reinforced at its reprise by bald octaves rather than being

EXAMPLE 3.1. Stephen Storace, "Cherokee March"

EXAMPLE 3.2. Stephen Storace, "British March"

harmonically enriched. Yet markers of difference are not as developed here as for the character Larry, whose role is that of the by then familiar stage stereotype, the "comic Irishman." Of course, it is a distinct advantage that he can easily be marked linguistically by his phraseology, such as "to be sure," and by "quaint" expletive vocabulary like "Hubbaboo!" and "Gramachree!"[14] He is also marked as "Irish" by having a girlfriend called Katy: comic Irishmen at this time nearly always have a girlfriend called Molly or Kate.[15] His music incorporates the usual signs of Irishness: a $\frac{6}{8}$ meter, drone fifths, and snap rhythms.[16] In contrast, Pocahontas has a sophisticated aria, "When the Midnight of Absence," which, with its elaborate form, shifting tempo and meter, and melody decorated with appoggiaturas and trills, is perfectly becoming for a princess.[17] Class overrides ethnic difference, as is revealed by the simpler music Bray provides for Alice and Kate. Here, as is often the case in Orientalist representations, the higher orders are less marked, if at all, by signs of the Other.[18]

FROM NOBLE SAVAGE TO BLOODTHIRSTY SAVAGE

The idea of the Noble Savage, the civilized Westerner's simpler, purer, but uncultured counterpart, had become widely known in the eighteenth century through the writings of Enlightenment figures such as Rousseau. As applied to the Native American, the Noble Savage trope, despite a few earlier instances, really belongs to the first half of the nineteenth century. Between 1820 and 1850, "noble" images proliferated in the arts.[19] Washington Irving wrote that the "solitary savage feels silently but acutely" and that his sensibilities ran steadier and deeper than those of the white man.[20] A few years after this remark there appeared James Fenimore Cooper's *The Last of the Mohicans* (1826) with the noble Chingachgook. It was not Cooper's novel, incidentally, but the film adaptation of 1936 that introduced what was to become stereotypical Indian grunting and dialogue of the "paleface make heap big mistake" variety. Some redress was achieved when Native American activist Russell Means got to play Chingachgook in the remake of 1992.

Michael V. Pisani mentions that thirty-five "Indian plays" were produced in North America between 1830 and 1850, though little of the music has survived. They were largely of the Noble Savage type. Alongside this, it should be noted that Pres. Andrew Jackson's Indian Removal Act of 1830 was being implemented by the military during that decade and Native Americans were being coerced to settle in Indian Territory (as Oklahoma was known in the nineteenth century).[21] Jon W. Finson, in discussing the Noble Savage trope in songs of 1835–51, has argued that the implication given in these songs that the Indian was unable to adapt to "civilized" life helped to justify the forced removal of Native Americans "by calling it both natural and mutually agreeable."[22] A significant literary publication of the late 1830s was Henry Rowe Schoolcraft's *Algic Researches,*[23] on which Longfellow's *Song of Hiawatha* (1855) is based (though Longfellow took the poem's meter from the Finnish national epic, the *Kalevala*). Longfellow's poem more or less concludes the literary vogue for Noble Savages. In the 1850s, parodies and burlesques had turned the Indian into an object of ridicule. However, it was the stage Indian that influenced "Indian" devices in concert music of the late nineteenth century according to Pisani, who concludes from a survey of such devices that they "originated on the stage and largely remained there" until composers like Edward MacDowell brought them to the concert hall in the 1890s.[24]

Henry Russell's "The Indian Hunter" has been called the first popular Indian song.[25] Henry Russell, a Jewish singer-songwriter from England, enjoyed much success when he visited New York in 1836[26] and had his first big hit with "Woodman, Spare That Tree!" (1837), a setting of words by George Pope Morris, editor of the *New York Mirror.* In the song "The Indian Hunter" (1842),[27] Russell sets words by Eliza Cook, an English poet and journalist, that suggest, through use of a first person narrative, that most of the hunting is done by the white man who follows the Indian "like the hound on the tiger's track." The subject of this song is a woods Indian not a Plains Indian—the dominant type in Hollywood films[28]—and he pleads to be allowed to live in peace in the forest. The Noble Savage trope in this song follows a typical pattern: the Other has no name (he refers to himself as "the hunter one"); he is defined in terms of place ("the forest shades are mine"; the "golden fields" of corn are the white man's) and skin tone ("my dark cheek" contrasted with the "white man"); he is close to nature ("the spirit that gave the bird its nest, / Made me a home as well") and innocent ("never did harm"). Another penchant of Noble Savages is to make sounds without meaning: here each stanza ends with some vocalizing on the syllable "yha," which, to be fair, actually comes closer than most to the vocables "hey ya" favored by several tribes (see Ex. 3.3).[29]

Beyond that, the song adopts a polite drawing-room style: a limited compass (major ninth), a touch of chromaticism, a couple of modulations, and a short vocal cadenza that precedes the refrain. These features are not dissimilar to those of Russell's better-known songs "A Life on the Ocean

EXAMPLE 3.3. Henry Russell, "The Indian Hunter"

Wave" and "Woodman, Spare That Tree!"[30] It is true that engravings of male figures with bare chests and thighs rarely grace the covers of such sheet music, but that one does so in this case is simply in order to provide one more sign of the Noble Savage. There is, interestingly, no trace of the black-face minstrel style of some of Russell's songs about African-Americans. The $\frac{6}{8}$ meter is a pastoral convention; the only suggestions of the Other, musically, appear in the leaping intervals of the excerpt quoted earlier, and in an earlier vigorous rhythm in the accompaniment—though that could also suggest agitation or the white man in pursuit (see Ex. 3.4).

An indication of the esteem felt for Eliza Cook's words is that they were set to a new tune (with the refrain changed to "Illy oh") by A. F. Knight and published as "The Song of the Red Man."[31] Russell is also credited with another Indian song, "The Chieftain's Daughter" (yes, it is Pocahontas again), with words by George P. Morris.[32] Another song popular in the 1840s might be considered a musical ancestor of Pocahontas's "Colors of the Wind," the hit song from the Disney animated film *Pocahontas* (1995).[33] It was Cora the Indian maiden's "The Wild Free Wind" (music by Alexander Lee) from Shirley Brooks's burletta *The Wigwam*. It begins, "Oh! the wild free wind is a Spirit kind, / And it loves the Indian well."[34]

EXAMPLE 3.4. "The Indian Hunter"

By the mid-1850s, readers, singers, and theater audiences had become bored with the Indian as Noble Savage. In the next decade this stereotype was supplanted by that of the Bloodthirsty Savage. Influential in the construction of this image were the tales of brutality circulated by frontiersmen who, of course, had a vested interest in persuading the government to remove any obstacles to their push westward. The discovery of gold in California in 1848 was a significant factor in the move westward and, at the same time, in ensuring that no treaties entitled Native Americans to land rights on the route to the Pacific. Moreover, 1860–90 was the period of the Indian Wars. In the frontier ballad "Sioux Indians," the bloodthirsty stereotype is fully formed, at least as far as the words go. The Indians in this ballad attack wagon trains for the sheer hell of it,[35] they are merciless, and they whoop and yell. An important distinction for stereotyping is made: cowboys have guns and Indians have bows and arrows, although for an unexplained reason the Sioux Chief has a gun. Pocahontas has not disappeared, either, since that is now the place name of the wagon train's destination. The song is in the Aeolian mode, which was to become a favorite signifier for Indian melody (see Ex. 3.5). Here it is uncertain whether any attempt is being made to present a melody of Indian character, since the Aeolian mode is also common in folk ballads. However, it is important to stress that even where such an intention exists, what we are given is usually a simulacrum, *a copy of an Indian melody that does not exist,* rather than a pseudo-Indian melody. When that kind of melody is recognized as Indian, it is recognized from familiarity with such simulacra alone, not from familiarity with Native American music.

The Bloodthirsty Savage is portrayed as even more violent and ruthless in "Haunted Wood." In this ballad, no sooner has a husband gone out to collect the mail than the Indians descend, throw his wife down the mountain

EXAMPLE 3.5. "Sioux Indians"

to die in agony on the rocks, and set fire to his "little dwelling" with the couple's babies left inside. Yet another song, "Texas Jack," concerns a massacre and scalping by Indians.[36] Not that scalping was an exclusively Indian activity; as early as 1755 the Council Chamber in Boston was offering £40 for male Indian scalps, reduced by half if they were taken from women or boys under twelve.[37] A rare voice of sympathy for Native Americans who have been driven westward only to find that the paleface's "great iron horse is now rumbling in the rear" is found in Henry Clay Work's "The Song of the Redman" (1868).[38]

FROM DISAPPEARING PEOPLES TO ECO-WARRIORS

In the early twentieth century, the perception that the American Indian was disappearing encouraged, in some quarters, a nostalgic return to the Noble Savage trope.[39] The person most prominent in lamenting the supposed passing of the Indian in the first two decades of the twentieth century was the anthropologist James Mooney, and, in the words of Brian W. Dippie, "his heresy became orthodoxy."[40] One factor Mooney failed to take into consideration was absorption, though the brief craze for songs about Irishmen marrying Native American women, prompted by the success of "Arrah Wanna" in 1906,[41] might create an erroneous impression about the extent of ethnic mixing.[42] The Bloodthirsty Savage was to continue to dominate in films, though there were exceptions. An early example of the latter was *The Vanishing American* (1925), and its title (that of Zane Grey's novel on which it is based) certainly did much to promote that enduring twentieth-century myth begun by Mooney, especially since the action was set during 1916–17. It is an irony that Indians only acquired legal status as American citizens the year before the film was released, when many people presumed them to be disappearing. Now it was a matter of providing the Indian with paternalistic care. Zane Grey put it thus: "The Song of Hiawatha is true—true for all Indians. They live in a mystic world of enchantment peopled by spirits, voices, music, whisperings of God, eternal and everlasting immortality. They are as simple as little children."[43] Grey's citing of Longfellow's *Hiawatha* illustrates the power of poetic forms to construct recognizable truths for particular readers. The song "Red Wing" of 1907[44] has no obvious Indian signifiers, but in its childlike simplicity it relates to the quotation from Grey and the perception of native peoples as being like children, an idea ideologically embedded in colonialist discourse. This is the innocent world of Red Wing, who is a "shy little prairie maid" with nothing to do but "while away her day" until her brave returns (though, predictably, he does not).[45] The melody was appropriated with knowing irony by Woody Guthrie for a song about a militant female trade unionist.[46]

   In contrast to the simplicity of "Red Wing," Rudolf Friml's music for "Indian Love Call" (1924)[47] is, in the main, a collection of diverse exotic signs that connote an ill-defined Other. It could easily be a representation of the East, but then, as Gilles Deleuze and Félix Guattari remarked, "America reversed the directions: it put its Orient in the West, as if it were precisely in America that the earth came full circle; its West is the edge of the East."[48] For "America," read the whole of North America; indeed, *Rose Marie,* the musical from which this song comes, is set in Canada. A feature of this song that was to prove common was that the verse rather than refrain plays the larger role in signifying the Other. The verse makes use of angular melodic intervals and whole-tone movement joined to chords with augmented fifths to represent the "love dreams" of "Indian maidens."[49] The refrain has pentatonic inflections, the odd moment of pounding fifths, and, often ignored in performance, a melisma that the printed music shows should be performed by continually restressing the vowel sound "oo." Since it would have been a simple matter to exchange this for one long line that indicated a syllable extension, it is clearly intended as a special effect (see Ex. 3.6).

The Indian enters the ballroom in "Indianola" of 1917.[50] This "instrumental novelty," as it calls itself, opens with percussive chords that signify "Indian drums"[51] and, later, introduces pounding drone fifths while making an effort at an Indian melody—with a *style hongrois* raised fourth (see Ex. 3.7). It is important to remember that meanings arise from the *interrelations* of signs; that is how we recognize this dance piece as a representation of American Indians. Otherwise, taken as a whole, it could be thought an unaccountable mixture of one of Brahms's Hungarian Dances, a powwow, and a fox-trot. It was, after all, merely a novelty item: one of its two composers, S. R. Henry, is credited on the sheet music as the composer of "By Heck," which suggests a reputation for depicting the English North West rather than the American Wild West.

This was not the only occasion on which ballroom dancing was given an Indian dimension. Twenty years later, Ann Dvořák, who performed movingly as the young Indian heroine in the film *Massacre* (1934), raised more than a few eyebrows when, shortly afterward, she sought to popularize a new ballroom dance called the Sioux Stomp.[52]

In the swing era, Indian devices were accommodated into syncopated rhythms. An example is "Big Chief 'Swing It'" (Mitchell-Pollack, 1937). In the excerpt from the verse given in Example 3.8, the Indian signifiers consist of pounding fifths, flattened seventh, chromatic descending bass, and *accia-*

EXAMPLE 3.6. Rudolf Friml, "Indian Love Call"

When I'm calling you____ oo_ oo____ oo-oo - oo!____

EXAMPLE 3.7. S. R. Henry and D. Onivas, "Indianola"

cature. The intention of the latter is made clearer when, later on, the words "Indian whoop" are written above them on the sheet music (see Ex. 3.8).

The last bar of the musical example introduces a minor chord with a major sixth added above its root; just before the coda, this same dissonant harmony is pounded out (see Ex. 3.9). This chord is also an Indian signifier,

EXAMPLE 3.8. Sidney D. Mitchell and Lew Pollack, "Big Chief 'Swing It'"

EXAMPLE 3.9. "Big Chief 'Swing It'" chords

though it bears no relation to anything in Native American musical practice. It is a demonstration that musical signs, cuckoo calls aside, share the arbitrary character of linguistic signs, since this chord has acquired its connotations only through use in Indian pieces of a similar stylistic code. It can found, for example, in the previously discussed "Indianola" (see Ex. 3.10). In slightly altered form (as a dominant ninth) but with similar effect it can be found even in Viennese operetta, set to the same rhythm as in "Indianola" and joined to other familiar signifiers—an "Indian drum" and Phrygian inflections (see Ex. 3.11).[53]

The refrain of "Big Chief," as usual, has less of the Other and features elements of swing more prominently. The song concludes with a *sforzando* chord to accompany the shout, "Ugh!" It would be remiss of me to leave readers with the impression that this song was typical of Indian music in jazz. Charles Barnet provides a marked contrast: his celebrated 1954 recording of Ray Noble's "Cherokee" (1938) is free of obvious Indian signifiers.[54] It met with sufficient admiration, in fact, for him to be honored with membership in the Cherokee Nation. This same piece also was the launching pad for Charlie Parker's early improvisational experiments in 1939 that led directly to bebop, the musical style that replaced swing.[55]

Since, in the nineteenth century, as Michael Pisani found, the stage was the main source of musical signs for the Indian, it is no surprise to discover that, in the twentieth century, film music functioned in a similar way. These signs, it must be stressed, are not clichés, as some people may assume. A cliché has lost its meaning. "Pull the other leg; it's got bells on" is now simply a tiresome way of saying "don't take me for a fool." The Indian signs, however, may be routine stereotypes, but they certainly do possess meaning, and a dehumanizing meaning at that. This can even be the case when the Indian signifier is derived from Native American musical practice. The way

EXAMPLE 3.10. "Indianola" chords

EXAMPLE 3.11. Emmerich Kálmán, "Rose der Prairie"

such material is arranged and the use to which it is put are crucial to the way it is received. The Native Americans in Max Steiner's score to that celluloid eulogy to Custer *They Died with Their Boots On* (1941)[56] are represented by what the composer terms an authentic Indian tune (which he claims to have taken down by ear).[57] However, it receives a treatment similar to the theme associated with the film's devious villain, Sharp. Furthermore, its prominent tritone can easily be interpreted as a conventional marker for evil—an illustration that *even if material is incorporated from a Native American practice, its meaning may still be interpreted in terms of white Western cultural experience.* This is particularly likely to happen since Steiner elsewhere opts to characterize Indians with typical Orientalisms such as "snaking" woodwinds.

For most of the time the semiotics of the film are at the basic level of pounding drums (signifying Indians) and raucous bugles (signifying cavalry). Thus, in the end, Steiner's music embraces the ideological values of the film.[58] The Indians are portrayed as bloodthirsty savages, with the exception of Crazy Horse (the Sioux chief), who is, significantly, played not by a Native American actor but by Anthony Quinn. Nevertheless, we should not conclude that a straitjacket is thereby imposed upon reception: John Fiske has pointed out how the Australian Aboriginal population, for example, construct meanings out of "the white, colonialist ideology of the Western," evading the dominant message and taking pleasure "in the Indians' successes in the middle of the Western narrative," even though this pleasure is, in part, "dependent on their inevitable defeat at the end."[59] It is the end that fixes the film's relevance to the Aboriginal population's immediate social experience.

The impact of Hollywood film scores is seen in the expanded number of signs for Indians and the consistency with which they are used in popular songs. However, the old signs continue to exercise their attraction. The Aeolian mode of "Sioux Indians" reemerges in Hank William's "Kaw-Liga" (cowritten by Williams and Fred Rose), a number-one country hit in February 1953.[60] Kaw-Liga is a wooden Indian, an object that was once a common sight standing outside cigar stores (a convention begun in the nineteenth century).[61] The modal character of the song is especially prominent in the solo violin part, though there is an attendant problem in the lack of Indian associations linked to this instrument. Therefore, to compensate, we are given eight-to-the-bar tom-tom drumming, which would have made a considerable impact since drums were not a feature of Nashville country music at this time. The move from verse to refrain is accompanied by a shift to the major key and the adoption of a full-blown county style. This contrast finds an appropriate match in the lyrics: the verses narrate, apparently sympathetically; the refrain comments scornfully.

In "Running Bear" (J. P. Richardson), a big hit in 1960 and eventual million-seller, Johnny Preston sings of two lovers who belong to two tribes that "fought with each other," and so their love "could never be."[62] The lovers, Running Bear and White Dove, stand on each side of a raging river and die in an attempt to swim to each other—a tragedy relieved for us by the welcome assurance that they will now always be together in "that happy hunting ground." The story is indebted to *Romeo and Juliet* and acquires an added reminiscence of that play when we consider the name White Dove and recollect that Romeo called Juliet a "snowy dove."[63] A final confirmation that this song is not really about Native Americans will be found if one looks it up in Lee Cooper's magisterial guide to themes in American song lyrics. It features under the theme of "Suicide" as well as that of "Dating and Going Steady"[64] (I should point out that there is an entirely separate theme of "Sexual Activity," but that is not thought to apply in this case). The key is major, but simplicity or primitivism is connoted by the tune's construction out of pentatonic fragments (see Ex. 3.12). The eight-to-the-bar tom-tom drumming is present again but now joined by "hoomba hoopa" backing vocals. Once more, signs of difference are reserved for the verses and, just as "Kaw-Liga" moved to a typical country style for its refrain, "Running Bear" switches to a rockabilly style for its refrain. The direction "with a beat" in Example 3.13 may seem superfluous or odd unless it is taken to be an indication to the performer that the straight eights of the verse now give way to a boogie-type bass played with a triplet feel.

This song stands as a warning to those who would seek to find a correspondence between some of its features and actual Native American musical practices. The drumming does indeed suggest a resemblance to certain tribal war dances[65] (though how suitable that is for a song about dating and going steady is debatable), but the backing voices merely echo the familiar "ugh" and grunting sounds of the Hollywood Indian.[66] In fact, this song has a recognizable musical ancestor in the song "What Makes the Red Man Red?" from Walt Disney's *Peter Pan* (1952), which, besides the question in its title, memorably inquires, "When did he first say 'ugh'?" In Disney's film, this forms part of a song and dance interlude introduced by the Big Chief in

EXAMPLES 3.12 AND 3.13. J. P. Richardson, "Running Bear" verse and chorus

order to teach "paleface brother all about red man." Of course, it does nothing but confirm for paleface brother everything he "knows" already. The tune employs the Aeolian mode and is supported by a repetitive drum pattern and "onnawannagunda" chanting that eventually changes into equally meaningless hollering.[67] These nonsense syllables are not, of course, to be confused with the vocables that are substituted for sacred words when Native American songs are performed outside of their ritual contexts.

Signs for Indians had become so well established by the second half of the twentieth century that there was no difficulty separating friend from foe even in instrumentals. The stereotypical Indian enemy was the Apache, despite the fact that there was never a single political, geographical, or tribal group of this name, only a variety of nomadic families, some of whom banded together. In French slang, "apache" came to mean simply "ruffian." The notorious *danse apache* created by Mistinguett and Max Dearly at the Moulin Rouge in 1908 had nothing to do with Native Americans and used as its music an arrangement of the "Valse des Rayons" from Offenbach's ballet *Le Papillon* (1860).[68] In among the Indian drumming in the million-selling instrumental record "Apache" (Jerry Lordan, 1960) by the Shadows,[69] a cowboy presence is detected, intimating that relief from the foe is at hand. It is heard in the twangy guitar and sections in galloping rhythm—both well-established signifiers for cowboys.[70] It opts for the Dorian rather than Aeolian mode, although this would later prove ambiguous, since that mode became a favorite of MGM biblical epics, beginning with *Exodus,* released in the same year as "Apache." In the group's next Indian piece, "Geronimo" of 1963,[71] the combination of a more persistent gallop rhythm joined to brass interjections served, for the most part, to connote cavalry rather than Indians.

In contrast, Johnny Cash's recording of "The Ballad of Ira Hayes" (La Farge) contains no Indian signifiers; in fact, it exchanges them for the signifiers of the white soldier—especially the bugle but also, significantly, the snare drum, rather than tom-tom, that is heard at the very end.[72] The style is Nashville, too. In other words, Cash pays tribute to Ira Hayes by not characterizing him as Other, though the song describes Hayes with a challenging use of two contradictory images, that of a stereotype, "the whisky-drinking Indian," and that of "the marine that went to war." As a patriot, Ira Hayes cannot be given signifiers for Indian, since those may also connote "enemy." Hayes was a member of the Pima tribe who enlisted in the marines in 1942 and soon became a corporal. In 1945 he acquired fame after he appeared in a press photograph taken by Joe Rosenthal that showed him with five others helping to raise the flag on Mount Suribachi during the battle for the island of Iwo Jima:

> His struggle to raise the Stars and Stripes appealed to the sentiments of white America—Hollywood could not have created a better advertisement of a people united against a common foe . . . he personified the hoped-for assimilation of Indians into the mainstream of American life.[73]

Three and a half million war posters carried the picture, and it was also put on three-cent stamps. Yet, despite his heroic renown, Hayes died a destitute alcoholic, aged 33, in 1955. The song attempts to show the contradictions in the image of Hayes as "assimilated Indian" by focusing on white American greed and mistreatment, such as the stealing of water rights from Pima Indians in Phoenix Valley, Arizona. When Cash's record appeared, his emotional performance of the song would have no doubt been related to his own supposed Cherokee roots.[74]

A new Indian stereotype began to take over the popular imagination from around 1970 on, that of the Indian in harmony with nature, noncompetitive, nonmaterialistic, and profoundly wise about the universe.[75] The eco-warrior appeals today because of a wide range of environmental concerns—to name but a few, greenhouse gases, oil spills, acid rain, and toxic waste. Unfortunately, this image can prove no less dehumanizing and also has a tendency to imply that Native Americans are unable to cope with the grim practicalities of modern life. How shocking it is for some to see litter lying around on a modern reservation! The fear then follows that the Native Americans' culture is being eroded and needs to be preserved by white anthropologists.[76] In 1970 Dee Brown, in *Bury My Heart at Wounded Knee,* provided an Indian perspective on the American West, countered the ruthless savage myth, and expressed the hope that readers would "learn something about their own relationship to the earth from a people who were true conservationists."[77] A film that showed what it was like to be on the receiving end of an attack by General Custer was *Little Big Man* (1970), a satire that served an allegorical function in the context of U.S. involvement in Vietnam. A book that had an impact on awareness about what modern society was doing to the earth and, at the same time, established a firm link between Native Americans and environmentalism followed soon after; it was *God Is Red* by Sioux scholar Vine Deloria, Jr.[78]

In the 1980s there was a tendency to cast well-worn Indian signifiers aside. In "City of Dreams," David Byrne's subject is the legendary domain of the Caddo Indians who were wiped out by the Spanish when the latter moved into Texas.[79] The message of the song is if we can all live together this dream of the Caddo can come true. A perhaps surprising sympathy has been shown for the plight of the Native American within the genre of Heavy Metal. There is Iron Maiden's "Run to the Hills" (Harris), which deals with oppression and genocide, and Hawkwind's "Black Elk Speaks," in which Black Elk does indeed speak. The Iron Maiden song is notable for its adoption of two different enunciating subjects: the first two verses are given as if issuing from the mouth of a Cree singer, but then the viewpoint shifts to that of an onlooker who vents anger.[80] This is a subtle variant of the *verse = Other, refrain = Self* format found in "Kaw-Liga" and "Running Bear."

In the 1990s new signs became established as the Indian stereotype moved decisively to that of eco-warrior, in touch with nature and the vibrations of the universe. The film *Dances with Wolves* (1990) set the tone.[81] In a contemporary review, critic Dan Georgakas could not resist accusing the main character, John Dunbar, of spouting "New Age gibberish" such as "As I heard my Sioux name being called, I knew for the first time who I really was," but concluded his review approvingly: "Moviegoers in the United States have finally reached a state of consciousness where they applaud and identify with a daring individual who is willing to approach Native Americans as fellow human beings rather than as hostile Others."[82] It is an image, however, that not only conjures up New Age mysticism, as Georgakas recognized, but also demands a role in ambient dance tracks. In respect of these shifting attitudes, John Barry's romantic score was not as innovative musically as the film itself was in its representation of the Lakota Sioux.[83] Ry Cooder went further in his music to *Geronimo: An American Legend* (1993), having been asked by the director, Walter Hill, to find sounds to valorize cultures of both sides.[84]

The first album that was not originally a soundtrack and that most fully capitalized on the new (and desired) image was *Sacred Spirit* (1995).[85] It was a best-seller, and undoubtedly its carefully chosen title coupled to a cover that contained a Christ-like image of a Native American reproduced in nostalgic sepia contributed to that commercial success.[86] As part of the album's nonmaterialistic character, however, it came with a promise that a donation would be made to the Native American Rights Fund for each album sold. There appeared to be a widespread readiness to believe that a cognitive understanding of the meaning of the chants contained within its washes of atmospheric synthesized sounds was unnecessary, that one could understand them intuitively as a kind of nonrational communion with nature. One track from *Sacred Spirit* that includes samples of Native Americans chanting was advertised on British TV (Nov. 1995) as being part of a "great instrumentals" compilation album. That description is not without a certain logic, because the chant is packaged to be consumed as linguistically meaningless. The excerpt of chant played in the advertisement prompts no debate about logocentrism; it is, indeed, to be accepted as an instrumental. These Native Americans are producing sounds without meaning, thus signifying their closeness to the earth by identifying with nature rather than discursive meaning. Some of the romantic arrangements[87] on this disc recall Marjory Kennedy-Fraser's reinterpretations of Gaelic music making in *Songs of the Hebrides*. On the one hand, listen to the modal harmonies and romantic cello obbligato in "Wishes of Happiness and Prosperity" (track 7). On the other hand, "Celebrate Wild Rice" (track 4) is "housed up" with a looped Phrygian ostinato figure and other features that lend it the character of a dance piece for late-twentieth-century urban club culture. Sampling technology has undoubtedly allowed greater use to be made of Native American music in the 1990s, since features that once proved so difficult to reproduce vocally or instrumentally could now be sampled and looped into ambient or "chill out" music. It might have seemed that the potential of this music had been exhausted, however, when *Sacred Spirit Volume 2* abandoned Native American chants and attempted, instead, to create a fusion between classical music and the blues.[88] Again the album boasted a charitable purpose: support of the nonprofit Rhythm and Blues Foundation. However, other record companies were ready to satisfy the demand for more in the way of the first *Sacred Spirit*: the album *Raindance* used a title font with "As" made to look like tepees and styled itself "an ambient musical experience inspired by Native American chants."[89]

Since 1980, films and TV have reproduced a range of received ideas about Native Americans, many of which contradict one another. Even in *Dances with Wolves* there is a contradiction in the way the Pawnee are represented, compared to the Sioux (it carries a suggestion of bad Indian, good Indian). One of the most enduring images in American TV advertising is that of the "crying Indian"; it was first shown in the 1970s but was still being used as an image of environmental concern at the end of the century. When he died in 1999, the actor who played the Indian, widely believed to be Cherokee, was found to be the son of an Italian greengrocer.[90] Native Americans as objects of amusement rather than fear featured in a British TV advertisement for Mars chocolate bars in 1997. These confectionery treats were shown to have the same euphoric disorienting effect as the "firewater" of countless old westerns: an elderly member of the tribe tastes one and is suddenly seized with lust for "Little Flower."[91] Yet running concurrently with this was an Organics hair shampoo advertisement in which a "modern" Native American woman visits her wise, dignified mother and father on the reservation. Unfortunately, the advertisement's punning message about "needing to get to your roots" did little to complement the high-minded imagery. The favorite image, however, is the Indian as eco-warrior, the specifics of tribe, time, and place being of no great concern. As I write, in September 2000, the *New Internationalist Magazine* has been trying for some weeks to attract new subscribers by running an advertisement that quotes an anonymous Cree comment: "Only when the last tree has been poisoned and the last fish been caught will we realise we cannot eat money." Unfortunately, photographs of wise Cree elders must have proved elusive, for we are given instead a photograph of Wolf Robe, a Southern Cheyenne, taken in 1909.

Where songs of the 1990s were concerned, there was not the same willingness to tolerate stereotyping that can be found in earlier decades. In 1994 "Indian Outlaw"[92] sung by Tim McGraw, created controversy. The song borrows the violin solo from "Kaw-Liga" and quotes from Don Fardon's 1968 hit "Indian Reservation,"[93] but it was the lyrics that gave particular offense. Jo Kay Dowell, coordinator for the American Indian Movement of Northeastern Oklahoma, stated:

> Some people seem to think that those who practice our traditional culture don't exist anymore, but that's not true, and this song is offensive to those people that do. "Sitting in my wigwam, beating on my tomtom," this is the image we've been fighting against for the past 500 years.[94]

NATIVE AMERICAN PERFORMERS OF POPULAR MUSIC

That there are today more than 3 million registered tribal members spread across the whole of North America adds to the absurdity of the misconception that there was a homogeneous Indian culture that disappeared shortly after the last battle of the Indian Wars at Wounded Knee (1890). There has always existed a diversity of regional cultures, many of which not only survived the twentieth century but also have entered the twenty-first century revitalized. If, however, there is one shared quality among Native American cultures, it is a spiritual character coupled to an idea of a "life harmony" or balanced world. Native Americans remain active in environmental matters and have been at the fore in staging cultural events to raise awareness of their importance: for example, the Honor the Earth powwow that has been an annual event in Wisconsin since 1971. Native American cultures are not museum relics; they are living and changing. In the sociopolitical sphere, one could point to Wilma Mankiller, who became the first woman chief of the Cherokee Nation in 1987. In the economic sphere, one could point to the phenomenon of the Indian casino, an institution that flourishes as a result of reservations being exempt from state laws on gambling.[95] In the artistic sphere, there is no better example of the process of adaptability and change within Native American cultural traditions than the output of musicians. The Tohono O'odham tribe of southern Arizona, for example, started playing dance music of Mexican and European origin as long ago as the end of the nineteenth century.[96] Some uses of music are, indeed, intertribal (victory powwows and healing songs, for example), but the diversity of genres and styles found among the different Native American peoples increased, rather than narrowed or disappeared, during the twentieth century. Today Native American musicians will be found performing in all popular styles or fusing them with their own traditions. Some examples may be mentioned: Bill Miller with his country style, the jazz-influenced wooden flautist R. Carlos Nakai, Redbone with their Cajun style, the folky singer-guitarist Sharon Burch, the rappers WithOut Rezervation, Walela with their gospel-like style, the Latin-influenced trio Burning Sky, and the internationally esteemed Joanne Shenandoah, who mixes pop, country, and traditional in the songs she writes and performs. It should not be thought that the incorporation of traditional elements serves merely to provide a spicy ethnicity to otherwise familiar idioms. Shenandoah's music, for instance, is founded on a comprehensive knowledge of a huge collection of Iroqois music amassed by herself and her husband.[97] In 1997 Andy Bausch's film documentary *Rockin' Warriors* was premiered at the American Indian Film Festival in San Francisco, showing evidence of the extent of Native American involvement in rock, jazz, blues, and rap.

I have been reserving discussion of Buffy Sainte-Marie, one of the pioneers of fusion between folk, pop, and Native American musical practices, in order to collect some final thoughts together. She did, of course, write the title song for the film *Soldier Blue* (1970). She explained that its lines "Yes, this is my country" and "Can't you see there's another way to love her?" were to be understood in the context of the song's overall message, which "is not about loving one's own nation state; it's about loving the natural environment."[98] There is much Native American influence to be found in her songs. Sometimes, as in "Soldier Blue," it is located in the words rather than the music.[99] Other examples are the politically charged songs "Now That the Buffalo's Gone" (still relevant today as indigenous lands are once more being eyed acquisitively) and "Bury My Heart at Wounded Knee." Sometimes it is present in both words and music, as in the song "Starwalker." An uplifting example of her work is "Darling Don't Cry", which she cowrote with Edmund Bull and describes as a "cross-the-borders" pop song. On this song she is joined by the Red Bull Singers, and she says of it that she would "love the world to know about grassroots powwow music."[100] The "hey ya" refrain provides an interesting point of comparison with Russell's "The Indian Hunter." In "Darling Don't Cry" we see how a stereotype may be overcome: the drumming here does not connote the usual message of fear but stirs the body to excitement. It is, as Buffy Sainte-Marie emphasizes, the "heartbeat drum," a conception that lies within Native American culture but one blocked to outsiders who hear the "Indian drum" only through the distorting reminiscences of their own cultural representations.[101] This song offers an opportunity for myth to fall away, as pleaded for by Sioux author Vine Deloria, Jr.[102]

My intention in this chapter has not been to present a round condemnation of stereotyping.[103] Even stereotypes need not be entirely negative: their function as a critical stimulus in allegorical fantasy and in the *mundus inversus* of the carnival (as analyzed by Mikhail Bakhtin) is well known to cultural theorists.[104] However, I have been trying to demonstrate that most of the musical representations I have been discussing tell us only about the way white Americans and Europeans build their own sense of identity, and reveal little or nothing about the people who are supposedly the subject of those representations. Even carnivalesque inversions *enlighten us only about the persons whose values are being inverted*, rather than offering an insight into the culturally alien. The Buffy Sainte-Marie song just cited succeeds, I think, in communicating a deeper awareness of the cultural energy of those she identifies with as her people. Listeners with a white Western cultural background will, of course, hear it as a Western popular song that embodies difference. Yet, the raison d'être of that difference is not simply that it differs *from those particular listeners*, as was the case with so many earlier popular songs. Instead, it offers a positive insight into a different culture—a culture that, paradoxically, also happens to be Western.

INCONGRUITY AND PREDICTABILITY

IN BRITISH DANCE BAND MUSIC

OF THE 1920S AND 1930S

THIS CHAPTER WAS PROMPTED by a number of questions: How do we approach the study of British dance band music of these vintage years? Do they represent a golden age in quantity rather than quality? Is it possible to construct criteria for deciding what is good and bad in music whose social moment has passed? I am particularly interested in asking these questions of dance band music of the 1920s and 1930s because, despite the enormous attraction dance bands held for a majority of people in the United Kingdom between the two world wars and despite this period's mythic status as the "golden era" of the dance band (at least in the eyes of the publicists for the record industry), it is not uncommon to find dance band music neglected or despised (usually when compared to "real" jazz) even by writers normally sympathetic to popular music. How do we explain the contradictory response to an old dance band record summed up in the phrase "wonderfully awful"? Perhaps, in this particular case, the answer is that such things as humor and sentimentality are very period-specific; they quickly become dated, and so an old record often seems to lend insight into the way people felt at a specific time that, being past, in turn evokes nostalgia and a feeling of empathy with those whose lifetimes preceded our own. At the same time, it must be acknowledged that when we respond in such a manner the meaning of the music to us differs from its meaning to its original listeners—a neat illustration that history and aesthetics are not mutually exclusive categories.

Is it at all possible, then, to take any steps toward finding answers to the preceding questions in the current relativistic climate, or can we speak only of differences rather than aesthetic values? What methodology, distinct from that used in the study of Western classical music, is best suited to a consideration of the aesthetics of dance band music of the 1920s and 1930s? Two favorite attacks made by critics of commercial popular music are: (1) to claim it is cliché-ridden and (2) to condemn it for being badly performed. The first can be parried by considering the music from the point of reception (for example, certain structural parameters may be "standardized," but how predictable does the listener find the music as a whole?). The second can be countered by considering matters of incongruity. Incongruity is produced as the effect of conflict between stylistic codes, so that the conventional meanings of these codes are negated or thwarted. Alternatively, one might say that incongruity results when predictability is avoided by unstylish means. This may be unintentional and therefore likely to produce purposeless conflict or confusion of meaning or premeditated conflict, as is the case with parody, where a clash of codes is used deliberately so as to provoke critical awareness of style.

INCONGRUOUS MIXING OF STYLES

By the turn of the twentieth century, Britain had long adopted a European classical perspective on what constituted qualitative norms in music and was restaking its own claims as a major player in this field with composers such as Elgar, Holst, and Vaughan Williams. Moreover, there was a history of importing elite French, Italian, and German music to satisfy the tastes of the English, Scottish, and Anglo-Irish aristocracy. Now if we note that before the 1890s the only musical import associated with North America was blackface minstrelsy and that this was followed by a variety of other popular styles, such as the songs of Tin Pan Alley, ragtime, and jazz, the complexity of the reception given to jazz and of the cultural environment within which British dance bands emerged can easily be imagined. An immediate way in which the contradictory welcome given to popular music from the United States becomes apparent is in the urge to mix elite and popular styles. Yet this desire to elude the vulgar often creates incongruity, since what counts as "good" in elite music may not be regarded as being so in popular music, and vice versa. Consider the incongruous effect of quasi-operatic singing on some early dance band records[1]—even as late as Henry Hall's recording in 1936 of "It's a Sin to Tell a Lie," Elizabeth Scott is still "operatic" (perhaps an indication of how enduring an influence the BBC's efforts to encourage "highbrow" taste had been).[2] The incongruous mix of styles is also found in the United States (the Silver-Masked Tenor). What does it tell us about style? Is it not simply *good* singing? These singers certainly possess the skills to excel in one kind of music, but that proficiency is no more apt for this idiom than Frank Sinatra's for singing "On the Road to Mandalay" (Kipling-Speaks), which he once misguidedly did. The "classical" voice can be related to instrumental techniques and standards of beauty of tone production within that style. Dance band songs have their own range of associated vocal techniques that are not found in elite music—scatting, growling (both pioneered by Louis Armstrong), speaking, whistling, whispering, crooning, yodeling, and smearing or bending notes (and many of these can also be related to dance band instrumental techniques, for example the use of a plunger mute to create a growling sound on trumpet or trombone). Even the singer's pronunciation may be a crucial part of style: many British singers in the 1930s felt the need to adopt American accents to sing dance band songs stylishly, just as British singers in the 1970s felt it necessary to use an American southern accent for country music.[3] Some singers adopted the new crooning style, sometimes even a "dirty" jazzy style. Some performers developed more than one style of singing: Gracie Fields, for example, could sing in either her comic "cracked" voice or her "classical" voice, both with commercial success.[4] Two performers, each adopting a different singing style, can persuade the audience to think of the same song as belonging to two differing genre categories. Indeed, Charles Hamm has gone as far as to argue that the audience's perception of the meaning of a song, "shaped at the moment of performance by the singer's vocal quality, diction, and other nuances of delivery," is more important to definitions of genre in popular music than is formal structure.[5]

Any criticism of vocal style that fails to take account of the problem of incongruity is going to misfire. The classical listener may accuse the dance band singer of unclear vowels, exaggerated vibrato, insincere accent, nasal production, and so forth, in the mistaken belief that excellence is to be attained by adopting classical practices. However, a musical style is a discursive code that has developed from the solidification of conventions, and although it may be subject to further development and change, that process cannot be achieved by rupturing, negating, or contradicting its most important and defining attributes.

The mix of jazz and folk was something else that was tried out in the 1930s. This is a stylistic hybrid that returns periodically as a fusion that seems possible and, indeed, desirable to some.[6] Leonard Feather was the first to have the idea of jazzing up English traditional airs and recorded two arrangements in 1937. The next year he re-formed what he called Ye Olde English Swynge Band, which now included West Indian musicians Dave Wilkins (trumpet) and Bertie King (tenor saxophone), with the support of Harry Sarton at Decca.[7] Interest then faded, but further attempts along these lines were made by others after the war. The assumption was often made that because jazz and folk could both be fitted into the same ideological category of "authentic proletarian voice distorted by culture industry" there ought to be a similar fit between their musical idioms. The difficulty here is that, as Gino Stefani has pointed out, style codes are not only rooted in social practices but are also "a blend of technical features, a way of forming objects or events."[8]

Certain other stylistic fusions occurred as a result of shared repertoires, with varying degrees of incongruity in performance. The dividing line between the military band repertoire and that of the dance band or the light orchestra was not sharply drawn. In the 1920s, for example, Léon Jessel's "The Parade of the Tin [or Wooden] Soldiers" (1911) was commonly played by all three. The music is described as a "Fox Trot or March" but bears little resemblance to the former (besides, the origins of the fox-trot are normally traced back only as far as 1913). Even in the 1940s, the Squadronaires[9] played the occasional military band piece, such as "American Patrol" (Meacham),[10] and military bands sometimes played for dances (though they had to endure the grumbles and sarcastic comments of those dancers who found their style too rigid).[11] The "light classics" were another, and bigger, source of potential dance band repertoire: the popular song "Moonlight and Roses," for example, was adapted from Edwin H. Lemare's Andantino in D♭ (1892) by Ben Black and Neil Morét (1925). Ted Heath's band[12] played everything from "Olde Englyshe" airs to Debussy's "Clair de Lune."

INCONGRUITY BETWEEN MUSIC AND LYRICS

Occasionally an element that would appear to be incongruous with the verbal content of a dance band number is, nevertheless, pertinent to the musical style. Take the strangely withdrawn quality of male trios even where the mood of the words seems to dictate exuberance, a striking example of which occurs in Jack Hylton's recording of "Happy Days Are Here Again."[13] How happy do the singers sound compared to the good-humored trombone and the effect of joyous tap dancing with musical pitches created by the 16-bar xylophone solo? And how are we to understand the meaning of a trio singing as one person, as in Lew Stone's recording of "Zing! Went the Strings of My Heart"?[14] Again, this occurs alongside some otherwise readily grasped instrumental word painting ("zinging" strings on the guitar). These trios, as well as duets such as that on the Savoy Orpheans' recording of "Baby Face,"[15] challenge Peter Wicke's contention that it was the Beatles who introduced the collective "we" in opposition to the romanticized "I" of earlier love songs.[16]

INCONGRUITY BETWEEN DANCE BAND STYLE AND CLASSICAL STYLE

One of the most radical departures from classical vocal style in dance band records was the amplification of a soft voice. In classical style, where balancing sound is a matter for composers, not studio producers, such a voice tone would sound incongruous and suggest an artificial remedy had been sought for a lack of projection techniques. The change from recording horn to microphone with the advent of electric recording in 1924–25 made possible the popularity of the crooners "Whispering" Jack Smith, Rudy Vallee, and, in the United Kingdom, Al Bowlly. "Whispering" Jack Smith was a frequent visitor to Britain from 1926 to 1930, recording with Bert Ambrose[17] and Richard Caroll Gibbons.[18] Smith's version of "My Blue Heaven" was an enormous success and helped to establish the new crooning style.[19] It is still debated whether or not Smith crooned from necessity (a lung injury from a wartime gassing) or as a novelty (possible only with the new microphone technology). Crooning worked well for records, since it added to the intimacy of a musical commodity that could be consumed personally and privately in the home.

It is, in general, incongruous with classical style for instruments to be given priority over voices when both were used, but that such priority was for a long time the case with dance bands is shown by the anonymity of singers of vocal refrains on record labels of the 1920s and by Lew Stone's trick, even well into the 1930s, of asking band members to take vocal refrains. The individual identity of singers was deemed relatively unimportant until Al Bowlly built a following of admirers.

Recording technology was most notably exploited in matters of balance: only with the arrival of the microphone was the double bass able to replace the tuba, the former being all but inaudible on acoustic recordings. The "artificial" balance of the microphone recording opened up a new world of possibilities that inevitably conflicted with classical orchestration, the fundamental skill of which was to create a "natural" balance of sound among instruments (and voices). Recording technology could be used to create novel effects. Billy Cotton's record "I've Got Sixpence" (1941) has a fade-out ending; that is to say, it exploits the possibilities of sound recording to produce an effect that could not be reproduced in live performance.[20] The impression given by this record is that Cotton's band is marching toward the listener at the beginning and marching away again at the end, playing all the while. Henry Hall's record "Rusty and Dusty" (1936) has a similar fade effect, but on this occasion the song remains a complete musical entity: the fade is a technologically engineered *crescendo* and *diminuendo* that could just about be emulated live.[21] It demonstrates an initial reluctance to move beyond the bounds of what was possible in live performance, the reason for such reluctance being, perhaps, that commercial music was at this time thought of as a literate culture typified in commodity terms by the song sheet and not as an electronic oral culture typified by records. Evidence for this is given by the common practice of releasing simultaneously different band arrangements of new songs: consumers were expected to buy the interpretation they preferred. Only when sales of records began to overtake sheet music sales in the mid-1950s did a record that was particularly successful come to represent the Urtext of a song. This, in turn, gave rise to the practice of releasing budget-price recordings that closely copied an existing record, rather than offering an alternative interpretation.[22]

THE SOCIOCULTURAL CONTEXT OF DANCE BAND MUSIC

Since the problems of incongruity outlined earlier are as much involved with the historical and social context of the production of dance band music as with its technical features, we should seek to understand what was peculiar about the cultural context in which this new music emerged and established itself. For example, how important for the emergence of a distinctive cultural epoch, characterized as the "jazz age," was the decline in infant mortality rates during the first quarter of the twentieth century? After all, the "rock revolution" is often traced to the post–Second World War baby boom that produced the teenage market of the late 1950s. There was an unexpectedly large number of young people around in 1918 to take the place of those who had been slaughtered in the First World War, and many of those born in the new century would have been too young to have fought in that conflict. Furthermore, the psychological effect of being born near the start of the new century must have contributed to a sense of difference. A distinctive generation, therefore, was ready to identify with a distinctive and, in many ways, consciously oppositional music.

It is not surprising that this generation should favor songs with romantic, escapist, even frivolous lyrics, in reaction to the "improving" tone of drawing-room ballads and the association of the latter with the call of morality, duty, and patriotism for which so many lives had recently been lost in a questionable cause. Perhaps this explains why dance music, unlike the music hall, succeeded in winning over a large fraction of the middle and upper classes. In consequence, a figure such as Ambrose acted as a symbol of a broad class alliance, which stretched from the wealthy clientele of the Mayfair Hotel (see Fig. 4.1) to the working-class family who listened to his band

FIGURE 4.1. Bert Ambrose and his band at the Mayfair Hotel in 1932 (photo © Hulton Deutsch)

at home on the wireless. During the depression, for example, Ambrose's "The Clouds Will Soon Roll By," recorded at the Mayfair Hotel in 1932, could have been interpreted symbolically as a plea for patience and restraint and, if so, would have performed the hegemonic function of urging people to resist being drawn into class antagonism.[23] The years immediately after the First World War had witnessed some major political upheavals at home and abroad, troubling to both the Left and the Right: in the autumn of 1923, for example, Mussolini had consolidated his power (becoming Il Duce), and in December of that year Britain's first Labour government (under Ramsay MacDonald) was elected. Dole and the means test had been the fate of many after the First World War, and consequently the emotional temperature of the United Kingdom was running high.

PREDICTABILITY OF REPERTOIRE AND PERFORMANCE

The repertoire of some bands was more predictable than others. Accordion bands were inevitably drawn towards tangos, just as banjo bands found the blackface minstrel repertoire irresistible. Accordion bands were a feature of the 1930s; the most famous, Primo Scala (real name: Harry Bidgood) and His Accordion Band, was formed in 1934. Accordion bands, mandolin bands, and banjo bands all featured a rhythm section of piano, bass (sometimes bass banjo in banjo bands), and drums and often a xylophone (which provided an attractive percussive contrast with the reedy accordion tone).

Black performers found themselves affected by predictability—the audience's expectation that they should perform in a certain way. The history of the involvement of black musicians in British popular music of this period has been only recently the subject of research.[24] Small black bands, however, were not uncommon in London clubs by 1920, and these bands included not only African-Americans but also Africans and West Indians. The Versatile Four (two banjos, piano, and drums) performed in the clubs from 1913 and had some success in 1919 with their recording of "After You've Gone."[25]

The history of blackface minstrelsy weighed heavily upon black performers at the same time as it accounted for the continuing attraction of blackface performers such as Al Jolson and G. H. Elliot. Jolson was heir to the emotionalism and sentimentality of the U.S. postbellum minstrels, as Elliot was inheritor of the "refined" style of minstrelsy that dated back to troupes of the 1840s such as the Virginian Serenaders and Ethiopian Serenaders.[26] Much blackface minstrelsy and associated music had been misrecognized as a part of a real African-American culture rather than as an ideological construct: for example, Alfred Scott Gatty's *Plantation Songs* (published in the 1880s) represented a realistic picture of plantation life for many Victorians. When Sam Hague's all-black, ex-slave minstrel troupe toured Britain in 1866, he emphasized their "naturalness." Yet, like succeeding black troupes, they were not natural but working, instead, within white expectations of the genre. Black bands at first found themselves judged by minstrel standards, and early jazz musicians found it almost impossible to disentangle themselves from minstrel business. There was no obvious alternative to this way of performing to a white audience. As an example of confusion that concerned jazz and blackface one has only to think of the first talkie, *The Jazz Singer* (Warner, 1927), starring Al Jolson. It was a confusion that existed in the United States as well as Europe and was shared by both audiences and performers. Bing Crosby was regarded by many as a stylish jazz singer in the 1930s, yet David Brackett maintains that biographical evidence "strongly suggests that minstrel performers such as Al Jolson and Eddie Cantor were stronger influences on the young Crosby than King Oliver or Bessie Smith."[27]

As far as the music is concerned, however, it cannot be emphasized too strongly that while the score may appear predictable, the performance may not be so. The major figures in dance band music are generally performers rather than songwriters, a fact that indicates a particular musical emphasis. For we study the bulk of the commercial popular music of the 1920s and 1930s through recordings, whether live, radio, or studio recordings (the last often being one of several takes). In a survey of classical music we would examine scores; but even for a dance band record with little or no improvisation, the score of the arrangement is an inadequate representation of the music. To clarify the position, we might contrast the relative ease of studying a stage play from the printed page with the difficulty of studying a film from its screenplay. In the case of a film, the montage, the photography, the soundtrack, and an actor's performance may each at times take precedence over the script. There are those who, where dance bands are concerned, value recordings for the extent to which players *depart* from a literal reading of the score; this is a criterion for assessing value that is completely at odds with judgments on contemporaneous "art" music. As Rose Rosengard Subotnik has remarked, "The ideal of structural listening has made our perceptions and analytical concerns as musicologists almost completely dependent on scores, as if the latter were books."[28]

Most important, the nature of jazz improvisation must be considered. If transcribed, it will often produce complex notation (for example, five against three) and awkward-looking syncopation. Of course, it could be argued that "expressive" playing produces a similar effect on the rhythm of other kinds of music: a computer transcription of a concert harpsichordist playing the C-major Prelude from book 1 of Bach's *Well-Tempered Clavier* would not reveal a succession of even quavers. However, jazz flexibility differs in that it is part of a polyrhythmic structure. A predictable rhythmic pattern in an unchanging tempo may form the background to an unpredictable and rhythmically flexible improvisation. The question of how much of this flexibility is demonstrated by a dance band is therefore crucial for many jazz enthusiasts and can be used as a yardstick by which to judge the band's jazz credentials.[29]

In the late twenties a group of influential musicians and critics was determined to define jazz in a particular way. Indeed, but for the fact that "jazz" had stuck as a label for syncopated music, they would have preferred a more dignified term, such as "rhythm style," for the music they wished to privilege.[30] The key figures were Edgar Jackson, editor of the then monthly music paper *Melody Maker,* and bandleaders Bert Firman and Fred Elizalde. Jackson attempted to distinguish as true jazz music innovative in style, which contained improvised solos. He was as committed to the idea of progress as any modernist of the concert hall and heard evidence of progress in recordings of white rather than black musicians, interpreting performances by the former as innovative and polished and by the latter as retrogressive and crude. In his review of Duke Ellington's "Black and Tan Fantasy" in *Melody Maker,* in March 1928, Jackson states that he has considered previous records by Ellington's band to be "highly crude."[31] It is ironic that the tune he now finds "far above the average in melody" is Bubber Miley's minor-key version of the refrain of Stephen Adams's drawing-room ballad "The Holy City" (1892).

The influence of white American bands such as Red Nichols and His Five Pennies suffuses the early Zonophone recordings Bert Firman (b. 1906) made with his Dance Orchestra and, especially, with the Rhythmic Eight (not always eight in number). As musical director of Zonophone, Firman must have had enviable freedom of choice, and these 1926 recordings, with their improvised solos, lay claim to be the first British examples of jazz that complied with Jackson's redefinition of that term. Firman was first influenced by the two-beat ragtime style but moved to a four-beat style before the decade ended. The four-beat bar of "Painting the Clouds with Sunshine" (Dubin-Burke) recorded in 1929[32] allows greater variety of syncopation and a more interesting bass part. The first chorus sounds like classic New Orleans three-part polyphony, except that the front line is clarinet, trumpet, and, instead of trombone, tenor saxophone.[33] Hot as it is for British jazz of this period, it is still dominated by "paraphrase improvisation"—a term coined by André Hodeir to describe improvisation based on the original melody.[34]

Fred Elizalde (1907–79) started a jazz group with his brother at the University of Cambridge in 1927, then led a band at the Savoy that included ex-members of the California Ramblers. A "progressive" feature of some of Elizalde's recordings is their move away from paraphrase improvisation toward improvisation around chord changes. The technique can be heard in "Misery Farm" (Wallis) of 1928,[35] the singer on which is Al Bowlly (1899–1941), whose first engagement in Britain was with this band. Elizalde was voted number one in a *Melody Maker* poll in November 1928, indicating the paper had become a focal point for jazz enthusiasts. Opinions elsewhere differed: the BBC stopped broadcasting his band in the spring of 1929, and the Savoy management terminated his contract in the summer.[36] His music was not at home in the cultural environment of the upper-class hotel and was obviously regarded as morally suspect by the BBC, yet Elizalde's artistic aspirations for jazz extended to his writing concert suites.

Another important figure in British jazz at this time was Patrick "Spike" Hughes (1908–87), who recorded for Decca in the early 1930s with his Dance Orchestra (at first called the Decca-Dents, a name that pointed with punning humor to the disapproval some felt for the music). His band included Americans, and his records met all the criteria of the latest "real" jazz: "It's Unanimous Now" (Stept-Green), for example, is four-beat and full of improvisation around chords and contains jazz devices such as the two-bar chase (one solo succeeding another at two-bar intervals).[37] Hughes enthused about black jazz musicians, a symptom of a changing mood and future challenge to Jackson's theoretical paradigm. However, Hughes's idea of jazz stood as far outside the dominant musical aesthetics of the time as did Elizalde's. Nevertheless, an event in 1932 showed that there was a growing oppositional cultural formation given identity by the popular music paper *Melody Maker*. On Monday, 18 July, Louis Armstrong began his British visit by performing at the London Palladium. He came without a band of his own and was part of a variety bill. The reception ranged from surprised bewilderment to the ecstasy of *Melody Maker* readers whose excitement had been stirred up beforehand. When Duke Ellington and His Orchestra visited in 1933, *Melody Maker* arranged a special concert for jazz cognoscenti at the Trocadero Cinema, Elephant and Castle. Ellington wrote of that occasion in his book *Music Is My Mistress:*

> We were to avoid "commercial" numbers and apparently on this occasion we lived up to expectations because Spike Hughes, the foremost critic at that time, didn't criticize us at all. Instead, he criticized the audience for applauding at the end of solos and in the middle of numbers! That's how serious it was.[38]

Ellington had begun his visit as Turn Number 13, last on the bill, at the Palladium, something he took easily in his stride. His puzzlement at the Trocadero is another matter. As late as 1939 he was proclaiming, "Sure I'm commercial."[39] He seems to have remained unaware that being "uncommercial" was crucial to the arguments of Jackson and Hughes (the latter writing under the pseudonym Mike in *Melody Maker*), who were struggling to achieve recognition for jazz as a form of "art music."

In the early 1930s, despite efforts by Jackson, Hughes, and others, jazz was still being defined by reference to dance music: "I have played dance-music with genuine sincerity of purpose," claimed Jack Hylton, "for I believe that in many ways clever and melodious 'jazz-music' portrays the spirit of this age."[40] This is not to say "jazz" was being used as an undiscriminating term. The criteria that underlie the aesthetic values of Stanley Nelson's *All about Jazz* (1934), for example, may seem very different from Jackson's, but all these criteria are alike in that each writer sees jazz evolving along approved lines. Nelson makes the revealing comment: "From the jungle to the ballroom is a long step and jazz has undergone a refinement in keeping with such a transition."[41] Jackson's own notions of progress and refinement marginalized the efforts of many black musicians. Constant Lambert, in 1934, argued against jungle metaphors but stated: "The next move in the development will come, almost inevitably, from the sophisticated or highbrow composers," because they alone can rid jazz of its "nightclub element," the way Haydn rid the minuet of its "ballroom element."[42] It is difficult to imagine how this would work with Ellington's "Hot and Bothered," which Lambert so admired. He was merely replacing one disparaging label ("jungle music") with another ("nightclub music"). Elizalde, in contrast, pleaded for jazz to be thought of as "an art apart, and not in any way comparable to the classics."[43]

THE PREDICTABLE, THE FUNCTIONAL, AND EXTRAMUSICAL NECESSITIES

In order not to confuse the predictable with the functional, it is important to weigh the importance of differing extramusical necessities when considering the musical output of the *palais* (or dance hall) band, the show band, and the radio band. In trying to understand how the popular music of this period was consumed, the importance of the dance is not to be underestimated. The primary function of much of this music was what anthropologists term conative, its main object being the regulation of physical movement. In the 1960s, the dance as a set piece for couples that demanded many prelearned movements declined in importance and young people began to dance *at* bands rather than *to* bands. This is not to say that ballroom dances were so rigidly codified that space was unavailable for individual freedoms: quicksteps, for example, offered skillful dancers an opportunity for fancy footwork. Anyone who simply listens to old dance band records is not repeating the same experience of consumption as was had by those who were familiar with the functional side of the music. This is true even though there is no doubt that dance band records were also played simply to be listened to and many were not strict enough in tempo to substitute for the rehearsal pianist in ballroom dancing classes.[44] As Dennis Potter's TV drama (and, later, film) *Pennies from Heaven* demonstrated, it is when this music is choreographed and connected to the body that it really comes to life. It is significant that when the Original Dixieland Jazz Band (ODJB) first appeared in Britain, at the London Hippodrome on 7 April 1919, they performed with a male and female dancer.

The predictability of dance rhythms must also be weighed against their effect (deliberate or otherwise) as a counter to sentimentality. An illustration would be "Whispering" Jack Smith's recording of "My Blue Heaven," where the strictness of the tempo acts as a foil to the sentiment of the words. Instead of the text's being subjected to a range of conventional classical devices for evoking sentiment (for example, a generous rubato or the lingering emphasis of a pause or *ritardando*), the unchanging pace (and, it must be added, Smith's crooning) creates an impression of understatement.

Show band numbers often involve a visual element that needs to be considered as a vital part of the experience. (See the photograph of Harry Roy's band [Fig. 4.2].) A show band was to be looked at, hence the routines: for example, Jack Hylton and His Band "sank on stage"[45] at the end of "He Played His Ukulele As the Ship Went Down" (le Clerq), and Jack Payne's band[46] positioned themselves around a model of a locomotive to play "Choo Choo" (Trumbauer-Malneck). Billy Cotton's band evolved from *palais* band to show band and later moved from variety theater to TV (where he was given his own show). Since people were watching, not dancing, show bands were less predictable in matters of tempo than the *palais* bands.[47]

The medium of radio was as important to the production and reception of items by BBC radio bands as was the visual element to show bands and the dance to palais bands. In Henry Hall's recording of "Rusty and Dusty," the fade-in beginning and fade-out ending are effective on radio and reminiscent of the listener's own activity of tuning into the station and turning the volume control. It also differs from a typical dance hall number in being a song for children. Like "The Teddy Bears' Picnic," it caters to the radio

FIGURE 4.2. Harry Roy and his band performing in 1934 (photo © Hulton Deutsch)

FIGURE 4.3.   Henry Hall and his orchestra broadcasting from a BBC studio in 1932
(photo © Hulton Deutsch)

"family audience." Another obvious radio entertainment is Henry Hall's "I
Like Bananas," the evidence here being the quantity of spoken humorous
material (see Fig. 4.3).[48]

PREDICTABILITY OF LYRIC CONTENT

Not all the lyrics of popular songs of this time were of the "moon and June"
variety, which they are often caricatured as being. There were "jilt songs,"
such as "It's the Talk of the Town" and "I've Got an Invitation to a Dance."[49]
Even the delicate subject of separation and divorce is touched upon in "In a
Little Second Hand Store."[50] There was the occasional song about current affairs. By 1931, as a result of the slump in world trade and the subsequent
trade war, the economy had sunk into deep recession, prompting U.S. pres-
ident Herbert Hoover to propose a holiday from all war debts to achieve a
world recovery. In England, Horatio Nicholls (Lawrence Wright) wrote a
song about it, titled "We're All Good Pals at Last." German anti-Semitism is
criticized in "Leave Abie Alone" (Pearson) of 1933, a song that, unfortunately,
does not entirely shake itself free of anti-Semitism, since it contains the re-

grettable lines, "Tho' he's only a Jew, he's a man the same as you." It should be stressed, however, that care is needed when selecting songs to characterize responses to social upheaval: the anthem of the depression in the United Kingdom was not "Brother, Can You Spare a Dime?" (Harburg-Gorney) but the buoyantly cheerful "Sing as We Go" (Parr-Davis). Gracie Fields, who made the latter song famous, was resiliently and optimistically "one of us" in the eyes of the British working class.

PREDICTABILITY AND MUSICAL SIGNS

Certain musical and verbal signs are used time and again to evoke a particular sociocultural location in the imagination of the listener. Since such signs rely upon a conventional association between signifier and signified, they can be adopted by any songwriter. Jimmy Kennedy and Michael Carr, one of Britain's most successful songwriting partnerships, furnish many examples. In Jack Harris's recording of "On Linger Longer Island," the presence of a Hawaiian guitar added to a melody suggestive of the sliding parallel chord shapes idiomatic to that instrument (see Ex. 4.1), the mention of "wicky wacky," the greeting "Aloha," and even the word "linger" in the title tell us instantly it is a tropical island and not, say, a Hebridean island, even without our being given the confirmation of the place name Waikiki (itself the most popular choice in songs of this type).[51]

The word "misty," however, in "Misty Islands of the Highlands" is just what one would expect to find as a description of the Hebrides. The song contains references to the glen, heather, and a crofter's cabin (*sic*—perhaps "bothy" was thought insufficiently familiar outside Scotland), and there are lots of sentimental appoggiaturas.[52] In fact, it continues a "Scottish nostalgia ballad" tradition that dates back to the times of the Highland clearances, when crofters were being evicted to make room for sheep.

In addition to the misty Celtic romanticism of Marjorie Kennedy-Fraser (*Songs of the Hebrides*, 1909–21) and Duncan Morison (*Ceol Mara*, 1935), who had turned Hebridean melodies into drawing-room ballads, there had developed another kind of pseudo-Celtic music, illustrated by the Jimmy Kennedy and Michael Carr song cited earlier and their "Did Your Mother Come from Ireland?" An Irish song aroused certain expectations, and this one satisfies most of them: there are references to the shamrock,

EXAMPLE 4.1. Jimmy Kennedy and Michael Carr, "On Linger Longer Island"

blarney, Kerry pipers, and Saint Patrick; the music features a solo fiddle (in Billy Cotton's version[53]) and modulates to the relative minor for a contrasting middle section, a device that can be traced back to several well-known "Irish" ballads of the nineteenth century.[54] "Did Your Mother Come from Ireland?" arrives as the continuation of a 150-year-old cultural history of commercial Irish song that brought its own necessities. Jimmy Kennedy, who *was* Irish, and Michael Carr, who moved to Ireland as a child, could no more ignore those necessities than Louis Armstrong could suddenly shake off a history of expectations associated with blackface minstrelsy. "If You Want to Touch an Irish Heart" (Castling), for example, treats Claribel's "Come Back to Erin" as an "authentic" Irish song. This type of pseudo-Celtic song has to be distinguished from deliberate attempts at caricature, as in Flanagan and Allen's "That's Another Scottish Story," where a "mean Scot" stereotype forms the running gag.[55]

Some subjects prompt the production of an instantly recognizable chain of signifiers. In "The General's Fast Asleep" and "The Handsome Territorial," arpeggio shapes and repeated notes are used to connote bugle calls.[56] "South of the Border" uses a bass pattern that signifies cowboys or a trotting horse (see Ex. 4.2).[57]

Similar patterns are also found in Kennedy and Carr's "Sunset Trail" and "Ole Faithful."[58] The illusion of "South of the Border" being a cowboy song was enhanced when Gene Autry began to sing it—yet as a screen cowboy he was no more a *real* cowboy than it is a *real* cowboy song. Once more, as in chapter 3, we find ourselves in Baudrillard's world of third order simulacra. As a less extreme and more theatrical form of simulation, Duke Ellington's band at the Cotton Club was often having to pretend to be in the jungle (though some of the club's clientele probably believed they were hearing *echt* jungle rhythms). British bands usually found themselves pretending romantically to be in the Wild West or the South Seas.

EXAMPLE 4.2. Jimmy Kennedy and Michael Carr, "South of the Border"

MIXTURES OF INCONGRUITY AND PREDICTABILITY

Predictability and incongruity mingle together when use is made of what Barthes in *Mythologies* labeled a "second order semiological system": "That which is a sign (namely the associative total of a concept and an image) in the first system, becomes a mere signifier in the second."[59] In the case of music, we need to consider how the associative total of a concept and a *sound* is made to function as a signifier.

Ambrose's recording of "Ho Hum" opens with a quotation of Mendelssohn's "Spring Song."[60] It is not there to function simply as a sign that combines a signifier (sprightly, "innocent," lyrical theme) and a signified (springtime). It is being used, as a quotation of the music of the classical composer Mendelssohn, to signify an artistic, poetic, and elevated vision of spring. The effect then achieved is that Mendelssohn is mocked by what follows—music markedly different from his own.[61] We are being told with humorous effect, even a hint of naughtiness or subversion, that *that* music is nothing like *this* music. The technique could be compared to that of montage in film, although here it is a juxtaposition of two different sound images, or to the startling juxtapositions found in surrealism or subcultural bricolage.[62]

In Jack Hylton's recording of "Meadow Lark," a similar effect to that described earlier is created by its opening quotation of Grieg's "Morning" from *Pier Gynt*.[63] This is not intended to simply signify morning by using a conveniently already-composed pastoral pentatonic theme; it is intended to signify morning as represented in elite or art music. An immediate contrast again follows and draws our attention to its incongruity in this context, to the difference of what is Hylton's music—and the assumption is that the latter is also *our* preferred style of music. The classical quotation was by no means a peculiarly British affair; in the song "Bill," from Jerome Kern's *Show Boat* (1927), the introduction quotes from Beethoven's *Leonora* Overture no. 3 and does so with a certain sourness, since its connotations of heroism (associated both with Beethoven's opera and, indeed, with Beethoven's own character) only serve to emphasize that Bill is neither a hero nor a person who would "appreciate" Beethoven.

What has been written here concerning classical quotations should not be taken to apply to all quotations: for example, the quotation may be assimilated into the song as the same sort of music, as happens when Stephen Foster's "My Old Kentucky Home" (1853) is quoted in Jack Hylton's recording of "Speaking of Kentucky Days."[64]

Sometimes audience expectations are challenged. In Lew Stone's recording of "My Old Dog," Nat Gonella is not singing in a Cockney accent for humor, even if the song by comic songwriter Leslie Sarony is, in many ways, a typical vehicle for a comedian in "tearful clown" mood—and Cockney, Yorkshire, and Lancashire accents are usually "good for a laugh" in parody songs or songs that concern working-class manners. Many sublimely ridiculous things seem to have been introduced deliberately into this recording:

for example, the romantic "virtuoso" piano accompaniment to words that describe roses growing in the corner of the garden where the dog lies (dog roses?) and the chorus whistled in unison by several members of the band (you whistle for dogs, of course). The band appears to be adopting the sophisticated strategy of sending up the song by being serious.[65] This is a strategy well known from Gilbert and Sullivan operetta, but because the style of those works is incongruous with that of dance band music, the use of similar devices will not necessarily produce similar effects. For example, the use of a chorus to echo ends of lines is, for Gilbert and Sullivan, a common humorous device, but listen to Roy Fox's recording of "Calling Me Home" where, in the sentimental context of boy treble, muted trumpet, and sustained saxophone chords, that same feature is intended to be taken seriously.[66]

PREDICTABILITY OF RHYTHM AND HARMONY

Some additional words are necessary concerning predictability as it relates to rhythm and harmony. To the classically trained musician, much dance band music appears to consist of repetitive rhythmic patterns bound into a metrical straitjacket. Often the attention of the classical musician has been arrested by a kind of repetition that is used regularly in this style *instead of* the kind of repetition found in classical style. The device of the riff will serve to illustrate the point. Richard Middleton[67] takes up the term "museme" coined by Philip Tagg[68] and refers to the riff as an example of a museme, a unit of musical expression that cannot be broken down further without losing meaning (this is not an exhaustive definition, and it is doubtful whether one can be found). Western music, Middleton explains, is normally characterized by "discursive" repetition, repetition that operates from the level of the phrase to longer units. Musematic repetition shows the influence of African-American music, and musematic techniques become increasingly common in twentieth-century dance music, reaching a peak in swing tunes and arrangements. There are earlier examples of musematic repetition, such as "Yes Sir, That's My Baby" (Kahn-Donaldson, 1926), but what was rare in the 1920s became typical of the dance band music of the late 1930s and early 1940s.

There was a preponderance of heavy two-beat feel in 1920s dance music, which could prove unyielding with little syncopation and a tuba remorselessly pounding roots and fifths of chords, as in Jack Hylton's recording of "Yes Sir, That's My Baby."[69] Even complex syncopations may bounce off this basic pattern (for example, "Fascinating Rhythm," by Ira and George Gershwin); that is, they work around a divisive meter. The newness of the Charleston was that it was not just the melody that was syncopated, but an additive meter (3 + 3 + 2) was created as a result of syncopating all parts (including those playing accompanying harmony) simultaneously. The Savoy Orpheans' recording of "Charleston" contains a spoken introduction by Ramon Newton that points out its novelty: "This record is unique, in that it features a distinctly new syncopated rhythm called the Charleston."[70] The remark stands as testimony to the paradoxical value of unpredictability in a capitalist society; there are always potentially large profits to be made from a mass-marketed "unique" commodity. The additive rhythm used in the Charleston is not, in itself, "distinctly new"[71]—but it received greater emphasis than ever before.

Around 1930, there was a change from two-beat to four-beat,[72] a merging of ragtime two-beat and blues four-beat that offered greater swing. Duple meter of the 1920s was likely to be emphasized by a banjo as two semiquavers plus three quavers per bar, or two quavers plus two semiquavers plus one quaver per bar.[73] There was not yet the backbeat emphasis of one quaver plus two semiquavers plus two quavers. In 1933 Feather was complaining about the lack of jazz in triple meter, yet the ODJB had $\frac{3}{4}$ tunes in their repertoire: for example, "I'm Forever Blowing Bubbles," and "Alice Blue Gown."[74] It is not surprising that Feather would become the first to compose a $\frac{5}{4}$ blues ("Bass Reflex").[75]

While there often does seem to be a high degree of predictability regarding the overall shape of a song arrangement (introduction, instrumental chorus, vocal chorus, instrumental chorus), it rarely applies to the disposition and duration of instrumental solos. The imagination shown in some arrangements is considerable: for example, Lew Stone's moody arrangement of Reginald Foresyth's "Garden of Weed"[76] and Sid Phillips's many inspired arrangements for Ambrose.

However, the characteristic parallel motion of dance band harmonies can in some hands result in awkward voice leading; in such cases, the unpredictability of individual parts is scarcely a matter for praise. Consider the lower violin part in "When Day Is Done" (Katscher–de Sylva, 1924) in a dance band arrangement of 1926 made by Walter Paul (see Ex. 4.3). Note, for example, how the desire to write sweet parallel sixths results in awkward augmented fourths for the lower violin during the phrase "in my arms" (immediately followed by an ungainly leap of a major seventh). The fondness for parallel motion means that consecutive fifths also feature as a matter of contingency rather than deliberation; thus, the effect they produce is again born of accident rather than imaginative usage. See the extract from Jack Mason's 1938 arrangement of "Alexander's Ragtime Band" (Berlin, 1911) given in Example 4.4. In instances like these, the unpredictable elements are merely random by-products of an overly rigid treatment of one musical parameter at the expense of others. There is no purposeful design to stimulate or delight; they issue instead from a pursuit of stylistic practice in which the mechanical has overridden the imaginative.

Absorbing the commercial 32-bar Tin Pan Alley song form into jazz did not have all ill effects, whatever some may have feared: for example, it brought a more complex harmonic vocabulary that extended the possibilities for improvisation and melodic *Affekt,* thereby offering opportunities for imaginative avoidance of the predictable. "Honeysuckle Rose" (Razaf-Waller, 1929)

EXAMPLE 4.3. Robert Katscher and B. G. De Sylva, "When Day Is Done"

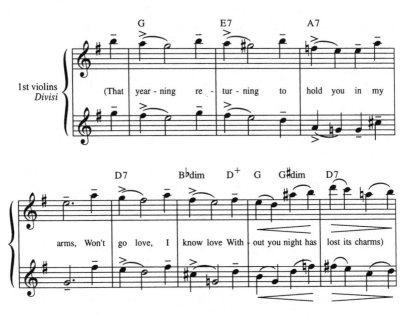

shows how melodic *Affekt* is transformed by use of extended harmonies rather than simple triads, which here (i.e., the predictable ones) would steadfastly affirm the home key with alternating IV and I chords instead of building expectation (by delaying the tonic) with alternating chords of II^7 and V^{13}. Note also that the tune continually outlines a D-minor triad, yet Waller does not use this chord once in the entire song. In this song unpredictability is clearly linked to musical imagination (see Ex. 4.5).

EXAMPLE 4.4. Irving Berlin, "Alexander's Ragtime Band"

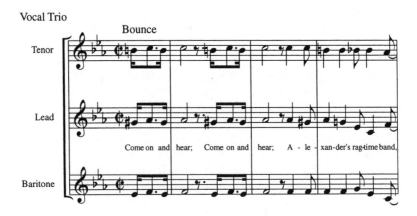

EXAMPLE 4.5. Andy Razaf and Fats Waller, "Honeysuckle Rose"

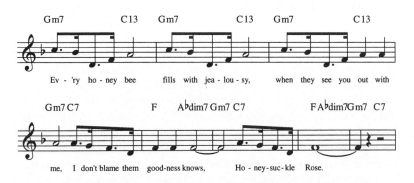

As far as 32-bar structures themselves are concerned, it is possible for the overall number of bars to be predictable, but not their phrasing within the 32-bar chorus: in "Let's Put Out the Lights" (Hupfeld), for example, the 32 bars divide into 8 + 7 + 9 + 8.[77] Even songs that fall out as 8 + 8 + 8 + 8 do not necessarily have foursquare phrasing within the eight-bar periods. What is more, the effects of syncopation can be enormous: in Irving Berlin's "Puttin' on the Ritz" the opening 4 bars of the chorus contain a syncopated rhythm that metrically displaces the sixteen crotchet beats so that, instead of a grouping of 4 + 4 + 4 + 4, they fall into 3 + 3 + 4 + 3 + 3. Not all songs use the 32-bar chorus: "Valencia," a "one-step" recorded by the Savoy Orpheans (billed on the recording as the Savoy Havana Band), is constructed in the main of ten-bar melodic sections (dividing into 2 1/2 + 7 1/2 bar phrases).[78] Finally, if the 32-bar chorus was in itself such a successful formula, why has it been of so little importance to rock?

CONCLUSION

Apropos of music hall, Raymond Williams remarked that some performers brought "new kinds and areas of experience which the 'legitimate' drama neglected or unreasonably despised."[79] It might be argued similarly that the dance band provided a musical experience the concert hall despised (though not all concert hall composers—Vaughan Williams titled the third movement of his *Partita* "Homage to Henry Hall"). Some scorned this music for being riddled with musical "errors" and being poorly performed when what was really at issue was the incongruity between its stylistic practices and the conventions of classical music.[80] Others were content to condemn this music because they assumed, as did Theodor Adorno, that it epitomized in practice the kind of advice given in Abner Silver and Robert Bruce's *How to Write and Sell a Hit Song* (1939).[81] This second line of attack amounts to a condemnation of predictability, which is seen as the inevitable outcome of basing a musical practice on the notion that there is a formula for success. To draw a parallel in the classical field, no one was keen to suggest that the success of the second English musical renaissance was directly linked to the explanations of classical "good practice" given in Ebenezer Prout's *Applied Forms,* because classical good practice was thought of as placing emphasis on individual imaginative reworkings of musical forms and devices (this allows a fox-trot to be accused of standardization but not a classical minuet).

Such matters as the ubiquity of formal devices like the 32-bar chorus and the need to tailor musical items to fit 78 rpm records have indeed raised the issue of standardization. It is better, though, to think of the problem from the angle of reception rather than production, as a problem of predictability rather than standardization, since the latter concept works against the perception of a dialectical relationship between the production and consumption of this music by suggesting that the listener's role is passive and that a formula for commercial success (if, indeed, such a formula were to exist) lies with the producer alone.

part three

THE SACRED AND THE PROFANE

Lux in Tenebris: BRUCKNER

AND THE DIALECTIC OF

DARKNESS AND LIGHT

BRUCKNER IS OFTEN REGARDED as that rare phenomenon among nineteenth-century composers—the "pure" musician.[1] This supposed musical autonomy did not prevent the appropriation of Bruckner by the Nazis, and, what is more, the aim of the International Bruckner Society in the 1930s to cleanse (*reinigen*) Bruckner's works easily slipped into ideas of purifying them of the corrupt influence of both well-meaning Jewish friends and hostile Jewish critics of his music.[2] After the Second World War, however, the key to understanding Bruckner was no longer in terms of peasant roots, *Blut und Boden* (blood and soil), and affinity with nature but instead to recognize him as the "king of absolute music."[3] The reception of his music today is undoubtedly affected by this abstract conception of his compositions. His music certainly poses marketing problems for record companies: no Bruckner appears on any of the EMI *Classical Moods* albums, which include *Passion, Melancholy, Dreams, Celebration, Spiritual, Tranquillity, Romance,* and *Power.* Bruckner is not seen as a typical classical composer—he does not appear on any of EMI's four double albums titled *The Classic Experience*—nor is he seen as a popular figure (Castle Communications' five-CD set *100 Popular Classics* contains no Bruckner).

Bruckner also presents hermeneutic difficulties for critical musicologists engaged in the ideological critique of sexuality and gender in music. The issue of gendered themes and the erotic character of the climax in tonal music suddenly seem irrelevant or inappropriate when discussing Bruckner. In fact, New Musicologists and Critical Musicologists of every hue appear reluctant to discuss Bruckner or offer any explanation of his famously massive climaxes. Yet Constantin Floros, one of the few scholars to call for the development of hermeneutic strategies for understanding meaning in Bruckner, has asked that the symphonies should not be classified as absolute music in any circumstances, arguing that they are far removed from the formalist aesthetics of Eduard Hanslick.[4]

This chapter is an attempt to provide further critical insight into the meaning of Bruckner's music. The strategy I am adopting is: (1) to establish the sacred character of Bruckner's music and show how he inherits religious signifiers for darkness and light; (2) to show how he uses these signifiers; (3) to explore the appropriateness of the darkness/light trope, with all the connotations it would have for a deeply religious composer; and (4) to put forward a theory of "transfiguration of themes" in Bruckner, as distinct from Liszt's transformations, and assess the appropriateness of the idea of there being plateaus of intensity in his music rather than peaks. It is also my purpose, with reference to the words *Lux in Tenebris* in my title, to consider whether the applicability of the Hegelian dialectic to Bruckner (in the way it has been applied to Beethoven) is open to challenge. In doing so, I shall take advantage of the turn away from dialectics and hermeneutics presented by Jacques Derrida's philosophical project of deconstruction.

THE SACRED CHARACTER OF BRUCKNER'S MUSIC AND THE FORMATIVE INFLUENCES ON HIS SEMIOTIC MARKINGS

Bruckner's deeply religious character and submissive attitude to authority have been explained by "the entrenchment of Catholicism in the rural districts of Austria during the *Vormärz* (the period preceding the revolution of 1848)."[5] He was born in Ansfelden, near Linz, in an area of peasant farming land during "a period of deepest reaction and intolerance" when the "iron grip of the State was reinforced by the authority of the Roman Catholic Church."[6] Between the ages of 21 and 31 he lived in the seclusion of the Abbey of St. Florian, one of Austria's "most majestic edifices in pure baroque style—'Jesuit style.'"[7] Any freedoms gained by the revolution were short-lived; thus, when he left, in 1855, he may not even have been aware of any change. That year he began his studies with the conservative and exacting Simon Sechter; it was also the year of the Concordat, which "in effect handed over the whole educational system ... to the representatives of Rome."[8] The narrowness of Bruckner's intellectual curiosity is indicated by his personal library: but for two books, it reputedly consisted entirely of music and religious works.[9]

The formative influence on Bruckner's semiotic markings was Austrian church music and the works of the Viennese classical composers. He became familiar with Mozart's Masses and Haydn's *Creation* during the year (1835–36) spent with his relation and godfather Johann Baptist Weiss, organist at Hörsching. Bruckner's Missa Solemnis (1854) is indebted to Mozart and Haydn, reminiscences of whom are also occasionally found in his early symphonies. Robert Simpson, for example, points out that the continuation of the opening of the slow movement of the Third Symphony recalls in texture and mood the introduction to Haydn's *Seven Last Words*.[10] This movement also contains at bar 13 a *Marienkadenz,* a feature common in Viennese sacred music that appears in some of Bruckner's choral music, for instance, the seven-part *Ave Maria* of 1861. Still earlier sacred musical influences are in evidence: the Sanctus of his E-minor Mass builds on a theme from Palestrina's *Missa Brevis*.[11] Several of his motets are written in the old church modes: *Pange Lingua* (1868) is Phrygian; *Os Justi* (1879) is Lydian.[12]

More generally, his compositions rely on our knowledge of a sacred music paradigm, so that we recognize, say, the use of a choralelike theme, a *Marienkadenz,* or other signs established within the discursive code he uses (such as the connotations of major and minor). In Hans-Hubert Schönzeler's opinion, Bruckner achieves "moments of utter sublimity" with his chorale themes; they can be climactic on brass or *pianissimo* on strings, "providing moments of repose, of peace and meditation."[13] Deryck Cooke remarks: "The liturgical character of some of the chorale themes in the symphonies arises out of their simultaneous melodic and harmonic reliance on the archaic church progression from tonic to subdominant and back."[14]

Sometimes Bruckner makes his sacred intentions unambiguous, as with his characteristic expression mark *Feierlich* (meaning "solemn") and by planning to dedicate the Ninth "An meinen lieben Gott." Elsewhere, we are left to make the appropriate connections: for example, bare fourths, fifths, and octaves may be associated with organum, hence the sacred character of the opening of the Te Deum. Liszt's Missa Solemnis (1855) plays with the same associations, opening with the sound of a bare fifth. Providing further evidence of a larger sacred paradigm, the vision of an angelic choir is easily conjured up at such moments as the conclusion to *Psalm 150*.[15] This image may also be evoked by the symphonies: compare the "Hallelujah" conclusion to *Psalm 150* with the end of the Eighth, where there is much in common— even a similarity in violin figuration. Compare, likewise, the conclusions of the Te Deum and the Third (though the latter is in D major, not C major).

Bruckner's move from Mass to symphony was made, perhaps, in order to explore additional sacred possibilities in music. Explaining why Bruckner wrote no more Masses after 1868, Schönzeler remarks: "He was able to sing his *Gloria,* his *Credo* and his *Benedictus* in the wordless, all-embracing, absolute music of his gigantic symphonic movements."[16] The opening notes of the Second Symphony, for example, make up a characteristic Brucknerian phrase for "Benedictus" (cf. the Benedictus of his E-minor Mass). Symphonic form, however, offered fresh opportunities, especially that of a massive affirmative ending not suited to the Mass because of its concluding humble prayer. Bruckner was more aware of liturgical propriety than most: Crawford Howie comments that the first and last movements of Bruckner's D-minor, E-minor, and F-minor Masses, "in contrast to those of the Classical composers, were inspired by the penitential tone of the text."[17] Cooke suggests that the theme of the third movement of the Ninth "is too full of a peculiarly personal anguish for Bruckner to have used in a liturgical context"[18] and that the polka/chorale of the Third presents related liturgical problems. However, Dika Newlin asserts, "the spiritual content of his works deepened but remained essentially the same."[19]

Bruckner's inclination toward self-quotation is evident in his earliest symphonies: for example, the Andante of *Die Nullte* (Symphony no. 0) contains two quotations from the Qui Tollis of his E-minor Mass, while the Finale quotes the Osanna from his Requiem (letter A) and his seven-part *Ave Maria* at the junction of the development and recapitulation. The slow movement of the Second Symphony quotes (at bar 137 and following) the Benedictus from his F-minor Mass in the correct key; at bar 180 it returns following a key change that again enables it to appear in its original key, disposing us to attribute hidden significance to this tonality.

Let us explore possible meanings of some of Bruckner's borrowings and self-quotations with reference to the Third Symphony. In the first movement, bars 262–65 of the 1873 version, the *miserere* of his D-minor Mass is quoted (see the Gloria, bars 100–103). This sacred quotation at the end of the exposition may remind us of the Kyrie quotation (from the F-minor Mass) at a similar point in the Finale of the Second Symphony. The close of an exposition is obviously felt to be an appropriate place for piety, whereas sin, in the shape of Venusberg references introduced in the revision of 1877, appears just before the recapitulation. Bruckner clearly added these references for a purpose; he had known *Tannhäuser* for years,[20] so there is no reason that they could not have appeared in the 1873 version. Perhaps, in a transitional work such as this, Bruckner was attempting to bring a moral and religious character to sonata principle, before realizing that the sonata structure he had inherited was itself incapable of accommodating his musical vision. The coda contains an ostinato pattern that shows the lingering influence of Beethoven's Ninth (cf. the codas to the first movement of *Die Nullte* and the Finale of the Second). Another Wagner quotation in this symphony is the sleep motive from *Die Walküre* just before recapitulation of the first movement (and in the coda of the second movement). Again, I would suggest that Bruckner finds the approach to a recapitulation a suitable point to present a darker side. Sleep is associated with darkness and death, because it eclipses conscious thought.[21] Bruckner has removed all traces of magic and phantasmagoria from the Wagner, strengthening the darker connotations.[22]

The urge to self-quote continues to the end of Bruckner's symphonic career and therefore functions as a means of asserting a unitary sacred paradigm for his compositions. In bars 181–84 of the Adagio of the Ninth, he again quotes the *miserere* of his D-minor Mass. The second theme of the Adagio begins with an inversion of this motive (bar 45), and the rocking viola accompaniment resembles passages of the Benedictus in the F-minor Mass (bars 23–24, sopranos and altos; bars 98–99, tenors). The movement opens with an approximate inversion of the fugue subject of the Finale of the Fifth and, later, contains more specific references to the Seventh and

Eighth Symphonies. Bruckner's sketches reveal, too, that the string figure from the opening of the Te Deum was to return in the Finale of the Ninth.[23]

If we accept, then, that these are religious symphonies (with the arguable exceptions of the First and Fourth) or, at least, that the religious element is of enormous importance,[24] it is important to examine religious signifiers in music of a similar stylistic code. Before Bruckner, the minor triad and key had changed in its signification. In the early Baroque, minor tonality (as distinct from the modal) was too recent to have acquired the conventional character of a signifier. The affective code for grief in the seventeenth century is shown by the chromaticism, angular intervals, and dissonance of "When I Am Laid in Earth" from Purcell's *Dido and Aeneas.* Contrast this with Purcell's use of the minor key in the marriage hymn in *The Fairy Queen* and "Ah! Ah! How Happy Are We" from *The Indian Queen.* Minor could still signify happiness (in the sense of contentment) as late as 1742 (see the aria "Happy Is the Land" from Bach's *Peasant* Cantata). Major gradually became an opposition to minor in the Baroque. "The People That Walked in Darkness" from Handel's *Messiah* shows the use of unison, minor key, and angular chromatic melody for darkness and thickened harmonic texture, major key, and diatonic melody (given added stability and predictability by containing a repeated phrase) for light. "Total Eclipse" from Handel's *Samson* is quoted in Deryck Cooke's *The Language of Music,* where he remarks upon the use of minor for "all dark" and major for "the blaze of noon."[25] The chorus "O First-Created Beam" from the same oratorio anticipates Haydn's famous chorus in *The Creation,* moving from low pitch and minor to loud C major after the words "Let there be light!"

Turning to representations of darkness, in "He Sent a Thick Darkness" from Handel's *Israel in Egypt* we find unpredictable and ambiguous tonal movement and so are led to equate the lack of tonal clarity with darkness. This convention persists into the nineteenth century: a minor key, chromaticism, and angular intervals (especially the tritone) are heard during the opening of act 2 of Beethoven's *Fidelio,* before Florestan's first words: "Gott! welch' Dunkel hier!" The key then changes to major as he puts his trust in God.

BRUCKNER'S SIGNIFIERS FOR DARKNESS AND LIGHT, AND THE MEANING OF DARKNESS AND LIGHT IN HIS RELIGION

Bruckner's early familiarity with conventions for signifying light can be seen in the "Domine Jesu Christe" section of his Requiem of 1849. Immediately following an agitated setting of "ne absorbeat eas tartarus, ne cadant in obscurum," the C minor of "tartarus" is exchanged for C major for the words "sed signifer sanctus Michael repraesentet eas in lucem sanctam" (see Ex. 5.1).

A similar change from minor to major occurs at the word "lux" in the Agnus Dei of the same work. In another early work, the Missa Solemnis, he moves from minor to major at "Deum de Deo, lumen de lumine." The semi-

EXAMPLE 5.1. Requiem

otic code he adopted in his early works proved as enduring as his own character, which was not changed by his move to Vienna in 1868 or by any growing liberalism in Austrian politics.

The use of low and high pitch as signifiers is evident in the B♭, D-minor, E-minor, and F-minor Masses, in each of which the words "judicare vivos et mortuos" are given a high pitch for "living" and low for "dead," as Beethoven treated them in his Missa Solemnis, Haydn in his *Nelson* Mass, and Schubert in his A♭ Mass of 1822. This helps us to locate the historical specificity of Bruckner's semiotic code; one would expect to find this feature in most eighteenth- and nineteenth-century Masses but not in earlier Masses. Indeed, William Byrd's Mass for four voices rises in pitch at the word "mortuos."

It is well known that light and darkness have important sacred connotations. As a religious signifier, light may be *lux sancta* or a trope for the divinity/godhead—God of God, Light of Light: Lux mundi.[26] As such, it is associated with goodness, morality and, importantly, salvation: a psalm of David begins: "The Lord is my light and my salvation."[27] For Bruckner, light is not associated with reason as in the eighteenth-century Enlightenment; instead, it is *lux sancta,* the holy light of salvation for the believer. In contrast, darkness has connotations of immorality (especially lust), evil, and Hell. The association of darkness with lust is confirmed by linking Jude's statement (in his New Testament Epistle) that the fallen angels are "in everlasting chains under darkness unto the judgment of the great day"[28] to the explanation in the apocalyptic Book of Enoch that the main cause of their fall was lust. Saint John makes a direct association between darkness and evil by claiming: "Men loved darkness rather than light, because their deeds were evil."[29] In Bruckner we encounter yearning but not the lusting for climax found in, say, Wagner's *Tristan.* There is calm at figure T only a dozen bars before the massive climax of the Adagio of the Eighth Symphony (Nowak edition). The spiritual character of Bruckner's yearnings appears to be confirmed by the fact that they are frequently followed by tranquil sections—which signify, perhaps, meditation or prayer. Besides, you can never be certain of the outcome of a buildup of excitement in Bruckner: for example, the positive-feeling approach to figure Ss in the Finale of the Eighth (Nowak edition) leads to the grim return of the "annunciation of death" (Bruckner's description[30]) theme. The Scherzo of the Ninth opens with the "Tristan" chord, but how unlike that of Wagner is Bruckner's treatment of it! It is as if Bruckner were saying, "No, this chord of desire is evil!"[31] In this context we may recall the prominent trumpet and upper wind tritone—*diabolus in musica*—as the first movement drew to a close.

Life is associated with light—"the light of life"[32]—as death is with darkness (the "shadow of death" being a common image).[33] We find associations of C minor with death in the "funeral marches" in the slow movements of the Fourth and the Sixth (its third theme); Simpson remarks that before the latter commences "the light of C major fades slowly."[34] We really know what the climax of the Adagio of the Seventh represented for Bruckner: the *non confundar* theme of the Te Deum is quoted, and he described the beginning of the coda as "funeral music for the Master."[35] Here the C-major climax has connotations of light, God (*In te, Domine, speravi*), and glory.[36]

According to the Bible, darkness existed *before* God created light, and after creating light God "divided the light from the darkness."[37] It was the latter image that Michelangelo placed on the ceiling of the Sistine Chapel immediately above the altar; it is the birth of form. Bruckner's tremolando beginnings have often been interpreted as birth tropes: Max Auer, for example, wrote of "thematic structure" raising itself "out of nothingness,"[38] and August Halm remarked: "We think we are inhaling something like the breath of creation, when we are enveloped in the first tones of his Seventh, Ninth, or Fourth Symphonies."[39] Derek Watson writes of "the evocation of creation itself" in these beginnings.[40] Sometimes the music emerges literally from nothing: the first bar of the Scherzo of the Ninth is empty; nothing is heard until the third beat of the second bar.

THE DIALECTIC OF DARKNESS AND LIGHT: STRUCTURE AND MEANING IN BRUCKNER

Auer's description of the openings of most Bruckner symphonies as "an awakening from unconsciousness and darkness to light and clarity"[41] could also be applied to most codas. These are especially helpful for showing the appropriateness of the darkness/light trope, because they are tonally static (note the use of pedals and ostinati). Simpson commented that most of Bruckner's ultimate passages open "in darkness."[42] So they move from darkness to light, but it is not achieved as in the Hegelian dialectic, through struggle and reconciliation, and the end presents us with only a contingent victory. There is no reconciliation of contradictions: in a word, light cannot be reconciled with darkness.

Bruckner's dialectic is of a peculiarly nonmuscular character. It is in some ways epitomized by the lack of struggle between the polka theme and the chorale theme in the Finale of his Third Symphony (see Ex. 5.2). Here a Hegelian dialectic cannot work because there can be no reconciliation between life and death.[43] More of a conflict *could* have been suggested; we have only to think of the third movement of Mahler's First Symphony. Bruckner's polka-chorale that signifies life juxtaposed with death or, rather, "In the midst of life we are in death"[44] is antidialectic.

In attempting to understand Bruckner's *lux in tenebris*,[45] we should note that the initial term of the opposition light/darkness is privileged over the other: darkness is absence of light; light is not absence of darkness.[46] Although light/darkness is not itself a metaphysical opposition (since darkness does differ *naturally* from light), its connotations, with the exception of life/death, are metaphysical: for example, night can suggest the feminine, lust, and evil. Therefore, it offers itself up to Derrida's deconstruction, which is concerned with demonstrating the privileging of one term over another in metaphysical oppositions.[47] Moreover, light/darkness is metaphysical in Bruckner, because it exists only as *representation*. Meaning is created by differing and deferring (Derrida's *différance*): a musical illustration of this in Bruckner is that minor does not simply differ from major; it is governed by major. Therefore, the minor opening of the Third Symphony is not mistaken for the dominant term of the opposition major/minor; we know major will triumph, though its triumph is deferred. Minor is *always* the antithesis—but not a true antithesis, because Bruckner *privileges* major over

EXAMPLE 5.2. Symphony no. 3, 1877 version, Finale, bars 65–72

minor. In Bruckner's music, *major is the commanding term for ideological and not structural reasons:* major connotes light and minor connotes darkness; or, we might say, minor is major with a lack, as darkness is light with a lack. There is no structural reason that minor should not command major: for example, in Mahler's Sixth all light is extinguished (adumbrated early on by the major triad's turn to minor). The fact that light does not shine forth in the revised first movement of Bruckner's Eighth is what makes it so exceptionally doom-laden.

APOCALYPTIC VISION IN BRUCKNER'S MUSIC

The religious meaning of the term "Apocalypse" is "unveiling" or "disclosure."[48] I would argue that Bruckner's treatment of structure can often be understood as a process of revelation, thereby presenting us with a musical form of apocalyptic vision. Consider, for example, the unexpected revealing of the tonic at the point of recapitulation in the first movement of the Seventh Symphony (see Ex. 5.3) or slow unveiling of the tonic in the first movement recapitulation of the Eighth (in both case effected without struggle or drama). Also, consider Simpson's description of the Finale of that work as the "cathedral" Bruckner has been trying to envisage during the course of the symphony: "One by one the impediments have been removed, until the image is clearly revealed."[49] Liddell and Scott's *Greek-English Lexicon*[50] gives "an uncovering, (revelation N.T.)" as its definition of ἀποκάλυψις. Again an analogy may be found with Bruckner's formal method: for example, Simpson described Bruckner's music as having a tendency "to remove, one by one, disrupting or distracting elements, to seem to uncover at length a last stratum of calm contemplative thought."[51] Ernst Bloch maintained that in Bruckner's finales

> the listener is released from the pressure of the temporal world in a contemplative review of the passions, territories and the established primary colour of the whole performance, in the expectation of visionary prospects and with the consciousness of standing at the birthplace of that which is lyrically essential in the symphony.[52]

Instead of Beethoven's version of the Hegelian dialectic in his middle-period sonata form movements, where there is dramatic conflict of key and material in the exposition, struggle in the development section, and reconciliation in the recapitulation, Bruckner's dialectic of darkness and light involves slow discovery rather than muscular striving, and resolution without reconciliation. For while we do have opposing forces, there is no sense of Hegel's "inadequate thesis" versus "inadequate antithesis" finally reaching a higher reconciling synthesis or sublation (*Aufhebung*) that preserves what is rational in them, canceling out the irrational. As an illustration of Hegelian sublation applied to sonata form, here is Rose Rosengard Subotnik explaining the reconciliation of dialectical opposites in middle-period Beethoven:

EXAMPLE 5.3. Symphony no. 7, Nowak edition, bars 275–82

Through the recapitulation the subject seems not only to bring together within itself, but actually to derive from within itself, the
principles of dynamic development (historical change) and fixed,
eternal order (unchangeable identity) and to synthesize the two into
a higher level of reality.[53]

In the dialectic of darkness and light we cannot move toward a higher synthesis. Apocalyptic literature emphasized the dualism of good and evil, gave
structure to the notion of Heaven and Hell, and created the idea of the "final
judgment." Good cannot achieve a higher synthesis with evil, nor Heaven
with Hell; thus, the very existence of a dialectical conflict is questioned. This
also holds for darkness and light: as stated earlier, darkness is understood as
absence of light *and not vice versa*. The first theme of Bruckner's Third Symphony does not undergo a tonal struggle to become "light"; light (in the
form of major tonality) is merely absent from it until the end of the symphony. Changing the order in which major and minor appear makes no difference: in Bruckner's Seventh, where the opening theme is major, we do not
interpret the dark inverted minor form of the theme midway through the

movement as dominant, because we do not perceive a lack, a desire for darkness, in its original major form.

Bloch expresses concern about the "profound problem . . . of the musical finale as *happy ending*" in Bruckner and Beethoven.[54] While agreeing that "climax and resolution are necessary," Bloch insists that the "through darkness to light!" or the joyous ending "does not stem from the music-making itself in an inexorable way."[55] As I have argued, there is no innately musical logic for Bruckner's Third to end in D major rather than D minor. Bloch is seeking an inner human essence that makes itself felt in the musical processes themselves, so that joy is achieved by the work itself and not just by the will of the composer: he speaks of "a birth of faith out of music, coming from the quietest, innermost, farthest depths of the musician's soul," which could "finally strike up the *Sed signifer sanctus Michael*."[56] But there *is* no inexorable logic about darkness moving to light, and in the Christian religion the movement from darkness to light is interpreted precisely as a matter of free will. Bloch's search for deeper unity and organic growth in music is motivated by his need to find logical explanations for what is happening on the surface. Today we must recognize that postmodernist theory, poststructuralism, and deconstruction have strongly challenged notions of organic unity and the composer's expressive presence within his or her music.[57] Because of the presence of multiple versions of his music, concern with "deep structure" in Bruckner gives rise to something similar to demands for the "director's cut" in film—the Haas editions are just such an attempt to provide the originary, univocal creations of the "master artist." It is instructive to read Subotnik on Theodor Adorno's opinion that exaggeration enters Beethoven's preparations for recapitulation as he begins to realize that "the principle of reprise . . . arises from no logical necessity within the subject."[58] She explains:

> By contrast with logical implication, as embodied in the syllogism, musical implication, as Adorno understands it to occur in the classical style, is a temporal rather than a formal process. . . . musical implication makes itself fully known only in terms of an actual and hence subsequent resolution.[59]

However, Adorno regarded nineteenth-century music as lacking implicative power.[60] As an example of our not understanding an implication until re-

EXAMPLE 5.4A. D-minor Mass, Gloria, bars 100–103

EXAMPLE 5.4B. Symphony no. 9, Adagio, bars 45–48

vealed, note that the third bar of the fugue subject to *et vitam venturus* in the F-minor Mass moves stepwise up a fourth, but its meaning is deferred, and it only becomes clear that this is an inversion of the Kyrie motive during the last dozen bars of the Mass.[61]

In Bruckner, imbalance is created between tonal forces without the physical struggle associated with Beethoven. Simpson remarks of the first movement of Bruckner's Seventh: "Throughout the whole first part of the movement B major takes over, as it were, by stealth, in a manner remote from the muscular action of sonata."[62] I would argue that this is why the metaphors of darkness and light so often work in Bruckner—because darkness does not *struggle* to become light. Instead, night is *gradually transformed* into day (Bruckner's gradual "unveiling") or a light *suddenly shines* in the darkness. There may be a crisis at the inversion of the main theme in the C-minor middle section of this movement (bars 233–36), but it is not treated as part of a process of tonal tension and release. As a result, the home key does not feel stable at the recapitulation. While the C-minor passage may readily be interpreted as the dark antithesis of the movement's opening (this key carrying, as it does, connotations of death), it should be emphasized that inversion itself does not work as an opposite in musical semiotics. Consider what happens when the *miserere* motive from the Gloria of the D-minor Mass appears in inverted form in the Adagio of the Ninth (the A♭ theme at bar 45); it does not become *jubilate* (see Exx. 5.4a and 5.4b). Moreover, notice that when the fugue subject of *Psalm 150* is inverted it is still sung to the same words. The inverted theme in the Seventh Symphony does work as an opposite because musical *descent* has been established by convention as an opposite to ascent in music of this style and period and the inversion of this theme produces an unwavering descent (see Exx. 5.4c and 5.4d).

EXAMPLE 5.4C. Symphony no. 7, 1st movement, bars 3–6

EXAMPLE 5.4D. Symphony no. 7, 1st movement, bars 233–36

Since many musicologists have commented on the gendered character of nineteenth-century sonata structures, we should consider the applicability of such ideas to Bruckner. Susan McClary summarizes the argument thus:

> In sonata, the principal key/theme clearly occupies the narrative position of masculine protagonist; and while the less dynamic second key/theme is *necessary* to the sonata or tonal plot (without this foil or obstacle, there is no story), it serves the narrative function of the feminine Other. Moreover, satisfactory resolution—the ending always generically guaranteed in advance by tonality and sonata procedure—demands the containment of whatever is semiotically or structurally marked as "feminine," whether a second theme or simply a non-tonic key area.[63]

McClary is discussing what she regards as a typical narrative and what she describes elswhere as "tonal striving, climax, and closure."[64] Bruckner's climaxes, however, are not really reached by tonal striving—the E♭ climax of the Adagio of the Eighth did not have to be in E♭ (as we know, it was in C major in the first version); there is more in the way of tonal *balancing* in Bruckner. I am referring here to balanced tonal masses rather than a balance of power. In a rudimentary musical structure, for example, a move from tonic to dominant may be balanced by a flat-side move to the subdominant. This does not mean that the tonic does not remain the commanding tonal area; the tonic chord was the *Generalissimus* for Bruckner.[65] Constantin Floros has remarked: "For all Bruckner's modulatory flexibility, the harmonic design is always lucid and methodical."[66] Equal attention is devoted to balancing his phrase structure, building short blocks into huge formal designs.[67]

TRANSFIGURATION OF THEMES

I am not the first to recognize the appropriateness of the word "transfigure" to Bruckner's music. Crawford Howie claims: "In no other settings of the Mass is one so aware of the transfiguration of the contrite mood of the opening *Kyrie* into the confident mood of the final *Dona nobis pacem*."[68] Edwin Doernberg speaks of "two delicately transfigured greetings from the

EXAMPLE 5.5A. Beethoven, Symphony no. 9, 1st movement, bars 218–23

EXAMPLE 5.5B. Beethoven, Symphony no. 9, 1st movement, bars 469–74

EXAMPLE 5.5C. Bruckner, Overture in G Minor, bars 23–27

EXAMPLE 5.5D. Bruckner, Overture in G Minor, bars 282–85

Eighth and Seventh Symphonies" at the close of the Adagio of the Ninth.[69] As long ago as 1907, Willibald Kähler described the Adagio of the Eighth as "solemnly transfigurative."[70] I wish to use "transfigure" in a more specific sense, however, in what I have to say here. By describing any theme or motive as transfigured, I mean that it acquires a new "radiance" while its rhythmic identity remains unchanged.[71] This radiance may be created by an alteration from minor to major, from low to high pitch, or from chromatic to diatonic, and in each of these cases a change in texture is usually involved. Examples are found as early as the coda to the G-minor Overture (1863) and, in this piece, the "transfiguring" may derive from Beethoven. Just before the coda of the first movement of Beethoven's Ninth (bars 469–76), the development's minor fugue subject (bars 218–23) changes to major, resembling a procedure adopted in Bruckner's Overture in G Minor (see Exx. 5.5a, 5.5b, 5.5c, and 5.5d).

Beethoven's coda, however, reasserts darkness, and nowhere else does the light shine upon this theme or upon any of his dark themes. To have concluded his Ninth Symphony with a loud tonic major version of the first subject of the first movement would have been out of the question. A resolution in Beethoven's dialectic has to be reached by agreement, even if this can only be attained with bitterness and after hard struggle. In contrast, Bruckner often presents a sudden outright victory, but with a sense that the conflict may recommence.[72] Sometimes a theme seems to epitomize *lux in tenebris:* the revelation of the final bars of the Third, for example, is that the trumpet theme has from the beginning been designed for transfiguration by the tonic major chord (it is accomplished by the alteration of a single note). Light is absent at first but destined to shine in the darkness at the end. I think the most likely prototype for this type of Brucknerian transfiguration occurs at the end of Wagner's *Der Fliegende Holländer,* where the Dutchman and Senta appear *in verklärter Gestalt* (in transfigured form) as they ascend to Heaven. The Dutchman's motive is lit by major harmony without any change to its melodic structure, thus demontrating a remarkable resemblance to what happens in Bruckner's Third Symphony (see Exx. 5.6a and 5.6b).[73]

Bruckner does not transform his themes by changing tempo, meter, and rhythm (like, say, Liszt in *Tasso*); he transfigures by changing pitches and

EXAMPLE 5.6A. Wagner, *Der Fliegende Holländer,* the Flying Dutchman's motive at the beginning of the opera

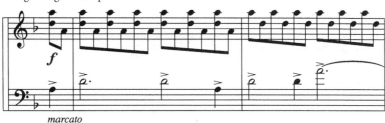

EXAMPLE 5.6B. Wagner, *Der Fliegende Holländer,* the Flying Dutchman's motive at the end of the opera

harmony. Carl Dahlhaus remarks that "Bruckner's symphonic style . . . is primarily rhythmic rather than diastemic, and thus seems to stand the usual hierarchy of tonal properties on its head."[74] When Bruckner changes the pitch structure (the meaning of diastemic) of his motives, "there is no need to search for an overriding thematic process to legitimize the change"[75] as one would seek to do with Brahms. In certain cases, pitch is important: inversions, for example, are not accidents. However, Bruckner does not abide by the musical logic of the Brahmsian "developing variation" for which pitch structure is the crucial parameter. Bruckner, it may be noted, uses inversion, augmentation, and diminution but not retrograde, which drastically affects rhythm.

Let us examine various kinds of transfigurations in the later symphonies. In the coda of the first movement of the Sixth, the theme that, for Simpson, originally heaved "darkly in the depths"[76] now "rises and falls like some great ship, the water illuminated in superb hues as the sun rises, at last bursting clear in the sky."[77] The theme is here transfigured by an alteration in shape, a transposition upward in pitch, "glowing" brass timbre, and a new accompaniment of religiously symbolic plagal harmony (see Exx. 5.7a and 5.7b). At the close of the symphony, the theme is transfigured by a change from Phrygian mode to diatonic major (see Ex. 5.7c) while, above it, the string figure from bars 29–30 of the Finale returns transfigured by a change from chromaticism to diatonicism. These changes conform to my earlier definition of transfiguration as a process in which rhythmic identity is re-

EXAMPLE 5.7A. Symphony no. 6, 1st movement, bars 3–6

EXAMPLE 5.7B. Symphony no. 6, end of first movement

EXAMPLE 5.7C. Symphony no. 6, end of Finale

tained while other parameters are altered in a way that marks them semi-otically as "elevated," "glowing," and so forth.

Watson speaks of the "grim darkness" of the C-minor inverted statement of the main theme in the first movement of the Seventh.[78] It is in marked contrast to the close of the movement, when E major "shines forth."[79] A parallel may be found in Raphael's *Transfiguration* (1517–20), in the Vatican Museum, Rome (see Fig. 5.1). This painting, which Bruckner may well have known, is based on Saint Matthew's description of Christ's transfiguration: "His face did shine as the sun, and his raiment was white as the light."[80]

Raphael's *Transfiguration* is interpreted by Linda Murray as follows:

> The contrast between the divine radiance of the vision and earthly confusion and sorrow, between the means of salvation in which one must believe rather than just witness, and the blindness and suffering of unregenerate human nature, made insensible of its state by possession of sin, seems to be the programme behind this work.[81]

Raphael depicts a light/darkness opposition, which Murray reads metaphorically as "vision" and "blindness." The clear-cut division into faith and sin would no doubt have appealed to Bruckner.

FIGURE 5.1. Raphael's *Transfiguration*

The main motive of the first movement of the Eighth is identical in rhythm to the first subject in the opening movement of Beethoven's Ninth, as Doernberg points out.[82] This is more than simple coincidence, for although they have only rhythm in common, this is the crucial parameter for Bruckner. The motive is, in fact, restricted to a single pitch for the "annunciation of death," but is transfigured as a C-major broken chord at the symphony's close. The "annunciation of death" is followed by what Bruckner labeled the *Totenuhr*.[83] Rather than "hour of death," this refers to the *Klopfkäfer* (knocking beetle), whose sound was a sign, in folklore, for impending death.[84] The negative impact of the ending of the first movement is counterbalanced by the extremely positive effect of four simultaneous thematic transfigurations at the symphony's close. Moreover, the transfigured main themes from each movement are joined by a fifth transfiguration: it is of a figure that appeared in C minor at the beginning of the coda and now resounds in C major.[85] After the first performance of the Eighth, no wonder Hugo Wolf felt impelled to write that it was "the absolute victory of light over darkness."[86]

Transfigurations are not restricted to the endings of movements. In the Adagio of the Ninth, the "flaming light"[87] that shines at letter A is a transfiguration of the first bar of the movement. Then "darkness returns" again for the "Farewell to Life"[88] at bar 29.

PLATEAUS OF INTENSITY

Bruckner's music presents us with plateaus of intensity rather than orgasmic releases. His method of breaking off, replacing, then reinstating is not the typical tonal process of tension and relaxation. Because there is no reconciliation in Bruckner's dialectic, the resolution of conflict needs massive emphasis and yet may still be heard as uncertain, conditional, abrupt. In a commentary on St. John 1:1–5, A. E. Brooke explains that in men "life takes the higher form of 'light,' moral and spiritual life" of which God is the source, and that the "fight between this light and its opposite, the moral darkness of evil, has always been going on, and the light has never been conquered."[89] The phrase "lux in tenebris" affirms that light has never been conquered—but, then, neither has darkness. In this context, consider Martin Kettle's warning: "The biggest error you can make with a Bruckner symphony is to mishear its emphatic sounds and believe they are conclusive . . . His symphonic writing aims at a distant resolution, but when it arrives it only does so through contingent climaxes."[90]

Perhaps all climaxes for Bruckner are contingent until the *tuba mirum* sounds for judgment day. Until then, darkness cannot be completely and forever vanquished by light. The fact that darkness so often returns at the beginnings of his codas shows the provisional nature of his climaxes. If brightness can be eclipsed at this late stage, what sense of finality is really

achieved in the concluding blaze of sound? Bruckner seeks a spiritual closure in his codas, but it is never more than provisionally attained, because
any sense of a *telos* (or final goal) has been displaced by a multiplicity of
break-flows and reversals.

For Watson, the C-major climax of the slow movement of the Seventh
is "a most wonderful letting in of the light."[91] Yet in the bar prior to this blaze
of light, we are poised on the dominant of C♯ minor, the movement's tonic.
Halfway through this bar, the dominant harmony is interpreted enharmon-
ically as a German sixth in C major/minor, facilitating an abrupt shift of
tonal direction. The massive C-major climax in this C♯ minor movement
satisfies an *ideological,* not a *structural,* need. Its meaning must be sought in
an intertextual field of reference; it is not to be found embodied in some
purely compositional logic. The climax of the Adagio of the original Eighth
was also C major, a key that had already been loudly proclaimed at the end
of the original first movement. Like Watson, I assume that when Bruckner
revised the loud C-major ending of the first movement, he changed the climax of the Adagio for same reason, to maximize the impact of the C-major
climax to the Finale. Watson is surely wrong, however, to claim that the original first movement ending "weakens the overall tonal pattern."[92] The revised ending is also in C major, although it may not feel much like it (and
the last nine bars are hollow fifths). The devout Bruckner could not allow
what he himself termed, with its religious connotations, an annunciation of
death to be followed by a nihilistic minor conclusion as Tchaikovsky or
Mahler might have done. In the original version it is the *triumphal impact* of
C major at the symphony's conclusion that is weakened, not the symphony's
overall tonal pattern.

Bruckner's main climaxes resonate darkly as *quantus tremor, dies irae,*
or the "shadow of death" or blaze radiantly as *rex gloriae, Gloria/Hosanna in
excelsis,* or *lux sancta.* The Finale of the Fifth, which Simpson labeled "one
of the greatest climaxes in symphonic music,"[93] is a climax of the Gloria/
Hosanna type. The first fugue subject is 3 bars long, like that to the words
"Alles was Odem hat" in *Psalm 150,* and the two are clearly related. There are
no erotic Tristan climaxes in Bruckner; he does not build climaxes with
"yearning" appoggiaturas but by accretion of motives, and his climaxes end
far too abruptly. While a tragic climax, complete with "aching" or "despair-
ing" appoggiaturas, sometimes occurs,[94] it is never the movement's, or symphony's, *main* climax. Bruckner avoids the heroic climax, too, and this is
not to be put down solely to an absence of percussion and rhythmic figures
suggestive of drums. The endings of Liszt's *Tasso* (see Exx. 5.8a and 5.8b) and
Les Préludes, for instance, are heroic transformations of material, not Brucknerian transfigurations.

Eero Tarasti comments that the "fanfare theme" of *Les Préludes* "moves
in the Beethovenian tonality of triumph, C major, but whose dotted rhythmic figure, the unison sound of heavy wind instruments, cellos and basses
as well as plagal harmonies give this theme an ideal and sublime hero-

EXAMPLE 5.8A. Liszt, *Tasso*, Adagio, bars 62–67

EXAMPLE 5.8B. Liszt, *Tasso*, Moderato, bars 535–42

mythical quality typical of Liszt."[95] It was not inappropriately used many years ago as incidental music to the film serial *Flash Gordon Conquers the Universe*. The endings of Tchaikovsky's Fifth and Mendelssohn's Third Symphonies are no more Brucknerian, despite their victories of major over minor.[96] They sound too comfortable with their march rhythms and "heroic" brass. Bloch would undoubtedly argue that an impression is given of assertion for its own sake. Beethoven, much admired by Bruckner, is associated with the hero-mythical, typified by the *Eroica* Symphony.[97] Sometimes Bruckner elevates the hero-mythical to the sacred: for example, the Wagner tribute in the Adagio of the Seventh.[98] To use Tarasti's semantic vocabulary, there is a sacred isotopy in Bruckner's music into which other mythical semes merge. In the Fourth, it could be argued that the nature-mythical and the pastoral dominate; indeed, in this work Martin Pulbrook claims that there is evidence of Bruckner's making a conscious effort to move away from "specifically religious inspiration."[99]

Simpson declares that the typical Bruckner finale is

> not really a summing-up, despite the immense climaxes that end the Fifth and Eighth symphonies. Such climaxes, far from being driven by the accumulated energy of a vividly muscular process (as in a classical symphony) or by the warring of emotive elements (as in the purely romantic work), are rather the final intensification of an essence.[100]

For Cooke, too, a Bruckner finale is not "the culminating high point of the symphony"; its function is rather to "simply ratify the world of the first three movements on a larger scale."[101] Simpson's and Cooke's comments provide evidence for my contention that it is more appropriate to speak of plateaus in Bruckner's music rather than peaks.[102] The typical Bruckner climax is attained as a plateau of intensity, as distinct from the more usual nineteenth-century process of arsis, climax, and catharsis. The various stages of Bruckner's formal process, states Cooke, "are not offered as dynamic phases of a drama, but as so many different viewpoints from which to absorb the basic material."[103]

Gregory Bateson's idea of a "plateau of intensity,"[104] which he finds, for example, in Balinese culture, has been taken up by Gilles Deleuze and Félix Guattari. They explain this plateau as "a continuous, self-vibrating region of intensities whose development avoids any orientation toward a culmination point or external end."[105] The idea leads them to envisage a book that, instead of having chapters with culmination and termination points, is composed of "plateaus that communicate with one another across microfissures."[106] The Bible might already be thought to approach this description,[107] and so do Bruckner's nonculminative and fissured structures. Heinrich Schenker complained that Bruckner's musical thought "admits no inner need for a middle, a beginning, or even an end,"[108] and a later music analyst, Derrick Puffett, commented on "determinedly non-functional (dysfunctional?) harmony" in the Adagio of the Ninth Symphony and the ambiguous tonality found at the recapitulation.[109] The parallel should not be overdone—Deleuze and Guattari have a much freer assemblage in mind than a Bruckner symphony—but let us explore further. By "plateau," Deleuze and Guattari explain that they mean "any multiplicity connected to other multiplicities by superficial underground stems in such a way as to form or extend a rhizome."[110] Cooke's "ratifying on a larger scale" would suggest just such an extension. Furthermore, Simpson insists: "The massive endings of all Bruckner's symphonies are (with the exception of that of the Fifth) not really culminative in the old sense; they are formal intensifications that blaze with calm. Even in the Fifth there is ultimately this sense of a calm fire."[111]

I have argued that the Bruckner climax is provisional and would suggest that the lack of synthesis in his work is made evident by the lack of, or difficulties in obtaining, closure. Darkness keeps returning. For example, after the climax at letter F in the Finale of the Second, there is an abrupt silence, then a *pp* quotation (bar 200, Haas edition) from the Kyrie of the F-minor Mass (bars 122 onward) and the exposition concludes in this mood (with a plagal cadence). The Kyrie is quoted again (bar 547, Haas edition) shortly before the coda; it is again *pp* following an *fff* climax and 8 unexpectedly quiet intervening bars. The coda itself fails to achieve closure at its first attempt. I cannot agree, therefore, with Newlin's view that "Bruckner's ideal finale is one in which all that has happened in the preceding movements is synthesized" and that such a synthesis "is symbolized in the citation of themes from previous sections of the work."[112] In the closing bars of the Sixth, two themes from the Finale are presented simultaneously with a transfigured version of the main theme of the opening movement, yet Simpson remarks, rightly it seems to me, on its inconclusiveness. The "nocturnal mystery"[113] with which the Finale opens has passed and "the A major sun is high in the sky," but the ending "leaves dark questions unanswered."[114] I assume he has in mind the turns toward B♭ minor at letter X and at bar 397, which are too close to the movement's end for comfort.

Ernst Kurth notes perceptively that harmonic and instrumental darkenings frequently occur "at the moment of achieved apexes" in Bruckner's music.[115] Kurth sees it as symptomatic of Bruckner's anxiety in the midst of exuberance. However, anxiety can suddenly become exuberance. Doernberg, remarks of the end of the Second Symphony: "When a defiant C minor ending seems inevitable, there is a striking change to the major and the symphony ends with positive confidence."[116] Confidence, however, is never secure. Bryan Gilliam writes of the first movement of the Eighth: "As Bruckner originally conceived it, the movement's chief dramatic event was a final presentation of the tonally ambiguous opening theme—at the very end of the coda—now resonantly clarified into an unambiguous tonal context."[117] Indeed, the coda of the first version concludes with 17 loud bars of C major. Gilliam claims that Bruckner "clearly intended the coda as an apotheosis"[118]; therefore, the revision "represents a fundamental change from his original structural concept."[119] One might also add that it represents a fundamental change of mood. Bruckner, from the G-minor Overture on,[120] is always at his least secure when trying to attain closure, which is why his music lends substance to Deleuze and Guattari's claim that "musical form, right down to its ruptures and proliferations, is comparable to a weed, a rhizome."[121]

Doernberg, commenting on the climax of the Adagio of the Ninth, remarks that "no solution is offered to the paroxysm of dissonance and restlessness."[122] The music is shattered at this point, yet it revives—like Deleuze and Guattari's rhizome, it "may be broken, shattered at a given spot, but it will start up again on one of its old lines, or on new lines."[123] Examples are legion in Bruckner's symphonies: at letter N in the first movement of the Eighth (after the third *fff* statement of the main theme), the music splinters into fragments but then begins to reconstruct itself; at letter D in the Finale of the Eighth, the music starts up on new lines after having broken off (at I and between P and T there are other examples).[124]

CONCLUSION

It has not been my intention to argue that Bruckner's music is solely about darkness and light; neither has it been my contention that Bruckner's music is sacred to the exclusion of all else. Constantin Floros sums up the contradictory elements embraced in the cosmos of the Bruckner symphony as "the sacred and profane, the ceremonial and the intimate, religious and romantic, drama and lyricism, march and funeral march, the *Ländler* and the chorale."[125] *Ländler* rhythms can be found in the Scherzos of the Third and Fifth Symphonies. Bruckner was once in demand as a fiddler at village dances, loved dancing himself, and wrote dance music for piano. He was disappointed in love many times and was far from uninterested in romance. His love interests probably spilled over into his songs and piano music, for example, "Mein Herz und deine Stimme" and *Steiermärker*). He referred to his First Symphony as " 's kecke Beserl," which, according to Newlin, was "a favourite expression of Viennese students designating a bold young girl."[126] Ludwig Finscher regards this symphony as a secular work in contrast to *Die Nullte* (Symphony no. o), which conforms to the sacred paradigm.[127] Bruckner often described a lyrical second group of themes in his scores as *Gesangsthema* or *Gesangsperiode*,[128] and it is possible that feminine connotations may be found here. Ludwig Wittgenstein considered this section of a Bruckner symphony the "wife" to the "husband" of the first subject.[129] Nevertheless, it is important to recognize a distinction between a gendered theme and a gendered sonata structure, and there is something strangely apposite about the Bruckner monument in the Volksgarten, Vienna, which shows a bare-breasted muse raising her arms toward him while he stares in another direction.[130]

I have argued that darkness and light proves to be a productive trope for understanding certain structural and ideological processes in Bruckner's music; and this is partly, of course, because darkness and light are themselves not just about darkness and light. Both terms are rich in the connotations, especially of a religious kind, that were deep concerns of the composer. The darkness and light trope reveals Bruckner to be a man of religious doubt. The blaze of light that follows the repetitions of the "Non confundar in aeternam" theme in the Adagio of his Seventh Symphony turns quickly to darkness: 3 bars after a massive climactic assertion of C major (bars 177–82) we are cast into a despondent C♯ minor. Bruckner cannot be sure whether he will be confounded or not. His friend and ex-pupil Carl Hruby claimed that Bruckner was "a perfect example of speculative Christianity: he wanted to be insured against every eventuality."[131] Two years before his death, his private diaries reveal him meditating on the words of the anatomist Hyrtl: "Is that which Faith calls the immortal soul of man only an organic reaction of the brain?"[132] Enormous imaginative richness and variety of detail can be encompassed in a journey from darkness to light. For further exemplification of the variety of possibilities available, one has only to compare Bruckner's symphonies with the darkness-to-light journeys of the Second, Fifth, and Seventh Symphonies of the temperamentally very different Mahler. Newlin suggests that "certain stylistic traits" are persistent in all Bruckner's symphonies and may be thought of as symptomatic of a "higher unity among the works."[133] This is, perhaps, the reason a light/darkness trope works so consistently. It is the case, sadly, that Bruckner has even been pilloried in terms of darkness and light: Hanslick, after the first Viennese performance of the Seventh in 1886, complained: "In between the lightnings are interminable stretches of darkness."[134]

6

Diabolus in Musica:

LISZT AND THE DEMONIC

ONE PURPOSE OF THIS CHAPTER is to present a typology of the demonic in the music of Franz Liszt (1811–86), but I am also seeking to answer a number of related questions that concern the role Liszt played in the establishment of demonic genres, the techniques he employed in representing the demonic, and the impact they had on his stylistic development as a composer. Do demonic elements appear even where Liszt has not chosen to indicate their presence by title? A wider issue is how we interpret the demonic in Liszt and whether this subject matter brings with it certain structural constraints for the composer.

It is scarcely a coincidence that two of the most celebrated evocations of the demonic that precede Liszt's efforts are both found in operas: Mozart's *Don Giovanni* (1787) and Weber's *Der Freischutz* (1821). A staged spectacle is an efficient means of establishing particular connotations for musical devices, following which they may acquire a degree of independence as musical signs that can be employed in instrumental programmatic forms. Liszt believed that musical form was enriched and enlarged precisely by "those who make use of it only as one of the means of expression."[1] He admired Berlioz for subordinating musical structure to the poetic idea and not cultivating "form for form's sake."[2]

Seeking out demonic devices in act 2, scene 5, of *Don Giovanni*, we find a *fortissimo* diminished seventh chord (with prominent trombones) at the sudden appearance of Commendatore, then dissonances, syncopations, chromaticism (which includes the sharpened fourth), an insistent rhythm, a slow chantlike delivery by Commendatore, tritones after his second call for Don Giovanni to repent, and a slithering bass line. Liszt produced his Reminiscences of *Don Juan* in 1841, making much use of the Commendatore's music of act 2. In the Wolf's Glen scene of *Der Freischutz,* we find tremolo strings, low clarinets, a chromatic descending bass, trombones, shrieking woodwind, unexpected harmonies, jagged motives, diminished sevenths, slithering bass lines, ostinati or ostinatolike patterns, a tritone on the appearance of Samiel, "ominous" soft timpani strokes, and acciacaturas (horns from bar 338). Liszt's demonic music is saturated with such devices, to which he added many more of his own.

NEGATION

In constructing the demonic, the primary musical technique for Liszt is that of *negation:* negation of the beautiful so that it becomes the ugly, of nobility so that it becomes vulgarity, of grace so that it becomes awkwardness, of tranquillity so that it becomes perturbation, and so forth. The secondary technique is parody, though qualities are often negated and parodied (or mocked) at the same time. There is a sense that the demonic is not just malevolent but gleefully malevolent. In music, terms that form binary oppositions are rarely of equal status. One term is usually the negative rather than the opposite of another, its identity is, as it were, that of the other term with a minus sign. Dissonance is a lack of consonance, yet consonance is not a lack of dissonance. This is clear when we look at the etymology of those words: the "dis" in "dissonance" is taken from the Greek prefix δυσ—which carries the notion of "unlucky" or "bad" (a δυσαγγελος is a messenger of ill tidings). The "bad" connotation of "dis" is why some prefer to speak of themselves and others as "differently abled" rather than "disabled." Chromaticism and whole-tone scales negate diatonicism and, in doing so, negate tonality. Again "tonality" is the dominant term; we do not think in terms of lacking *atonality.* Here Liszt's late piece "Bagatelle ohne Tonart" (Bagatelle without tonality) underlines the point and, since this was originally intended as the Fourth Mephisto Waltz, suggests that it is the *ohne* or the minus sign that we should be looking for in his representations of the demonic. That Liszt himself conceived of the demonic in this way is evident from his description of Satan (of Milton's *Paradise Lost*) as a spirit of darkness who casts rays of negation and death.[3]

When seeking out demonic signifiers it is important to remember that it is only as signs relate to other signs that their meaning is recognized. Acciacaturas, for example, are common in elfin representations, but in Baroque harpsichord music they merely function as a way of giving a rhythmic accent to a note, since no dynamic accent is possible on that instrument. Hence, it is important to locate chains of signifiers (syntagmatic chains) that, in representing the demonic, will link together some of the following: minor key (especially D minor), chromaticism, dissonance (especially involving diminished seventh chords and augmented triads), angular melody (especially tritones), syncopation and tempo fluctuation (creating a disintegrating effect on meter and tempo), sacred or noble signifiers in the "wrong" context (trombones in Mozart's *Don Giovanni*, the Dies irae in Berlioz's *Symphonie fantastique* and Liszt's *Totentanz*), glissandi, acciacaturas, slides, and chromatic "slithering" (having a disorienting effect on pitch). In general terms, my argument is that the demonic sign is one that is read as destructive, negating, or mocking because it attacks a particular musical parameter, for example, pitch, regular rhythm, and consonance.

A TYPOLOGY OF THE DEMONIC

The various demonic types involve musical representations of grotesque dancing, shrieking, malicious laughter or cackling, blaspheming or cursing, and malevolent parody. Among them, the tritone has long represented the devil in music by negating a sense of modal or tonal stability. Originally, it acquired the name *diabolus in musica* because of its disruptive effect on the concordant fourths and fifths of Western European medieval music: the interval B to F needed to be "corrected" by flattening the B or sharpening the F.[4] As a counterpart to the tritone, Liszt had a more personal sacred sign, his "cross motif" taken from the first three notes of the Gregorian chant "Crux fidelis," which he used in several of his works. Liszt mentions his use of Gregorian melodies in his compositions in a note to the score of St. Elizabeth.

The idea of music without tonality probably emerged from Liszt's experience of composing using whole tones: the passages of whole-tone scales and whole-tone derived chords (like augmented triads) of *Der Traurige Mönch* had already been described by Liszt in 1860 as "tonartlosen Dissonanzen."[5] Liszt was not the first to make use of whole-tone music: Chernomor is characterized with descending whole tones in Glinka's *Ruslan and Lyudmila* (1842) though seldom, as Serge Gut notes, with augmented triads.[6] Moreover, daring beyond anything in Glinka is the descending whole-note scale from D to F♯, each note harmonized as the root of a major triad, towards the close of Liszt's *Dante* Sonata.

A whole-tone theme opens the last movement of *Von der Wiege bis zum Grabe* (1881), and Liszt goes on to make use of whole-tone derived chords (bars 316, 320, 323–24, etc.). This shows the consistency with which he coded his representations, since his first use of whole tones with augmented triads was in an earlier contemplation of death, *Pensée des morts* of 1852. Whole-tone motion and augmented triads are also important in his late piano piece *Unstern!* and would thus appear to imply that death is part of the "disaster" of its title.

Another catalyst for composing music without a key came from the chromatic-melodic implications of Liszt's harmonic predilections. The four possible augmented triads provide all twelve notes of the chromatic scale (cf. the first theme of the *Faust* Symphony), as do the three possible diminished seventh chords. As Liszt approaches the choral ending of his *Faust* Symphony (1854), he presents a broken diminished seventh chord in the bass, treating each note as the root of a triad after the manner of his treatment of the whole-tone scale toward the end of the *Dante* Sonata.[7] Besides this, some of Liszt's demonic music is so chromatic that a key signature is unhelpful. Hence, although the "Inferno" movement of the *Dante* Symphony is, overall, in D minor, Liszt omits the key signature.

In contrast to chromatic and dissonant harmonies but lending a Gothic dimension to the demonic is Liszt's use of bare fifths. They carry connotations of medieval church ritual, but this is negated by a demonic context—turning, as it were, mass into black mass. The sacred and demonic were never far apart in the Middle Ages (consider the demonic gargoyles of Notre Dame Cathedral in Paris). Bare fifths open Beethoven's Ninth Symphony and the key is D minor, but these do not constitute a chain of signifiers sufficient to represent the demonic and communicate, rather, hollowness or emptiness. A more demonic context for bare fifths is found in Schubert's song "Der Doppelgänger" (1828), and a tritone sounds as the singer confronts his double (bar 44). However, in the context of the variations on the Dies irae heard in Liszt's *Totentanz* (1849), bare fifths create a different and striking effect, a kind of Gothic horror. In the third variation, for example, they are employed as the norm, the thirds of triads being produced only as a matter of contingency by the melody of the Dies irae (see Ex. 6.1).

The "Csárdás macabre" (1881–83) takes fifths to extremes, but this is parallelism of the organum type (see Ex. 6.2). It is macabre because the incongruous mixture of "ancient" harmony and "modern" chromatic motion creates a weird, uncanny effect (a quotation from the Dies irae follows a little later in the piece).

Liszt's interest in fifths no doubt suggested to him the idea of quintal harmony. The harmony of the opening 25 bars of the First Mephisto Waltz is constructed by layering fifths on top of each other (see Ex. 6.3). This is the harmony that results if all four strings of the violin are sounded together. The violin is, of course, commonly thought of as the devil's instrument. The devil's partiality to the violin is of a considerably older vintage than the rumors that surrounded Paganini and it was an idea that crossed a variety of

EXAMPLE 6.1. *Totentanz* (Var. 3)

EXAMPLE 6.2. "Csárdás macabre"

cultures. For example, Tartini's *Devil's Trill* Sonata was supposedly inspired by a dream or vision of the devil playing, as was "Fanitullen" (The devil's tune), a traditional Hardanger fiddle tune from Norway.[8]

Liszt also uses quartal harmony for demonic effect. An early example is found in the chord on which the opening of the *Malédiction* Concerto (1840) is based (see Ex. 6.4), but quartal harmony makes a more extended appearance in the Third Mephisto Waltz of 1883 (see Ex. 6.5).

"Liszt's choice of keys," insists Alan Walker, "is frequently determined by a higher expressive purpose, and is rarely the result of random selection."[9] He gives as examples the association of the divine with F♯ major, love with A♭ major, and Hell with D minor. The Magnificat of the *Dante* Symphony (1856), for example, begins in F♯ major. Moreover, its high pitch (musical texture pitched above the bass clef) contrasts with the low-pitched texture of the demonic first movement (implying Heaven is on high, Hell down below).

Liszt's orchestration is rich in demonic signifiers; some of them, as we have noted, have been inherited, but others are of his own devising. A subtle example is the harp diminished seventh glissando in the "Inferno" movement of the *Dante* Symphony, bar 393; the effect was reused in Mephisto Waltz no. 1 at bar 878. It is another example of negation—it denies the harp its idiomatic diatonic scale. Liszt instructs that if no harp is available for the diminished seventh cadenza in the *Dante* Symphony it is to be omitted rather

EXAMPLE 6.3. Mephisto Waltz no. 1, bars 9–13

EXAMPLE 6.4. *Malédiction* chord

than played on a piano. On the piano the effect would be lost: the harp is characteristically diatonic, the piano not. The arpeggio is achieved by re-tuning strings to enharmonic equivalents through use of the harp's pedals (see Ex. 6.6).

The question is sometimes raised concerning Liszt's intellectual owner-ship of the orchestral effects he employed. Peter Raabe concluded from lengthy examination of the many extant manuscripts of Liszt's orchestral music that whatever scoring suggestions had been made by the likes of Peter Cornelius, Joachim Raff, and Johann Conradi, these occurred at draft stages. The final versions were written in Liszt's hand and were undoubtedly af-fected by his experience of working with the Weimar orchestra.[10]

Some orchestral effects were part of a Romantic general currency, and Berlioz's *Grande traite d'instrumentation et d'orchestration modernes* (1843) provides insight into their origins and how they were received in the mid–nineteenth century. For example, the "slides of short notes, preceding longer ones" on double bass found in the Hades scene, act 2 of Gluck's *Orfeo,* at the description of the howling of Cerberus,[11] can be seen as a source for the opening of the "Mephistopheles" movement from the *Faust* Symphony. In each case, the slide is a tritone in compass (see Exx. 6.7 and 6.8).

EXAMPLE 6.5. Mephisto Waltz no. 3, bars 6–11

EXAMPLE 6.6. *Dante* Symphony, harp cadenza

Liszt's *Dante* Symphony begins with a recitativelike setting for *fortissimo* trombones, tuba, and lower strings of the words (from canto 3) written over the gateway of hell. Regarding the timbre of trombones, Berlioz states: "In fortissimo it is menacing and terrifying, especially if the three trombones are in unison, or at least two are in unison and the third takes the octave of the same tone."[12] He cites the Chorus of Furies in act 2 of Gluck's *Iphigénie en Tauride* (incidentally, it is in D minor) and Alceste's aria "Divinités du Styx" in *Alceste*, act 1. It is clearly a lesson Liszt has learned. Moreover, he chooses to punctuate this instrumental recitative with rolls on two timpani and strokes on a tam-tam. To cite Berlioz again: "The gong or tamtam is used only in compositions of a mournful character or in dramatic scenes of the utmost horror. Its powerful, vibrating sound combined with heavy chords of the brass (trumpets and trombones) has a truly awful effect."[13]

The passage culminates in a chantlike monotone (except for the final note) of "Lasciate ogni speranza, voi ch'entrate" on trumpets and horns against a string tremolo (see Ex. 6.9). Then a representation of the whirlwind (marked *tempestuoso*) begins in cellos and basses accompanied by a bass drum roll (a bass drum roll had featured in the "Songe d'une nuit du Sabbat" of Berlioz's *Symphonie fantastique*, 1830), and a theme appears that descends chromatically and gives emphasis to the tritone (see Ex. 6.10). The devices of *accelerando* and *stringendo* in this movement can be interpreted as being designed to have a negating effect on steady tempo.

A particularly demonic passage occurs after the "Lasciate ogni speranza" theme returns at letter Q, complete with a newly acquired tritone ending. The orchestration of the bars that follow (269–75) serves to illustrate another comment from Berlioz's treatise:

EXAMPLE 6.7. *Orfeo*, act 2, Hades scene

EXAMPLE 6.8. *Faust* Symphony, "Mephistopholes"

The combination of the low tones of the English horn with those of the clarinets and French horns during a tremolo of the double-basses produces an effect as characteristic as it is novel; it is particularly well suited to cast a menacing color upon musical ideas in which fear and anguish predominate. This effect was known neither to Mozart nor to Weber or Beethoven. A magnificent example is to be found in the duet in the fourth act of "Les Huguenots"; I think Meyerbeer was the first to have used it in the theater.[14]

Here we can see clearly how a signifier that is given a concrete signified in opera is able to establish itself as a convention. Furthermore, these bars from "Inferno" contain *fortissimo* runs of notes on the piccolo, something Berlioz pronounced excellent "for violent and incisive effects—for example, in a thunderstorm or in a scene of fierce or infernal character."[15]

Liszt states in the score that the trills in clarinets and viola, bars 404–24, represent mocking, scornful laughter and are to be very sharply marked[16] (see Ex. 6.11). Once more, Liszt is indebted to a sign born of opera. Berlioz attributes to Weber the use of the low register of the clarinet to produce "those coldly threatening effects, those dark accents of quiet rage."[17]

To summarize other demonic signifiers present in this movement, there are sforzandi and accented notes; expression markings such as "violente," "tempestuoso," and "frenetico"; extremes of tempo (it opens *lento,* at letter G

EXAMPLE 6.9. "Inferno," bars 12–17, "Lasciate" theme

EXAMPLE 6.10. *Inferno*, bars 22–25

is *presto molto,* and at Q is back to *lento*); plenty of tritones; short, dry *sforzandi* from heavy brass; descending chromatic lines; bare fifth harmony for the last statement of the "Lasciate" theme; D minor but much tonal ambiguity (the "Lasciate" theme is first announced over a chord of C♯ minor); two timpanists; and *violente* strings and a snarling low horn created by its being stopped yet played *forte* for the 5 bars that lead to letter B.

It might be thought from the foregoing that Liszt relied heavily on the orchestra for his demonic effects. However, the *Dante* Sonata (1837–49)[18] shows that Liszt could achieve novel demonic sonorities even without the timbral resources of an orchestra. Liszt asks for unorthodox pedaling for the "lamentoso" theme, requiring the pedal to be held down continuously for first 5, then 4 bars. It is intended to represent the tumult of Hell as described in lines 22–30 of canto 3:

> Quivi sospiri, pianti e alti guai
>> risonavan per l'aere sanza stelle,
>> per ch'io al cominciar ne lagrimai.
> Diverse lingue, orribili favelle,
>> parole di dolore, accenti d'ira,
>> voci alte e fioche, e suon di man con elle
> facevano un tumulto, il qual s'aggira
>> sempre in quell'aura sanza tempo tinta,
>> come la rena quando turbo spira.

EXAMPLE 6.11. *Dante* Symphony, bars 410–13

(There sighs, lamentations and loud wailings
  resounded through the starless air,
  so that at first it made me weep.
Strange tongues, horrible language,
  words of pain, tones of anger,
  voices loud and hoarse, and with these the sound of hands,
made a tumult which is whirling
  always through that air forever dark,
  as sand eddies in a whirlwind.[19])

Evidence for his representational intentions is found in a copy owned by Liszt's pupil Walter Bache, which contains annotations that he may have made on the basis of information from the composer.[20]

As early as February 1840, a critic who commented on Liszt's *Dante* Sonata in the *Allgemeine Theaterzeitung* sees a whole future in the techniques the composer uses to capture the *diabolische Element*.[21] At this time, Liszt himself was not using the term *Zukunftsmusik* ("music of the future") to describe his compositions; Alan Walker attributes the coining of this term to Carolyne von Sayn-Wittgenstein in the 1850s.[22] I would certainly not claim that *all* Liszt's innovations result from his desire to represent the demonic in music; however, I am arguing that some of the most striking and adventurous techniques he develops can be related to that desire. In support of this argument, I refer the reader to Serge Gut's remarks on the number of original elements in Liszt's musical language that were put to the service of works like the *Dante* Sonata, the Sonata in B Minor, the *Faust* Symphony, and the First Mephisto Waltz.[23] It will be noted that three of his four examples have an overt demonic context.

DEMONIC GENRES

Building on the work of his predecessors and contemporaries, Liszt plays an important part in establishing particular demonic genres, such as the *danse macabre,* the demonic scherzo, the demonic ride, the "vision of horror" (the "Inferno" movement of the *Dante* Symphony), and the more abstract studies like *Unstern!* (a dark counterpart to the *méditation religieuse* genre). In so doing, he was to bequeath a fertile legacy to Saint-Saëns, Franck, Dvořák, Mussorgsky, Balakirev, and others.

In 1838 Liszt made a transcription of Schubert's "Erlkönig" that became a favorite with the public.[24] It helped to establish the demonic ride as an instrumental genre. Berlioz includes a demonic ride, "La Course à l'Abîme," in scene 18 of *La Damnation de Faust* (1846), a work dedicated to Liszt. An example of one of Liszt's own demonic rides is "Wilde Jagd," no. 8 of the *Études d'exécution transcendante,* of 1851. Its tempo is *presto furioso,* and the piece features roaring bass octaves and irregularly placed chords interspersed with rapid five-note runs in octaves (the tuneful second subject, however, seems a little out of place). "Mazeppa," no. 4 of the *Études d'exécution transcendante,* contains traits related to the demonic ride, and these increased significantly in its orchestral version as Symphonic Poem no. 6.

Liszt also played a major role in establishing the genres of demonic dance and demonic scherzo. The demonic dance overlaps with the demonic scherzo as formerly the minuet overlapped with the scherzo: his Gnomenreigen no. 2 of *Zwei Konzertetüden* (1863), for example, is a round dance marked *presto scherzando.* Precursors of the demonic scherzo are found in Beethoven (the Scherzo of the Ninth Symphony and that of the String Quartet in E♭ Major, op. 74), Berlioz (*Queen Mab* Scherzo from *Roméo et Juliette,* 1839), and Mendelssohn (the Scherzo from his *Sommernachtstraum* incidental music, 1843).

In 1841 Liszt produced "Reminiscences of *Robert le Diable:* Valse infernale," with which he enjoyed great public success.[25] The piece focuses on the waltz sung in act 3 of Meyerbeer's opera (1831) by Robert's demonic father Bertram and a horde of evil spirits. This may have given Liszt the idea of composing a demonic waltz of his own. However, it was some time before he acted upon it, and Johann Strauss II beat him to both the composition of a waltz with a demonic theme, "Mephistos Höllenrufe" (Mephisto's summons to Hell) of 1851, and a polka, "Lucifer" of 1862.

In all, Liszt was to compose four Mephisto Waltzes and a Mephisto Polka. The First Mephisto Waltz was for orchestra originally, being the second of his Two Episodes from Lenau's *Faust* (1859–60), but Liszt created a piano version that differs in several respects. The orchestral version is titled "Der Tanz in der Dorfschenke" (The dance in the village inn) and represents Mephistopheles playing the violin—there is an explicit program attached to the score that quotes Nikolaus Lenau (1802–50), a Hungarian poet who usually wrote in German. The Second Mephisto Waltz was again for orchestra but also exists transcribed for piano. Leonard B. Meyer explains that the "satanic malevolence" in this waltz is delineated by "predominantly low register, loud dynamics, rapid tempo, discordant harmony and disjunct motion, and ironically irregular waltz rhythms."[26] The waltz makes dramatic use of the tritone at both beginning and end. Humphrey Searle regards the Third Mephisto Waltz of 1883 as one of the composer's finest achievements, which shows Liszt "at his most ruthless and savage."[27] Sacheverell Sitwell, too, valued it as "among his very finest and most powerful works."[28] That same year he wrote the Mephisto Polka, also for piano solo.

The "Bagatelle ohne Tonart" (1883–85) for piano was originally intended as the Fourth Mephisto Waltz. Its demonic character remains evident in its opening tritones and the series of unresolved diminished seventh chords with which it ends. The actual Fourth Mephisto Waltz (1885) for piano has an unfinished middle section. The outer sections are complete, however, and show Liszt's continuing interest in experimenting with tonality: its key signature is two sharps, but it begins and ends in an Aeolian C♯ minor.

A large-scale demonic concertante work is *Totentanz*. It is subtitled *Danse macabre*, which illustrated a common confusion between the latter and the "dance of death" in the nineteenth century. In the Middle Ages, the *danse macabre* was a processional dance toward death that involved all social ranks.[29] The dance of death, however, was supposedly performed by the dead rising from their graves at midnight (prior to seeking out new victims).[30] The first sketches were made in Pisa in 1839, and it has been argued that *Totentanz* was originally inspired by a fresco, *The Triumph of Death* (*Trionfo della morte*), in the Camposanto. The fresco was once thought to be by the fourteenth-century Florentine artist Andrea Orcagna but is now considered to be the work of Francesco Traini.[31] Death is portayed as a woman with a bat's wings swooping down on a company of nobles and swinging a scythe in her clawed hands. The personification of Death as a woman has a precursor in Petrarch's *Triumph of Death*, and this may account for the fresco's title. Yet why did Liszt choose "dance of death" rather than "triumph of death" for his own title?

Another theory is that the *Totentanz* relates to Holbein. Nineteenth-century editions of Holbein's woodcuts of 1538 were readily available. Sharon Winklhofer argues that Hans Holbein's *Der Todtentanz* (*sic*) was a more likely stimulus for Liszt's *Totentanz* and that the variations relate to characters depicted in that series of prints.[32] She suggests that the Camposanto fresco inspired, instead, the *Malédiction* Concerto. Yet the musical images most attached to the dance of death in the nineteenth century have been identified by Robert Samuels as the masked ball and the waltz.[33] It would seem that such images influence Liszt's Mephisto Waltzes rather than the *Totentanz*. The waltz was thought to stimulate sexual desire, and the masked ball offered opportunities for licentiousness; moreover, like the dance of death, it did not discriminate along the lines of social class. The linking of both masquerade and waltz to the dance of death can be seen in Charles Rowlandson's engravings *The English Dance of Death* (1814–16).

In deciding to use the Dies irae in his *Totentanz*, Liszt was no doubt influenced by Berlioz's "Songe d'une nuit du Sabbat,"[34] where it makes its first awesome appearance played by two trombones in unison, doubled at the lower octave by four bassoons. Later the dance theme of the "Ronde du Sabbat" is combined with the Dies irae to blasphemous effect (note that this works as a clash of styles even if the program is ignored). The Dies irae makes an equally daunting first appearance in Liszt's *Totentanz*, where it is pitted against a diminished triad ostinato hammered out by piano and timpani. This anticipates his later use (for example, in *Unstern!*) of a constantly repeated dissonant chord that makes no attempt to be reconciled with a theme being played simultaneously.

The demonic symphonic piece overlaps with all of the above but has its own distinctiveness as in, for example, the vision of horror that is the "Inferno" movement of the *Dante* Symphony or the venomous parody of the "Mephistopheles" movement of the *Faust* Symphony (which will be discussed in the next section). Arguably, the symphonic poem *Hunnenschlacht*, too, falls into the demonic category; Ben Arnold describes it as "a triumph of God over Satan, good over evil"[35] (it makes explicit use of the "Crux fidelis"). The *Dante* Symphony was originally intended to be a multimedia experience. Liszt planned to project slides made from Bonaventura Genelli's illustrations to the *Divina Commedia* during the performance.[36] A performance of the symphony with slides was eventually given in Brussells in 1984.[37] Liszt also wanted to use an experimental wind machine in the final section of the "Inferno" movement to depict Hell's whirlwind.[38] It was going to cost 20,000 thalers, a sum Carolyne von Sayn-Wittgenstein was prepared to provide,[39] but the idea was abandoned.

INTERPRETING THE DEMONIC IN LISZT

Lawrence Kramer suggests that "the satanic mystique of Paganini and the demonic/erotic aura of Liszt" were derived in part from a sense that "these musicians were driven to create works of superhuman difficulty—objects impossible to anyone but them."[40] This was, indeed, only part of the explanation, and sometimes the perception of demonic possession shifted from performer to audience if fearful critics thought the latter was responding with diabolic enthusiasm, as at Paganini's concerts at the Opera, Paris, in 1831. In the case of Liszt, his levelheaded pupil Amy Fay, who knew him as a human being rather than a concert virtuoso, wrote of his playing: "It gives *me* almost a ghostly feeling to hear him, and it seems as if the air were peopled with spirits."[41] While acknowledging that the younger Liszt's "uncanny skill" prompted ideas of the devil having aided him, Sacheverell Sitwell reminds us that Liszt played the role of Mephisto "to an ever-increasing extent in old age," when he looked like "a wizard, a Merlin."[42] Liszt, in fact, produced some of his most demonic pieces *after* he had given up public recitals.

The legend of Faust's compact with the devil, as reworked by Goethe, was an inspiration to many Romantic composers. Wagner's *Faust Ouvertüre* (1840), for example, was based on Goethe. Liszt conducted Schumann's *Scenes from Faust* at Weimar in 1849 and invited Berlioz to conduct *La Damnation de Faust* at Weimar in 1852 (though this merely borrows a few scenes from Goethe). In the early 1850s, Liszt had ambitions to compose a Faust opera to a libretto by Gérard de Nerval and Alexandre Dumas père. Nerval had published a French translation of Goethe's *Faust* in 1827, to which Berlioz introduced Liszt in 1830,[43] and had himself written four dramas based on the Faust legend.[44]

Serge Gut explains the appeal of this subject to Liszt by remarking that in the *Faust* Symphony "Liszt avait la possibilité de peindre musicalement la dualité de son âme: *Faust* et *Méphisto*."[45] Walter Beckett describes Liszt in his early twenties as being "torn between his strong impulse towards religion and his great and natural delight in worldly things."[46] We might consider also the well-known description "Mephistopheles disguised as an abbé" furnished by the historian Gregorovius after seeing Liszt in Rome in 1865.[47] Goethe represented Faust as having this duality in extremes:

Zwei Seelen wohnen, ach in meiner Brust,
Die eine will sich von der andern trennen;
Die eine hält, in derber Liebesluft,
Sich an die Welt mit klammernden Organen;
Die andre hebt gewaltsam sich von Duft
Zu den Gefilden hoher Ahnen.[48]

Two souls, alas, are housed within my breast,
And each will wrestle for mastery there;
The one has passion's craving crude for love,
And hugs a world where sweet the senses rage;
The other longs for pastures fair above
Leaving the murk for lofty heritage.[49]

Yet in the character study that forms the first movement of Liszt's symphony, Faust is not portrayed in a negative or vulgar way. In fact, he cannot be, since Liszt has chosen to give the role of negating and vulgarizing Faust's themes to Mephistopheles. Thus, it is only by taking the two characters together that we can come close to making up the sum of Goethe's Faust. Yet in doing so we would include a capacity for self-parody that Goethe's character does not possess and, at the same time, would remove the role of Goethe's agent of denial and destruction, Mephistopheles, who announces shortly after his arrival in Faust's study:

Ich bin der Geist, der stets verneint!
Und das mit Recht; denn alles was entsteht
Ist wert, dass es zugrunde geht.[50]

(I am the spirit that denies!
And rightly so; for everything that is created
Is worth destroying.)

In Goethe's view of evil, Alan P. Cottrell informs us, "the forces of denial do not enjoy coequality with those of divine goodness," though they remain "an indispensable attribute of the Creation."[51] Cottrell describes Mephistopheles's modus operandi as being characterized by two tendencies, illusion and denial. He encourages "flights of fancy, idle dreaming, vain rapture and the hubris of self-importance" yet proceeds to "mock man's sense of individual worth, ridicules his ideals," and "jeers at his struggle for freedom and dignity."[52] It is the second of these tendencies only that we find in Liszt's *Faust* Symphony (1857) and, as such, Liszt also departs from Goethe in his character study of Mephistopheles. Cynicism is the trademark of Goethe's Mephistopheles: he shows no principled preference for the material over the spiritual but, instead, a determination to use either as a means of temptation. Goethe suggests by this that both body and mind are vulnerable to the forces of evil. There is a parallel in Kierkegaard's contention that the demonic can take spiritual forms if such are needed to play a self-defensive role in denying faith and the eternal.[53] However, Kierkegaard's demonic is distinct from Goethe's. For Kierkegaard, George Pattison explains,

> that which in nature, in childhood and in the pagan world is experienced as innocent and thoughtless immediacy comes to be regarded as "demonic" when the Christian revelation establishes the goal of "higher" self-consciousness and ultimately self-responsible life as the true *telos* of human experience.[54]

For Goethe, it is art that makes order of nature and provides a defense against its destructive power.[55]

I am not citing Kierkegaard's philosophy because I believe it was something with which Liszt was familiar. Kierkegaard was little known in Europe before his "discovery" around 1920. My reason for making reference to his theory of the demonic is because it developed in the 1840s and throws useful light on the contemporaneous development of the demonic in Liszt. Kierkegaard's thoughts usefully illustrate the problem this subject matter holds for dialectic argument of the Hegelian kind, and this is not without its musical implications. The demonic character is, for Kierkegaard, not the opposite of the good but, rather, one that despairingly defies the good in fear of what is ultimately the source of personal salvation (thus resembling the condition termed "resistance" in psychiatry).[56] Kierkegaard's arguments therefore suggest reasons for Liszt's avoidance of dialectical struggle that leads to higher synthesis in his demonic compositions. In the *Faust* Symphony there is no higher synthesis of the characters of Faust and Mephistopheles, since the latter merely negates the former. The final *chorus mysticus,* though it sets Goethe's words, offers a Kierkegaardian solution to the musical struggle between Faust and the demonic. Here no "sublation" is possible; either Mephistopheles triumphs or Faust triumphs. For Gretchen, too, it is a matter of *gerichtet* or *gerettet,* judged or saved. Kierkegaard's antidialectical position, and his break with Hegelianism, is flagged up in the very title of his book *Either/Or.*[57] Faust's victory can only be achieved by redemption, an idea with which Kierkegaard challenges Hegel's dialectical thought. A moral choice is to be made between alternatives, rather than seeking a reconciling synthesis.

The first part of *Either/Or* contains a long essay on the demonic in Mozart, in which Kierkegaard advances the idea that music is "an imperfect medium," unlike language, and thus "cannot have its absolute object in the immediately spiritual."[58] This is not to claim that music is the work of the devil, but that music is available and suited to the sensuous and demoniacal because, while being of a much greater degree of abstraction than language, it is able better to depict mood and passion.[59] For Kierkegaard, Christianity is the Word made flesh and music is a communicative medium that does not have the same ethical and religious relationship to Christianity—in short, music is not part of a moral or ethical domain.[60] He refers to the many stories and legends in which persons are put under a musical spell by mermaids or mermen.[61] Breaking such spells often requires the music to be played backward. Similarly, the demonic character inverts meanings and negates the truth: "What the demoniac says is of such a nature that the truth is present as soon as the meaning is inverted."[62] Kierkegaard uses the legend of Agnes and the merman to sketch out further his ideas on the demonic in *Fear and Trembling* (1843)[63] and states that the demonic can "express itself as contempt for men."[64] This certainly accords with Liszt's musical representation of Mephistopheles.

For the demoniac there is only the choice between moving to faith and remaining within the demonic.[65] No reconciliation between the two is possible. We find a similar bind in the *Dante* Symphony. Heaven and Hell cannot be reconciled. In the "Inferno" movement, the only musical conflict presented is that between the restless and consuming love of Paulo and Francesca and the horrors of Hell.[66] Kierkegaard would argue, however, that the lovers are in Hell because they exhibit a demoniac absorption in one idea.[67] For Kierkegaard, Don Giovanni exhibited a demonic absorption in desire—in Geoffrey Clive's words, "his unwillingness to sleep or rest, his indefatigable loyalty to the sensual principle."[68] It is an idea that can readily be related to "obsessive" features in demonic music, like ostinati and the relentlessly repeated motives in late Liszt. Though Liszt was persuaded by Wagner not to conclude the *Dante* Symphony with a "Paradiso" movement, it would have been there that resolution of the anguish of the earlier music would have been found and, again, via the only means possible, that of redemption. This is why Ronald Taylor misjudges the work when he states:

> Open conflicts are subsumed in a predetermined aura of peace, and the balanced juxtaposition of contrasted forces, the structural principle on which the aesthetic satisfaction of any extended musical work depends, is undermined from the outset.[69]

It is a criticism that fails to recognize the particular structural problems posed by the subject matter of the demonic and the divine and instead implies that these are formal weaknesses due to either misjudgment or poor technique on Liszt's part.

Nevertheless, Taylor's criticism is no doubt one with which Heinrich Schenker would have concurred, though he avoided discussing the music of Liszt. One reason for Schenker's neglect of Liszt may have been, as John D. White has suggested, that Liszt was not part of the German tradition. However, since Schenker avoided Bruckner in equal measure, I would opt for White's second suggested reason for neglect, that Schenker found some composers "to be lacking in the kind of basic musicality inherent in his theories."[70] Part of the problem can be related to Liszt's interest in the musical possibilities of the tritone. For example, White demonstrates that a Schenkerian analysis of *Chasse-Neige* works plausibly but recognizes that Schenker would have had problems with the prolongation on E major in this B♭ minor piece—the tritone relationship being incompatible with his concept of the *Urlinie*.

It is now time to look at the *Faust* Symphony in closer detail, especially the "Mephistopheles" movement. You can read in countless places how, in this movement, Faust's themes are subjected to malicious parody. Sometimes simple assertions are given; sometimes musical quotations are presented as if they furnished transparent evidence. Here is Sacheverell Sitwell giving full reign to his imagination:

> The simple, blatant themes are tortured and twisted out of all semblance to themselves. They are given sneering, sarcastic shape; are corrupted and made evil and embittered; are presented in triumphant, exultant loudness: they sound forth in the guise of sardonic laughter: they mock and imitate: they travesty and burlesque the truth until the original themes can hardly be recognized behind their derision.[71]

What is needed is an attempt to account for why these meanings are found in the music and explain how such ideas are represented by the composer. For example, though Liszt's compositional procedure that involved the "transformation of themes" is well known, it is necessary to decide what distinguishes a particular variation or transformation of a theme as a parody of that theme and what makes a transformation of a theme communicate maliciousness. In Berlioz's "Songe d'une nuit du Sabbat," the Allegro proper begins with a parody of the beloved's theme, effected by means of acciacaturas, trills, and a bouncy $\frac{6}{8}$ rhythm. The small E♭ clarinet playing high in its range suggests a vulgarizing and trivializing of the formerly elevated violin theme. Liszt, perhaps, learns from this that acciacaturas and trills can be used to destroy a legato line and that a jigging rhythm can be used to turn music that connotes spiritual yearning into music that connotes physicality. He uses similar techniques to debase Faust's themes in the "Mephistopheles" movement of his *Faust* Symphony.

Chromatic slithers and *scherzando* comments are added to the symphony's mysterious opening theme (see Ex. 6.12). The *dolente* theme that becomes linked to Faust's love of Gretchen (first heard on solo oboe 1st mvt, bb. 3–5) becomes a comical staccato exchange between horns and bassoon (see Ex. 6.13). The *dolente* theme develops into the love theme (*affettuoso*) in the first movement but becomes a *sehr scharf markiert und abgestoßen* fugue subject in the "Mephistopheles" movement (see Ex. 6.14). Faust's *agitato ed appassionato* theme (D, p. 9) is turned into a dance (166–67), which denies the romantic status of Faust's yearning and relocates his desire in the body (see Ex. 6.15). Faust's *grandioso* theme (O, p. 43) becomes *giocoso* and is given a bucolic character with drone fifths in cellos, suggesting that Faust is dancing to the devil's tune (see Ex. 6.16). There is a particularly diabolic passage at letter Nn where Faust's *grandioso* theme is twisted into a tritone pattern that accompanies the former *dolente* theme alongside the sound of timpani

EXAMPLE 6.12. *Faust* Symphony

Faust movement, opening

Mephistopheles movement, Letter E

a tritone apart and woodwind trills. Faust is restored to dignity only after Gretchen's intervention: a bass ostinato on his *grandioso* theme is then heard against a shimmering C-major chord (letter K). In this symphony the feminine wins out, despite the "phallic striving" that takes place.

Liszt conveys the idea that Faust is torn apart by Mephistopheles by ripping his themes into fragments. This is suggested metaphorically by the use of rests and the dispersing of notes between different instruments, as in Example 6.13. Lawrence Kramer describes Faust's themes as "literally taken

EXAMPLE 6.13. *Faust* Symphony

Faust movement, bars 3-5

Mephistopheles movement, 1 bar after B

EXAMPLE 6.14. *Faust* Symphony

Faust movement, 3 bars after Letter Dd

Mephistopheles movement, Letter S

apart and tossed in fragments from one instrumental group to another."[72] Mephistopheles does not have themes of his own; he simply negates Faust's themes. His function is to *deny* the first term of the binary opposition good–evil. Therefore, there is no genuine opposition: one term, instead, draws its meaning from the other, which, effectively, commands it. The only new theme in this movement is taken from Liszt's *Malédiction* Concerto, where it is labeled "orgeuil" (pride). Paul Merrick finds it significant that the fugue in the *Faust* Symphony is preceded by the "orgeuil" theme: "Thus before the fugue starts Liszt points to the Devil's pride."[73] Pride was, indeed, responsible for Lucifer's fall. Merrick comments that the "curse" theme of the *Malédiction* Concerto is followed by a cadenza based on the triads of F and B major and then by the "pride" motif. He sees this as "psychologically speaking, the origin of Liszt's approach to programme music. If music is divine, then the purpose of men is to use it to return to God. The path to the divine is blocked

EXAMPLE 6.15. *Faust* Symphony

Faust movement, Letter D

Allegro agitato ed appassionato

Mephistopheles movement, 3 bars after Letter F

Allegro vivace

EXAMPLE 6.16. *Faust* Symphony

Faust movement, Letter O

Mephistopheles movement, 4 bars before Letter Y

by the Devil, who must be overcome."[74] This explanation, with its reference to overcoming, makes evident that no "higher synthesis" is possible here.

Does an examination of the demonic in Liszt shed interpretive light on his Sonata in B Minor (1852–53)? Tibor Szász interpreted the sonata as a struggle between God and Lucifer over the human soul.[75] Others, more commonly, have advanced the idea of a Faust program.[76] My concern is musical signs, not musical programs, and I intend to offer no such narrative explication of musical processes or structure in Liszt. However, as Vera Micznik has pointed out, if those signs that initially result "from the *ad hoc,* artificial combination of concrete signifieds articulated verbally in the programme with freely interpretable musical signifiers" eventually become conventions, these, too, turn into musical signs (independent of their original program).[77] Such signs are what I would claim can be found in the Sonata in B Minor, a work with no explicit program. Liszt uses devices that have a connotative dimension for listeners who are familiar with the way these devices have previously been used in program music and opera (and, once more, the role Liszt played in disseminating operatic music as *instrumental music* through his transcriptions and "reminiscences" is important). A variant of the "cross motif" (derived from "Crux fidelis") is present at the passage marked *grandioso,* though Liszt had not made the use of this motif explicit in any of his other music at this time (he was to do so in *Hunnenschlacht* of 1857).

David Wilde, in a Jungian interpretation, maintains that the sonata "is concerned with three archetypes: the Hero, the Anima and the Shadow."[78] In more traditional terminology, though it does damage to the subtlety of Jung's thought, the Anima and the Shadow might be spoken of as the soul and the devil. Rather than Szász's God versus Lucifer, then, Wilde sees the subject of the sonata as "Liszt's struggle with the Shadow."[79] The first three themes of the sonata he calls the melancholic, the heroic, and Mephisto. The "feminine" version of the "Mephisto" theme (see, for example, bars 152–60) he understands as woman "represented as temptress and servant of Satan."[80] Louis Kentner finds "the spirit of mockery, of negation and savage distorting caricature" in the Allegro energetico section of the sonata.[81] What Wilde terms the "Mephisto" theme is an active component in all this. There are certainly resemblances to be found between this section of the sonata and the fugal section that begins at Letter S in the "Mephistopheles" movement of the *Faust* Symphony.

The conclusion of the sonata was subject to a late revision; its original ending was a loud and extrovert B major.[82] The revised ending makes clear that there is to be no reconciliation at the end of this sonata, and, far from a confident dominant to tonic close, the final B-major chord is preceded by an F-major chord, the harmony a tritone away. As we shall see in the next section, a late work, *Unstern!*, also struggles to achieve closure in B major but, instead, remains hanging on the dominant seventh, the bass proceeding to step up a tritone from E to A♯ and down again without finding resolution.

LATE DEMONS

Bence Szabolcsi describes Liszt's late music as "haggard and sharp-featured, harsh and mordant, sometimes even caustic, yet, more swirling and nightmarish, more demonic and threatening than any music before."[83] His argument differs from mine, however, in that he is keen to interpret the late style in the context of Liszt's experimenting with Hungarian features. While acknowledging the importance of this experimentation, I am persuaded that many of these nightmarish and threatening features have their roots in Liszt's attempts to develop signifiers of the demonic. Szabolcsi sums up the features of late Liszt as hammering motifs incessantly repeated, the tendency to "fade out" or conclude on a dissonance, and an emphasis on the tritone and whole-tone scales,[84] to which might be added augmented triads, bare fifths, and an increased level of dissonance.

In the last decade of his life, Liszt produced demonic pieces that were not always virtuosic, one such being *Unstern!: Sinistre, disastro* (1880–86). The title raises a number of puzzling questions. The German might be translated as "dark star" or "evil star," and Liszt added a subtitle of French and Italian terms. Are they synonymous? As an adjective, the French "sinistre" can mean "evil" as well as "inauspicious"; as a noun it denotes "disaster." Yet the word "désastre" exists in French, so why use "sinistre"? Is it to ensure that there are three different-sounding though synonymous words in the title? Is it because "sinistre" connotes a natural catastrophe (e.g., flood or fire) while "désastre" is more abstract (e.g., a serious misfortune or fatal accident)? Was there a natural disaster with which Liszt was concerned?[85] Was the French chosen because of the quantity of melodic material given to the left hand? The German and Italian nouns (and for that matter the English "disaster") derive from the idea of an unfavorable or negative aspect of a star. *Unstern!* is another example of a positive term being given a negative twist. When you wish upon a star, Disney fashion, you pray it is not this one.

An impression of doom is conveyed by the tense use of dissonance and the "evil" tritone. Allen Forte comments that the opening passage of *Unstern!* is "remarkable and novel even in Liszt's innovative works because it exhibits a highly structured pitch-class set hierarchy" and includes the set 7-7, "one of only six heptads [seven-note sets] to contain three tritones."[86] The movement E–F–B with which *Unstern!* begins is "a pitch motto often found in the late works."[87] Bars 46–58 are based entirely on a whole-note scale. Then, at the reprise of the first theme of *Unstern!*, the tritone's resolution to C is frustrated (see Ex. 6.17). The grating discord here is not arbitrary: the F and B here *could* resolve onto E and C.

In the whole of the final section, which has a key signature of B major (bars 85–146), there is never once a B-major chord in root position. It begins with a second inversion B-major chord and another appears at bar 93, but there is no chord of B major for the remaining 53 bars. *Unstern!* appears, musically, to be about the unobtainable. Dissonance strives for release but is thwarted.

The augmented triads that are such a characteristic of Liszt's music are used in late pieces like this to eat away further and further at tonality. Humphrey Searle, apropos of the harmony found in Liszt's late works, comments that

> while he still used augmented and diminished chords and frequently used the whole-tone scale, he created new contrapuntal effects by playing themes and accompaniments against each other without any regard for the rules of harmony.[88]

In the late works, clashes often result from the use of ostinati. Perhaps these can be traced back to that striking early example, the opening of *Totentanz*. Chromaticism also becomes more daring.

EXAMPLE 6.17. *Unstern!*, bars 70–74

LISZT'S DEMONIC LEGACY

Allen Forte holds that, from the theoretical standpoint, what makes Liszt's experimental music

> so special and so interesting is not its unusual surface features— which are, of course, extraordinary—but the fact that it represents a systematic expansion of traditional voice-leading and harmonic models, an expansion that incorporates, as basic harmonies, sonorities (pitch-class sets) that are not part of the central syntax of tonal music, but that derive, in the most extreme instances, from a process of accretion to the augmented triad and the diminished triad.[89]

It will not now surprise the reader that it is my opinion that Liszt's efforts to represent the demonic were what stimulated his interest in these augmented and diminished sonorities. Liszt was himself convinced that musical innovations came about through the efforts of those who employed music "in accordance with the dictates of the ideas to be expressed" and that formalist composers merely popularized, subdivided, or reworked "what the tone poets have won."[90]

It must be borne in mind that little of Liszt's late experimental work was known during the first half of the twentieth century. Thus, though a case can be made for the influence on Bartók of demonic works like the *Dante* Symphony, any resemblances between Bartók's mature style and that of the late Liszt is coincidental. For example, Bartók did not see the London manuscript of *Csárdás macabre* until 1937,[91] twenty-six years after his *Allegro barbaro,* with which it may be thought to share certain resemblances.

Bence Szabolcsi claims that Dvořák's later compositions are "inconceivable without Liszt."[92] Certainly you can recognize Dvořák's indebtedness to Liszt in *The Water Goblin* (1896) and such passages as that which depicts the witch's appearance in *The Noonday Witch* (1896), bars 252–72. Liszt's association of whole tones and the demonic persists in the "Vaults" scene of Debussy's *Pelléas et Mélisande* (1902) and in Sibelius's *Tapiola* (1926). The "demonic ride" survives in Franck's *Le Chasseur maudit* (1882) and Humperdinck's "Hexenritt" (from *Hänsel und Gretel,* 1893). The demonic dance was taken up by Saint-Saëns (whose *Danse macabre* of 1874 opens with a tritone negation of the violin's open strings), Mahler (the First and Sixth Symphonies of 1888 and 1904, respectively), Stravinsky (the "Infernal Dance" from *Firebird* of 1910), and Vaughan Williams ("Satan's Dance of Triumph" from *Job* of 1930).

The demonic symphonic piece soon found a memorable successor in Mussorgsky's *Night on the Bare Mountain* (1867). Rimsky-Korsakov (in whose orchestration the work is best known) informs us in his autobiography that the piece was "begun under the influence of Liszt's Danse macabre, which Mussorgsky had heard in the March [of 1866]."[93] A brief summary of *Night's* demonic signifiers reveals the debt to Liszt: the tempo is *allegro feroce;* the key is D minor; the first woodwind theme outlines tritones; there is lots of staccato; it contains a low-pitched choralelike theme for brass and bassoons in unison; there are woodwind shrieks (piccolo prominent), acciacaturas, and mordent figures; it has prominent percussion, which includes tam-tam; and it makes use of bare fifths, ostinato figures, chromatic slithering, and trills. The demonic symphonic work lived on in Balakirev's *Tamara* (1882) and Sibelius's *Lemminkäinen in Tuonela* (1893–97), as well as *Tapiola*, and the Dvořák symphonic poems already mentioned. Finally, the influence of Liszt's demonic music on the twentieth-century horror film should not be ignored. It pervaded American horror films of the 1930s and 1940s—especially scores by Universal's composers Charles Previn, Hans J. Salter, and Frank Skinner. Its impact continued to be heard as long as orchestral music dominated soundtracks. In the 1950s and 1960s, for example, Liszt's demonic shadow fell upon Clifton Parker's score for *Night of the Demon* (1957) and James Bernard's music to *The Devil Rides Out* (1968).[94]

part four

IDEOLOGY AND CULTURAL OTHERNESS

ORIENTALISM AND

MUSICAL STYLE

IN WESTERN MUSIC, Orientalist styles have related to previous Orientalist styles rather than to Eastern ethnic practices, just as myths have been described by Lévi-Strauss as relating to other myths.[1] One might ask if it is necessary to know *anything* about Eastern musical practices; for the most part, it seems that only a knowledge of Orientalist signifiers is required. In the case of Orientalist operas, I had at first thought it might be important to understand where they were set geographically. Then I began to realize that, for the most part, all I needed to know was the simple fact that they were set in exotic, foreign places. Perhaps I should have remembered Edward W. Said's advice that

> we need not look for correspondence between the language used to depict the Orient and the Orient itself, not so much because the language is inaccurate but because it is not even trying to be accurate. What it is trying to do . . . is at one and the same time to characterize the Orient as alien and to incorporate it schematically on a theatrical stage whose audience, manager, and actors are *for* Europe, and only for Europe.[2]

Nevertheless, the state of affairs found in a work like Rameau's *Les Indes Galantes* (1735), where, for example, Persians are musically indistinguishable from Peruvians, was to change. Distinctions and differences developed in the representation of the exotic or cultural Other, and that, as well as the confusion that sometimes results, is my present concern. This confusion is most evident in the nineteenth century, when Western composers, especially those who worked in countries engaged in imperialist expansion, were torn between, on the one hand, making a simple distinction between Western Self and Oriental Other and, on the other hand, recognizing that there was no single homogeneous Oriental culture. Thus, even when different Orientalist styles had become established, they could sometimes be applied in a careless manner.

In this chapter, because of its broad span, I am looking primarily for changes in representation. As a caveat, I should stress that in a genealogical critique such as this a smooth linear narrative is impossible and, owing to the contingent nature of developments in Orientalist styles, a certain amount of lurching around on my part is unavoidable. To begin with an example of a significant change in representation, one might compare Purcell's young Indian with Delibes's young Indian.

J. A. Westrup stated apropos of Purcell's *The Indian Queen*: "For all the music tells us, the action might be taking place in St. James's Park."[3] His remark indicates that there is a historical specificity to musical Orientalism and thus helps to establish its beginnings. Consider the music sung by the Indian Boy, which concerns "native innocence," part of a favorite colonizing theme in which the indigenous peoples of conquered countries are looked upon as children—and here they are indeed a boy and girl (see Ex. 7.1). The

EXAMPLE 7.1. Purcell, *The Indian Queen*, Prologue

harmonic language and word painting here are typical of other compositions by Purcell. The minor key, although it later becomes a marker of ethnic difference, in this work can be used for contentment (for example, "Ah!
Ah! How Happy Are We"); unhappiness, another later connotation of the
minor, at this time was conveyed by chromaticism and dissonance (for example, "All Dismal Sounds" in the same work).

Lakmé's "Où va la jeune Indoue" (the "Bell Song" from Delibes's opera
Lakmé, 1883) is a tale of a young Indian girl's seduction by the divine Vishnu.
It begins with a wordless vocalise, a device that became common in representations of the "emotional" Eastener, the lack of verbal content pointing
to a contrast with the "rational" Westener. Carolyn Abbate remarks that
"such moments enact in pure form familiar Western tropes on the suspicious power of music and its capacity to move us without rational speech."[4]
Example 7.2, from slightly later in the piece, shows how developed exotic
signifiers had become in the two centuries after Purcell. Note the insistent
syncopated rhythm, the bare harmony with octave doubling, the Aeolian
mode, and the pedal point. Moreover, added to this is the timbre of double

EXAMPLE 7.2. Delibes, *Lakmé*

reeds, tambourine, and, later, little bells. Such features were all now an established part of an Orientalist musical code.

Style Turc AND *Style Hongrois*

The first type of musical Orientalism was the Turkish Style, which, according to Jonathan Bellman, "evolved from a sort of battle music played by Turkish military bands outside the walls of Vienna during the siege of that city in 1683."[5] He remarks that few had heard it and virtually no one remembered it and that "what became understood as Turkish Style was thus almost entirely the product of the European imagination."[6] It clearly gave pleasure but also a sense of superiority over the Turks. Why did the Turkish Style arrive as the first example of Orientalism in music? Was it because the Turks had dared to try to conquer the West? The successful lifting of the Siege of Vienna ended Turkish expansionism.

Typical Turkish Style of the eighteenth century would be: a $\frac{2}{4}$ march with a bass of reiterated quavers (often asserting a tonic pedal); a melody that is decorated with grace notes (often dissonant) and insists on the notes of the tonic triad but with an occasional raised fourth; and "crude" harmony, such as root position triads and octave doubling of melody.[7] The "Chorus of Janissaries" from Mozart's *Die Entführung aus dem Serail* (1782) is a good example (see Ex. 7.3). Alfred Einstein describes the unusual circumstances of the first performance of this work in London in 1827:

> To our astonishment, the prelude to this "Turkish opera" begins with
> the solemn strains from the scene of the men in armour in the Zauber-
> flöte . . . Next follows the flute and drum solo of the trial by fire and
> water. Only after this does Mozart's *presto* get under way.[8]

Evidently, the Egypt of *Die Zauberflöte* and the Turkey of *Die Entführung* lacked distinguishing codes in England at this time. My argument, however, is that musical Orientalism has never been overly concerned with establishing distinctions between Eastern cultures and that an interchangeability of exotic signifiers proved to be commonplace rather than astonishing.

The next style to arrive after the *style turc* in the genealogy of musical Orientalism was the *style hongrois*, which Bellman describes as "derived from the exotic-sounding music played by Gypsy bands (not actual Magyars) in Hungary and westward to Vienna."[9] When it emerged alongside the Turkish Style in the middle of the eighteenth century, there was no clear line between the two. The following pieces illustrate the cross over: Haydn's Rondo "In the Gypsies' Style" (the Finale of the Piano Trio in G Major, Hob. XV: 25); the Finale of Mozart's Violin Concerto in A Major (known as the "Turkish"), K. 219; and Beethoven's "Alla Ingharese" for piano (known as "Rage over a Lost Penny"). The *style hongrois* is marked by syncopation, dactylic and dotted rhythms, virtuoso violin or quasi-violin passages (the Gypsies were Hun-

EXAMPLE 7.3. Mozart, "Chorus of Janissaries"

gary's professional musicians), a more prominent raised fourth than in the Turkish Style, and the melodic interval of the augmented second. It becomes a more distinct style in the nineteenth century, and the augmented second is increasingly used to connote "Gypsy." The "Gypsy Scale" is then theorized by Liszt,[10] who emphasizes difference by choosing the raised fourth degree and omitting the equally common diatonic fourth degree (see Ex. 7.4).

"Hungaria," Symphonic Poem no. 9 (1854), has a conventional modulation to the dominant in bars 79–86 while retaining a transposed version of the "Hungarian" augmented second (see Ex. 7.5). What we have is a spiced-up major-minor tonality rather than music based on a different ethnic scale pattern—unorthodox augmented seconds but an orthodox modulation. In

EXAMPLE 7.4. Liszt's "Gypsy Scale"

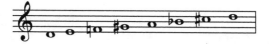

similar fashion, the old church modes were appropriated for representing the East and treated as if they belonged to major-minor tonality. The Dorian mode beginning on D, for example, can be regarded as the key of D minor, but with the colorful foreignness of a B♮. Treating modes as inflected major and minor scales means that one can modulate from, say, an Aeolian-inflected tonic to an Aeolian-inflected dominant, as Berlioz does in "The Flight into Egypt" from *L'Enfance du Christ* (1854).

THE MIDDLE EAST

Rimsky-Korsakov's theme for Scheherazade is in the Dorian mode, as is the opening of the "Dance of the Priestesses" from Saint-Saëns's *Samson et Dalila* (1877). Ralph P. Locke suggests that the "Bacchanale" of act 3 is based on the Arabic Hijāz mode, which provides a lower tetrachord that contains an augmented second (here the tetrachord is A, B♭, C♯, D); then, for the upper tetrachord, Saint-Saëns uses a transposition of this (i.e., E, F♯, G♯, A) (see Ex. 7.6). Locke says this is an option in Arabic music (Hijāz Kār) but thinks it more likely that

> Saint-Saëns's repeated insistence on the augmented second in the Bacchanale can be seen as an instance of the standard Orientalist practice (described by anthropologist Francis Affergan) of emphasising the "[sedimentary] residues . . . of what differs most" from Western practice; such an emphasis "reifies" the Eastener's "difference," thereby heightening rather than bridging the dichotomous gap between Self and Other.[11]

EXAMPLE 7.5. Liszt, "Hungaria"

EXAMPLE 7.6. Saint-Saëns, "Bacchanale"

f recitativo ad lib.

dim.

If Saint-Saëns was, indeed, concerned with the accuracy of the Arabic mode, it may strike an Arab listener as odd to hear the sound of castanets accompanying this dance. The whole thing becomes more bizarre when one considers that it was originally written, though not completed, as a *marche turque*.

Some nineteenth-century English and North American songs that concern Arabs, such as "I'll Sing Thee Songs of Araby,"[12] "A Son of the Desert Am I,"[13] and "The Arab's Farewell to His Favourite Steed"[14] are basically Western European in style. The melody of Caroline Norton's "No More Sea,"[15] however, is labeled "Arab air" (see Ex. 7.7). The description clearly had religious connotations at that time, no doubt because of associations with biblical Palestine. Forty years later, arranged as the "Hootchy-Kootchy Dance,"[16] this same "Arab air" signified seductive sensuality. In other words, when Orientalism appropriates music from another culture it is not used simply to represent the Other; it is used to represent our own thoughts *about* the Other.

The opening of Ravel's *Shéhérazade* overture (1898) illustrates the use of whole tones for exotic effect (see Ex. 7.8). They may have come from the Indonesian music he heard at the Paris World Exposition in 1889 or from Russian exoticism. Rimsky-Korsakov was also at the exposition performing rarely heard Russian repertoire. Whole-tone scales had been around in Russian music for some time; they appear as early as 1848 (in Glinka's *Ruslan and Lyudmila*[17]). The opening of Rimsky-Korsakov's *Scheherazade* (1888) has a whole-tone character. Russia was expanding into the Orient in the nineteenth century, occupying Samarkand and Bokhara in 1868, for example, and extending the trans-Caspian railway.[18] Richard Taruskin has argued that Borodin's *Prince Igor* is a "racially justified endorsement of Russia's militaristic expansion to the east."[19]

Ravel's other *Shéhérazade* consists of settings of three poems by Tristan Klingsor (real name: Léon Leclère) for mezzo-soprano and orchestra (1903). Klingsor was stimulated by the recent French publication of J. C. Mardrus's translation of *A Thousand and One Nights* and took the title of his hundred-

EXAMPLE 7.7. Caroline Norton, "No More Sea"

poem collection *Schéhérazade* from Rimsky-Korsakov's orchestral work. The very beginning of "Asie" from Ravel's Klingsor settings is a perfect summary of musical Orientalism at the turn of the century: consider how the signification of the first bars is confirmed by the word "Asie"; this is a Western musical epitome of Asia. Against the hushed expectancy of *tremolando* muted strings, the solo oboe plays a theme that contains a prominent augmented

EXAMPLE 7.8.   Ravel, *Shéhérazade* Overture

second, and at bar 3 the voice enters summoning Asia three times (the second time to an augmented second). Suddenly cymbals clash, the tempo quickens, and there is a downward rush of parallel motion chromatic harmony on strings as prominence is given to high woodwinds and a jingling tambourine. Perhaps Ravel went about as far as a Western composer could go with a conventional orchestra. Miklos Rozsa wanted to use the Ondes Martenot in his film score to *The Thief of Bagdad*[20] of 1940, but to his disappointment, Maurice Martenot, the only person able to play the instrument, was not available.[21] It is obvious that Rozsa wanted a weird-sounding instrument; his priority was not to find an ethnically appropriate instrument, but then neither was Messiaen's in *Turangalîla*. Rozsa had his limits, though: he refused to use "Adeste Fideles" for the nativity scene in his score to *Ben-Hur*.[22]

SPAIN

Spain seems to have been characterized first by dance rhythms, especially the fandango, as, for example, in Gluck's *Don Juan* ballet of 1761. Echoes of Spanish dance rhythms are almost all there is of a Spanish character to Weber's music to *Preciosa*;[23] the opening of the overture, for example, has the whiff of a fandango about it. Weber's Spanish Gypsies are characterized by the *style hongrois*[24] (a "Spanish" Gypsy style had to wait for Bizet). For a development of the Spanish code, one could compare Rimsky-Korsakov's fandango from *Capriccio espagnol* with the fandango from the act 3 Finale of Mozart's *The Marriage of Figaro*, which is, of course, set in Spain, though Mozart has borrowed the melody of his fandango not from Spain but from Gluck. Felicia Hemans's "Mother, O! Sing Me to Rest,"[25] from a collection of Peninsular Melodies that dates from the early nineteenth century, has nothing recognizably Spanish about it in either words or music. Compare the Spanish signifiers (quasi-guitar strumming and fandango rhythm) of E. Harper's "A Bandit's Life Is the Life for Me!" of 1872 (see Exx. 7.9 and 7.10).

The fandango became associated with bandits—"I Am the Bandolero"[26] is another example. It is noteworthy that when the plot of Beethoven's *Fidelio* was moved to Spain for censorship reasons, the composer felt no

EXAMPLE 7.9. Felicia Hemans, "Mother, O! Sing Me to Rest"

EXAMPLE 7.10. E. Harper, "A Bandit's Life Is the Life for Me"

EXAMPLE 7.11.   Rimsky-Korsakov, "Canto gitano"

urge to make musical changes. This was not an option for later nineteenth-century operas located in Spain, for example, Bizet's *Carmen* (1875).[27] However, some changes of location do not demand a change in musical style. So, it is ideologically significant that when Verdi's *Un Ballo in Maschera* was moved from royal Sweden to republican America to appease the censor, Swedes and Americans were presumed either to sound the same (*be* the same) or to be like Italians (in other words, "normal"). In Puccini's *La Fanciulla* American cowboys are Italians (that is, not represented as a cultural Other), and Verdi's Hebrew slaves (*Nabucco*) are Italians but not, for the most part, his Egyptians (*Aida*).[28] However, if we turn to a composer such as Sullivan, who was very aware of the semiotics of style, we find that in *The Gondoliers* the "Italian" style *signifies* Italy—this is different from using a style as a common language: there is an element of parody here or, at least, an acknowledgment of cultural specificity.[29]

In his "Canto gitano" from *Capriccio espagnol* (1887), Rimsky-Korsakov opts for Phrygian inflections rather than an augmented second between B♭ and C♯ (see Ex. 7.11). The Phrygian mode was to become a favorite "Spanish" signifier (a guitarist today can quickly and easily suggest Spain by playing a vigorous rhythm on the chord changes E major to F major to G major and back again). Bizet's "fate theme" from *Carmen* has Gypsy augmented seconds but moved around within Western-style sequences: they are not part of a mode; they form a motive fit for transposing. However, the transposing is not random: Bizet has the best of all worlds, using augmented seconds at all three of the favorite places for signifying the cultural Other within the space of an octave. He thereby produces something that approaches an Orientalist tone row (see Exx. 7.12 and 7.13). Debussy, however, decides that Liszt's Hungarian "Gypsy Scale" is good enough for his habañera "La Soirée dans Grenade" of 1903 (see Ex. 7.14).

Before we leave Spain, it is interesting to note that a TV advertisement for Spanish vacations (run in January 1996 on UK Channel 4) used an arrangement of Ravel's *Boléro* as background music. This must have been chosen because it was thought to signify Spain to potential British holidaymakers better than Spanish music does.

EXAMPLE 7.12.   Bizet, *Carmen*, Prelude

EXAMPLE 7.13.   Orientalist tone row

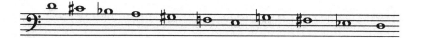

ETHNICITY AND ORIENTALISM

At this point, it is probably again useful to distinguish between ethnicity and Orientalism. To remain with Ravel, the point can be illustrated with reference to his *Rapsodie espagnole* (1907). The final movement, "Feria," contains castanets; but castanets are not necessarily evidence of Orientalism in themselves. It is only when they are used, in a manner we might label "castanet tokenism," to signify Spain. The presence or otherwise of "Spanish blood" in Ravel himself is not an issue here; it is rather his use of the devices of Western concert music to construct Andalusia as a romantic and mysterious landscape. A few examples must suffice: the augmented second in the clarinet theme after figure 2 in the prelude (which tells us this is an "Oriental" nocturne), the "très libre de mesure" cor anglais solo in the second movement, and the "cobra-coaxing" clarinet after figure 12 in the last movement. Finally, to underline the argument with which this chapter began (that Orientalist styles relate to themselves rather than ethnic practices), one might add to the example of Mozart's having borrowed his idea of Spanish melody from Gluck a deep suspicion that Bernstein was thinking of the theme at figure 6 in the aforementioned "Feria" when he wrote the music to "I Feel Pretty" for his Puerto Rican heroine in *West Side Story* (1957).

NORTH AFRICA

The next stop on our musical tour is Egypt. Rameau's "L'Egiptienne" (The Egyptian woman) from *Nouvelles Suites de Pièces de Clavecin* (1736) has no obvious Egyptian connotations today. But if we move once again to the nineteenth century and compare it with *Ballet égyptien* (1875) by French violinist Alexandre Luigini, we will find exotic signifiers are now in place.

EXAMPLE 7.14.   Debussy, "La Soirée dans Grenade"

Moreover, the opening theme of no. 8 from Luigini's ballet suite signifies strangeness with its whole-tone character. It is no doubt intended to convey stock notions of the mystery of Egypt: recently, for example, I received a travel brochure that invited me to "cruise down the Nile and experience the mystery and magic of Egypt" (Egypt's magic being economically illustrated by a photograph of the Sphinx and three camels). Handel's *Israel in Egypt* is not Egyptian, of course, but neither is Glass's *Akhnaten*. The latter may demonstrate a return to non-Orientalist treatment, that is, using a musical style typified by its own contemporary cultural-historical context rather than by any pseudo-geographical character of representation.[30] Andrew Lloyd Webber's *Joseph and the Amazing Technicolor Dreamcoat* is an example of a popular but non-Orientalist stage work.

The accepted genealogy of the Egyptian style is that Félicien David's *La Perle du Brésil* (note the location) of 1851 influenced Meyerbeer's *L'Africaine* (his last work, performed posthumously in 1865), which influenced Verdi when he was composing *Aida* in 1870.[31] Berlioz's "Flight into Egypt," mentioned earlier, has an Aeolian/Dorian modal character and prominent woodwinds, especially cor anglais, to add to its Oriental character. Yet, rather disconcertingly, he reverts immediately to the French pastorale for the Shepherds' Chorus.[32] The French influence behind the construction of the Egyptian style is understandable when one reads Edward Said's comment that "for something more than the first half of the nineteenth century Paris was the capital of the Orientalist world."[33] For the musical-technological world of today, Egypt would appear to be best connoted by an electronically "enhanced" cor anglais, which is what the "Egyptian Reed" setting on a Proteus synthesizer amounts to.

THE ASIAN SUBCONTINENT

Characterization of the Asian subcontinent emerged rather later in the nineteenth century. John Pridham's descriptive fantasia for piano, *The Battle March of Delhi* (1857), is without exoticisms, and even the purportedly genuine "Indian air" sounds as if the missionaries have already arrived (see Ex. 7.15).

In 1902 we find, Amy Woodforde-Finden's music to "Kashmiri Song" ("Pale Hands I Loved Beside the Shalimar")[34] has an "Indian" introduction and is heavily perfumed elsewhere (see Ex. 7.16). Whether this is the Phrygian mode or Rag Multani has no effect on its reception as Orientalism (that is, as "foreign sounds" understood only as signifying otherness to a Western listener). The Western listener does not need to recognize the Rag Multani (or the Phrygian mode, for that matter); he or she merely requires familiarity with the way signifiers of the East are handled in Western music. The convention is that the West always exerts power over those signifiers. Here the "foreign-sounding" intervals are countered by the reassuring presence of the piano (a triumph of Western technology and the "respectable" instru-

EXAMPLE 7.15. John Pridham, *The Battle March of Delhi*

ment of Western middle-class households), the equal-tempered tuning of
the piano, and the timbre of the piano. These are all of vital importance to
the way this song is received. Indeed, the cultural identity of the Rag Multani is open to question when played on the equal-tempered pitches of the
piano. A native of Kashmir would not recognize this song as anything other
than a Western masquerade, and that is before hearing the rich harmonies
that accompany its verses. There is an old recording of this song made by
Rudolph Valentino,[35] and if you are unaware that he is the singer it may be

EXAMPLE 7.16. Amy Woodforde-Finden, "Kashmiri Song"

tempting to describe the performance as poor. However, such a recording increases the impact of the song's Orientalism, because it adds Valentino's own persona to the music, thus affecting its reception for those who are familiar with Valentino as a sort of all-purpose exotic Other. Although Western composers take more interest in India in the twentieth century, the ethnic musical practices of the East, as we have had several occasions to observe earlier, count for little: meter, for example, will normally be organized as in Western practice rather than in the manner of an Asian tala.

THE FAR EAST

Finally, we move to the Far East, itself an ethnocentric label—it is far from *us,* and therefore the term relies upon a metageography for its meaning. Again an interchangeability of signifiers is commonplace. For example, the "Japanese" music of a late-nineteenth-century drawing-room ballad, "The Mousmee,"[36] was found by singer Franklin Clive to be eminently suited to the words of Rudyard Kipling's "On the Road to Mandalay," its "Oriental" character sufficing for Burma or Japan. In truth, by the end of the song's introduction we have not even left Hungary (see Ex. 7.17). (In the poem, Kipling reveals his own vague idea of geography, being under the impression that the sun rises in the west over China "across the bay" from Mandalay.)

Sidney Jones made the more common move from Japan to China when he followed up his musical success of 1896, *The Geisha,* with *San Toy* of 1899. Puccini moved just as easily from Japan to China (*Madama Butterfly* to *Turandot*). Ping, Pong, and Pang (*Turandot*) are Chinese stereotypes (whatever their satiric function): note, especially, their "Non v'è in China" toward the end of act II, scene 1, with its staccato chords, glittering timbre (harp, celeste, glockenspiel), pentatonicism, and singing in octaves rather than harmony. In accordance with the ideological assumption that the "lower orders" are more ethnically rooted than the "higher," lowly Liù is given the pentatonic

EXAMPLE 7.17. Walter W. Hedgcock, "The Mousmee" / "On the Road to Mandalay"

treatment, but not the Prince: see "Signore, ascolta!" followed by "Non pi-
angere, Liù!" from act 1.[37] Puccini's augmented triads, gongs, and such (from
Butterfly and *Turandot*) are inherited by Ketèlbey and paraded in his *In a
Chinese Temple Garden.*

Sir Edwin Arnold's *Light of Asia* (1892) is the inspiration for Fred
Weatherly's lyric to "Nirvana" (1900, music by Stephen Adams). The words
feature the "fallen civilization" theme of Orientalist writing ("The temples
old decay"). The song's message is that the Orient has mystic Nirvana; the
Occident has human love that aspires to the divine. Here chinoiserie is con-

EXAMPLE 7.18. Stephen Adams, "Nirvana"

structed by bare fifths, pentatonic melody, and the rhythmic pulse of the piano accompaniment. "The Sheik of Araby"[38] has a similar pulsation, but now, quickened in tempo and *alla breve,* it is associated with the decidedly unholy fox-trot (see Exx. 7.18 and 7.19). Pentatonicism and parallel fourths are the basic signifiers for chinoiserie; see Ravel's characterization of the China cup in *L'Enfant et les Sortilèges* (1925), especially from figure 37 in the orchestral score. (That the parallel fourths are played on the celeste is also significant.)

One of the twentieth century's most successful Orientalist musicals, prior to *Miss Saigon,* was *Chu Chin Chow* (music by Frederic Norton, 1916), loosely based on the tale of Ali Baba. The film version of 1934 opens with an image of an enormous cake in the shape of a domed palace or mosque. The Orientalist stereotype portrayed here is that of decadence and monstrous appetite. A little later there is an argument between husband and wife over who is to wear the jewels. The Orientalist stereotype this time is effeminacy. The falsetto voice of one male servant or slave is the only hint we are given

EXAMPLE 7.19. Ted Snyder, "The Sheik of Araby"

of the presence of eunuchs (it was obviously a delicate matter in 1934, but worth a quick laugh for the knowing member of the audience). Chu Chin Chow is a merchant Mandarin who is to visit Baghdad from China; on the way, he is robbed and killed together with his entourage by the Forty Thieves. By such ingenious means, the whole of the East is distilled into one plot.

Zahrat, the treacherous Egyptian slave girl, is played by Anna May Wong, looking distinctly Chinese. All accents, however, are 1930s received English (for example, "dazzled" pronounced as "dezzled"), with the exception of that of the leader of the thieves, Abu Hassan (whose accent suggests simply "foreign villain"). The Orientalism of the music is inconsistent, too. The chorus "We Are the Robbers of the Woods" could be a song for Robin Hood and his Merry Men. A female slave market scene is introduced that is not in the original *Arabian Nights* tale.[39] It provides another Orientalist stereotype: "They are sex mad." During the musical's first run, the Lord Chamberlain's Office became involved in investigating a complaint of "near nudity and non controlled breast movement."[40] The Orient is associated with sexual promise[41]: note its chocolate substitute in Fry's "Turkish Delight," which has long been advertised as "full of Eastern promise." *Chu Chin Chow* ran in London's West End for five years (1916–21) and was seen by nearly 3 million people. Oscar Asche, the librettist, said that he intended a "vision of the romance, the spendour, the inscrutable mystery of the East."[42]

In September 1989 *Miss Saigon* (Alain Boubil and Claude-Michel Schönberg, 1987) opened at the Theatre Royal, Drury Lane, London, and it went on to exceed the success and longevity of *Chu Chin Chow*. Its Orientalism is similarly erratic,[43] even though the orchestration makes use of a cor anglais and an "ethnic flute"[44] (whatever that may be). A few numbers are conspicuous for their Orientalist treatment: one of these ("If You Want to Die in Bed") is sung, predictably, by the "villain" of the piece. Ironically, this is the character who is convinced that the United States is where he should have been born.

The Far Eastern Orientalist style soon passed into dance band music and film music. An example of the former is Bert Ambrose's recording of "A Japanese Dream."[45] Roy Prendergast has remarked of the "Chinese" music in films of the 1930s and 1940s: "The Western listener simply does not understand the symbols of authentic Oriental music as he does those of Western music; therefore, Oriental music would have little dramatic effect for him."[46] An example of more recent pop chinoiserie is David Bowie and Iggy Pop's "China Girl" (1983).

ORIENTALIST MUSIC AS REPRESENTATION

There is a popular misconception to correct: Orientalist music is not poor imitation of another cultural practice: its purpose is not to imitate but to represent. Therefore, the Orient can begin in Spain if the intention is simply to connote a cultural Other.[47] However, as I was concerned to emphasize at the outset of this essay, there is not *one* Orientalist style: therefore, a chain of signifiers may be assembled to represent a more defined other culture, in which case Spain may be connoted in a more specific manner. Even then, there may be no distinction made between Spain, Mexico, and South American countries. A further refinement would come if such things as the differing musical characters of the Spanish and Argentine tangos were distinguished, but this is about as far as Orientalism can go, *because representations rely upon culturally learned recognition.* The peculiar achievement of Orientalism is, of course, that it gives rise to misrecognition. Imitation aims to duplicate; musical Orientalism has little to do with the objective conditions of non-Western musical practices—rather, it brings something new into being.

Here is a list of Orientalist devices, many of which can be applied indiscriminately as markers of cultural difference[48]: whole tones; Aeolian, Dorian, but especially the Phrygian mode; augmented seconds and fourths (especially with Lydian or Phrygian inflexions); arabesques and ornamented lines; elaborate "Ah!" melismas for voice; sliding or sinuous chromaticism (for example, "snaking" downward on cor anglais); trills and dissonant grace notes; rapid scale passages (especially of an irregular fit, e.g., eleven notes to be played in the time of two crotchets); a melody that suddenly shifts to notes of shorter value; abrupt juxtapositions of romantic, lyrical tunes and busy, energetic passages; repetitive rhythms (Ravel's *Boléro* is an extreme case of rhythmic insistence) and repetitive small-compass melodies; ostinati; ad libitum sections (*colla parte, senza tempo,* etc.); use of triplets in duple time; complex or irregular rhythms; parallel movement in fourths, fifths, and octaves (especially in the woodwinds); bare fifths; drones and pedal points; "magic" or "mystic" chords (which possess uncertainty of duration and/or harmonic direction[49]); harp arpeggios and glissandi (Rimsky-Korsakov changes the connotation of the harp with a mythical past to one of Oriental exoticism[50]); double reeds (oboe and especially cor anglais); percussion (especially tambourine, triangle, cymbals, and gong); emphatic rhythmic figures on unpitched percussion (such as tom-toms, tambourine, and triangle). The register of the melody can be important: for example the cor anglais connotes the East more emphatically than does the oboe. The use of a "frame" is often important: for example, Rimsky-Korsakov's "Canto gitano," mentioned earlier, is more than a song arrangement; its full title is "Scena e canto gitano," and the appearances of the song melody are framed by such things as free cadenza passages and *feroce* strings, which enclose its character and meaning within an Orientalist package. Whether or not any of the musical devices and processes listed in this paragraph exist in any Eastern ethnic practices is almost irrelevant. As Said explains, "In a system of knowledge about the Orient, the Orient is less a place than a *topos,* a set of references."[51]

ORIENTALIST MUSIC AND ITS MEANINGS

There have been arguments put forward to emphasize that there can be a positive as well as a negative side to musical Orientalism.[52] There is, for example, the well-known use of the "foreign" for purposes of social critique; for example, in Gilbert and Sullivan's *The Mikado,* Ko-Ko's list for execution is comprised wholly of irritating English characters. J. J. Clarke speaks of the East being used as a "mirror in which to scrutinize the assumptions and prejudices" of Western traditions.[53] For Orientalism, however, the mirror metaphor, is too simplistic: it is not a reflected East but a constructed East that is the issue. Moreover, the use of another culture as critique, no matter how well intended, can sometimes end up being dehumanizing (as we saw in the case of the "eco-warrior" stereotyping of Native Americans in chapter 3). A positive side to Orientalism is also found in the potential it offers for embracing difference (often with an erotic charge[54]) or for delivering a Bakhtinian carnivalesque inversion of dominant values.[55] Yet there is always a risk of encouraging notions not simply of ethnic difference but of racial difference. Singaporean violinist Vanessa Mae, for example, was presented at age 15 as sexy and sensual. It would have been impossible to market a teenage white all-American female violinist like this without outrage. There is also the real danger of Orientalism fixing devil-may-care attitudes of the "they're all foreign johnnies" variety. Amnesty International advertisements that followed a television documentary that concerned sales of torture equipment by British companies were headed with the quotation: "I don't really fill my mind much with what one set of foreigners is doing to another."[56] Said has described the limitations of Orientalism as those that "follow upon disregarding, essentializing, denuding the humanity of another culture, people, or geographical region."[57]

Orientalism describes the representation of the Eastern Other to the Western Self; it is not an impartial account of cultural difference, it is alter-ity understood in terms of fear and desire, terror and lack.[58] Notions of normativity and universality attach to the Western self-image, but when the Westerner is confronted with difference, strangeness, and a code of behavior that breaks with Western cultural prohibitions, desire is created (whether as Lacanian lack, Foucauldian incitement, or Deleuzian production). Since a transhistorical Western psychology is not being posited here, it is necessary to examine the changes in the historical, political, and economic determinants of human consciousness that explain the rapid rise of Orientalism in Western music of the nineteenth century. Its development should not be thought of simply as part of an evolution of musical style but, rather, must be located in its sociohistorical context. For the West, experiencing the rapid social change brought on by industrialization, the Orient must have exerted a fascination as a place that was conceived of as "synonymous with stability and unchanging eternality."[59] In the second half of that century, however, scientists of ethnology and anthropology were classifying races according to physical (especially craniological) and cultural characteristics, thereby breaking with the Enlightenment notion of the universal body. Moreover, Herbert Spencer's theory of the "survival of the fittest"[60] was a useful tool for determining "evidence" of weak and superior races. In Victorian Britain after around 1860, race, rather than social standing, was likely to be the predominant factor in deciding how a person was to be treated.[61] In the early twentieth century, eugenics and anthropometrics were concerned with the idea of "degenerate" races (the consequences of which we know all too well). Orientalism also provided "a kind of intellectual *authority* over the Orient."[62] This is already evident at the beginning of Orientalism in music, in the Turkish Style, which, with its constructed "crudities" and "errors," gave a sense of cultural superiority over the Turks. The related issue of the Oriental as "childlike"[63] and the "theory of Semitic simplicity"[64] finds a musical illustration in Hassan's song "There Was Once a Small Street Arab" from *The Rose of Persia* (Basil Hood and Arthur Sullivan, 1899) and connects back to Purcell's childlike portrayal of the Indian Boy.

In the eighteenth century, not only is there the cult of the Noble Savage to consider, but also the cultural elite were still able to regard the peasantry as a cultural Other. For a while this persisted even after the making of a working class, as shown by J. E. Ritchie's comments in *The Night Side of London* that the "costermonger race" is "alien" and their songs are not "ours" (addressing the reader as an assumed class equal).[65] Hence, the favored means of musical representation of a cultural Other prior to Orientalist music was the pastoral style. Pastoral conventions signify a rural Other in opposition to the courtly (later urban), in much the same way as Orientalist conventions signify an East in opposition to the West. However, though pastoral conventions, like Orientalist conventions, carry associations of nature as opposed to art, they do not function as signs of ethnic difference. Conventions for representing ethnic difference developed alongside the rise of an aggressive mercantile bourgeoisie and were usually first applied to neighboring countries over which they held sway. In England, where the breakup of feudalism came early, racial caricatures—Irish, Scottish, and Welsh—appeared in song at the time of Dibdin's Table Entertainments toward the end of the eighteenth century.[66]

The contradictory messages of Orientalist music can be found in its earliest manifestations, such as the *style hongrois*. Because of that style's association with Gypsies and because Gypsies were often viewed as untrustworthy, it was often used to suggest dissembling.[67] Yet Gypsies could be identified with as outsiders, which is what Bellman feels Schubert did.[68] The construction of Jewishness in Western music is perhaps the most fraught with contradictions. The musical Jew is sometimes the ordinary Western European—even an implied Christian Protestant. In Handel's *Judas Maccabeus* (1746), the Romans are the villains, suggesting the Roman Catholic Stuarts of the recently crushed Jacobite Rebellion to the English Protestant middle class. In other Handel oratorios, the Jews as "chosen people" again resonated with middle-class aspirations. A similar ideology is at play in the twentieth century in MGM's biblical epics (especially evident when Jewish heroes are played by Gentiles). Here, again, myth relates to myth: Hollywood film composers construct an identity for the Israelites that is more reminiscent of the Western medieval church than Palestine.[69] In its harmonic language and use of Aeolian, Dorian, and Phrygian modes this style owes more to a work like Vaughan Williams's Tallis Fantasia than any Middle Eastern culture; and it is found persuasive because the Israelites are regarded as being to all intents and purposes American Christians. In other words, the music tells us not about *them* but about *our attitude* to them. Set against this is a tradition that emphasizes difference. The Jew as Other is evident in the nineteenth century (for example, in Sullivan's *Ivanhoe*) and twentieth century (for example, Jerry Bock's music to the Broadway musical *Fiddler on the Roof*, 1964). Finally, there is the interesting case of "Der Juden Tanz" by sixteenth-century composer Hans Neusiedler. It became known to many from its publication in Archibald T. Davison and Willi Apel's *Historical Anthology of Music*, where it is described as having "shrill dissonances, otherwise unheard of before the adventurous experiments of twentieth-century music," that "produce an extremely realistic picture, not lacking a touch of satire."[70] That these remarkable dissonances are now thought to result from a misreading of lute tablature[71] raises the question: Why did it take so long for anyone to suspect anything was wrong? Had the piece not been titled "The Jew's Dance," would this have been accepted so readily as an accurate transcription?

Returning to more positive thoughts, how much does musical "impressionism" owe to musical Orientalism? Compare the way some impressionist painters moved away from light and shade, deep perspective, and other "realist" techniques to flattened form, bright, fresh colors, and decorative effects (the influence of Japanese prints from 1840) with the way some composers moved from major/minor tonality to the use of whole-tone scales (the influence of Java, Bali, etc.), an emphasis on timbre, and use of sequence and repetition rather than Beethovenian motivic development. Debussy's piano prelude *Voiles* is an example of whole-tone impressionism; does it suggest any connection with the *voiles violettes* of the ship that, in Klingsor's poem,[72] is about to depart for Asia? In the same poem, Klingsor refers to the sea's having "un vieux rythme ensorceleur" that could have appealed to the composer of *La Mer*. *Prélude à l'après-midi d'un faune* "proclaims a new musical cosmos," according to Hugh Macdonald,[73] but it is not a million miles from Orientalism (whole-tone movement, repetition, arabesques, etc.).

So how far have we traveled along the road of musical Orientalism since the eighteenth century? Let us return to Turkey and come full circle with the Pogues, whose mixture of punk and Irish folk is also able to embrace Orientalist musical constructions. In the music to "Turkish Song of the Damned" (MacGowan-Finer) of 1988, an augmented second falls between the second and third degrees of the scale and there is a flattened seventh in the upper tetrachord. These signs of cultural difference may not be identical to those used in eighteenth-century Turkish Style, but we can conclude from the background screams and menacing lyrics of this song that their connotations are very similar. Thus, our survey would seem to indicate that, in one sense, we have not moved at all.

Orientalism is never quite a case of "anything goes"; it is possible to mix signifiers of difference in a confusing manner: for example, it would be possible to write a calypso using Liszt's "Hungarian" scale. Moreover, Orientalist signs are contextual. For example a mixture of $\frac{6}{8}$ and $\frac{3}{4}$ is not a sign for Spanish in William Byrd's madrigal "Though Amaryllis Dance in Green," but it *is* in Bernstein's "I Want to Be in America" (from *West Side Story*). Likewise, the similarity between the close of the first movement of Anton Bruckner's Sixth Symphony and the theme tune of Maurice Jarre's *Lawrence of Arabia* does not create confusion. It is interesting, nonetheless, to wonder how much more stress on the Phrygian in Bruckner's coda would have been necessary to conjure up Sinbad for Donald F. Tovey, rather than Odysseus.[74] However, putting such matters as context aside, the geographical vagueness of much musical Orientalism remains. I will conclude with a final example, this time as it occurs in the labeling of "exotic" instruments: if we consult *Everyman's Dictionary of Music*[75] for a definition of "Turkish Crescent" we find "see Chinese Pavilion."

THE IMPACT OF AFRICAN-AMERICAN
MUSIC MAKING ON THE EUROPEAN
CLASSICAL TRADITION IN THE 1920S

THE REASONS THAT European classical composers were attracted to jazz during the early twentieth century were several and complex. A major social reason was the desire to put the First World War and prewar values behind them.[1] In Paris, composers were affected by the rage for *art nègre* and the fascination with Africa shown by artists such as Picasso. There were musical reasons, too. Jazz offered a way out of the Wagner impasse—that is, it provided an answer to the question: Where on earth do you go next after scaling the grand heights of *Parsifal?* The musical terrain of jazz presented fresh possibilities that were there for the taking. Jazz also offered a solution to the impasse caused by the supposed "exhaustion of tonal harmony," in that it was unmistakably of its time yet unrepentantly tonal. Furthermore, it provided a remedy for the malaise of "fin de siècle decadence." Ironically, this sometimes meant jazz features were employed in the construction of a new kind of decadence (a sort of middle-class "slumming"). Yet jazz could also function as a musical resource for replacing decadence with a new earthy vigor. Not least, jazz could be used to revitalize the classical tradition: jazz melodic features and syncopations allowed composers to return to writing something academically commendable, such as a fugue, while still sounding provocatively modern. It was even possible to take a Bach fugue and give it a syncopated lift, as did Hindemith in his "Ragtime" (1921), which is based on the C-minor fugue from book 1 of *The Well-Tempered Clavier.* Another reason for the appeal of jazz was that it suggested ways of obtaining rhythmic variety without the need for the irregular meters of *Le Sacre.* Jazz appealed to composers who were conservative in musical style as well as to those who prized innovative idioms. Some composers looked to jazz as a lifeline for the survival of the European classical tradition, in the same way as others looked to types of European music that stood outside classical practices. An example of the latter would be Bartók and Magyar music.

It is evident, however, that the appropriation of a handful of techniques associated with African-American music making for use in European concert music came to nothing as part of the modernist project. Ernst Krenek considered in retrospect that jazz was used in the 1920s as a last-ditch attempt to hide the disintegration of tonality.[2] Certainly, by the 1950s most modernist composers had taken the serial route. Jazz, in fact, challenges one of the crucial "grand narratives" of modernism: the end or dissolution of tonality. For these modernists, the tonal structure of jazz belonged in the cultural museum; it was not a case of "doo-doo-be-doo" but of "dodo, be gone!" Although jazz was to develop its own modernist wing, it should not in the early decades of the twentieth century be equated with modernism. Rather, jazz needs to be understood in relation to *modernity,* the novel and characteristic social features of which were cosmopolitanism and the alienated artist. In this context, the Jewish interest in jazz is significant, whether in bands, popular songs, musical theater, or the concert hall. Darius Milhaud, George Gershwin, and Kurt Weill were, of course, Jewish, as were the popular songwriters Irving Berlin and Jerome Kern.

One fundamental effect of the jazz invasion of Europe after the First World War was that it changed the European perception of Africa and Africans. In the 1920s, the continent of Africa would be typically characterized by African-American jazz and the typical image of an African would be of a black-skinned person who lived in the hot jungle areas. In the nineteenth century, it was the northern parts of Africa that sprang to mind first, and as late as 1890 the continent was still being characterized by Orientalist music, as Saint-Saëns's *Africa,* a fantasy for piano and orchestra shows (see Ex. 8.1).

THE APPEAL OF AFRICAN-AMERICAN MUSIC MAKING

In the 1890s, African-American music making was already beginning to interest the composer Frederick Delius, who as a young man in Florida was

EXAMPLE 8.1.   Saint-Saëns, *Africa,* op. 89

working during that decade as an orange planter. He confided to Eric Fenby that the urge to be a composer came from the African-American music making he heard there. He was very taken with the singing of African Americans on the plantation, and he particularly liked to hear his black foreman sing, often inviting him into the house and accompanying him on the piano.[3] Delius's first orchestral work was the *Florida Suite* of 1897, and it contains two black American dances, one in the first movement and the other in the third. It is significant that both of these dances start with a simple style that suggests innocence, then introduce disturbing, even threatening, Orientalist signifiers. Delius thus falls back on the conventional means of suggesting an ethnic Other. In the context of these brief remarks about Delius, there is a myth I would like to dispel. It is frequently heard that Duke Ellington's sometimes "impressionist" harmony is the result of his studying the music of Delius. Ellington, in fact, learned about harmony and arranging from Will Vodery, who arranged for the *Ziegfeld Follies.* However, there is an ironic twist, because Edvard Grieg, who influenced Delius's harmonic style, has been a strong influence on the harmonic style of Norwegian jazz.

At the turn of the twentieth century, the Anglo-African composer Samuel Coleridge-Taylor, who had leaped to fame with *Hiawatha's Wedding Feast* in 1898, was encouraged to take an interest in black American music by Fred Loudin of the Jubilee Singers.[4] Coleridge-Taylor composed an orchestral piece, "La Bamboula," and conducted it with the New York Philharmonic Orchestra in 1910. A *bamboula* was originally a type of African tambourine, but the name was adopted for a dance that became popular in New Orleans in the early nineteenth century. Coleridge-Taylor uses a tune of Creole origin.[5] The musical treatment Coleridge-Taylor gives to this tune, however, suggests Tchaikovsky rather than Creole music making (most strikingly in the *largamente* variation). Coleridge-Taylor did not see himself, nor was he viewed by contemporary critics, as the creator of a black style. In true classical fashion, he applies his musical ingenuity to developing and extending his material. Indeed, the *Daily Telegraph* had remarked in 1899 that his talent drew "the hope and expectation of all who wish well to English art."[6] The emphasis here is still on the expectations raised by what has become known as the Second English Musical Renaissance.

Before the 1920s, African-American music making was associated most strongly with ragtime and the cakewalk. The cakewalk had featured in blackface minstrel shows of the 1870s, but it was its performance by Charles E. Johnson and Dora Dean in *The Creole Show* (1890) that was to lead to its wider popularity. The cakewalk provided a novel dance to ragtime music of the 1890s: it soon became the rage in the United States, and then in Europe just after the turn of the twentieth century.[7] Lehár included a cakewalk in his operetta *The Merry Widow* (*Die lustige Witwe*) of 1905, though it contains no syncopation and thus resembles a Sousa march (the well-known "Stars and Stripes Forever" of 1897, for instance) more than a ragtime. Ironically, Sousa's band did play arrangements of syncopated dance music as well as marches. Characteristic ragtime syncopation is found in Debussy's "Golly-wogg's Cake-Walk" from his *Children's Corner Suite* of 1906–8, yet there is also quirky use of a very untypical "blue note," the flattened sixth. Moreover, the "crudity" of the added-note chords and the mocking tone is difficult to judge. We cannot be sure, for example, that Debussy is poking fun at Wagner with the *Tristan* quotation in the middle section; he may be suggesting that "quality" music sounds absurd in such a context—a context that, by implication, is thus revealed as trivial. It is by no means certain, either, that Debussy has African-American music in mind. It is possible that here, as in his first book of *préludes,* he is thinking of blackface minstrelsy. Debussy may have been given the idea of writing a ragtime piano piece by hearing his friend Satie's *Le Picadilly* of 1904. Debussy's cakewalk bears a more striking rhythmic resemblance, however, to a popular New York ragtime song of 1899, "Hello! Ma Baby" (Howard-Emerson).

Ragtime began to have an impact on British popular song after the visit of the American Ragtime Octette in 1912. Music hall artists responded to the challenge: even Marie Lloyd recorded a ragtime song, "The Piccadilly Trot" (David-Arthurs) in 1912.[8] In George Formby senior's song "John Willie's Ragtime Band" of 1913,[9] there is a reference to "Hitchy-Koo,"[10] a nonsense song (and therefore morally suspect) with which the Octette had scandalized respectable Edwardian society. For the "respectable" music press, "Hitchy-Koo" was "the last word in aimless, brainless rottenness."[11] The Formby song is satirical, suggesting that ragtime had become so popular that even a northern brass band is playing it. Jazz, in fact, remained controversial for brass bands for many years, even to as late as 1996, when Philip Wilby composed a championship test piece called *Jazz.*

A few words of historical background need to be added that concern the blues. A blues idiom is hinted at in "A Negro Love-Song," a pentatonic melody with blue third and seventh in Coleridge-Taylor's *African Suite* of 1898, many years before the first blues publications. These are often credited to W. C. Handy, the so-called Father of the Blues, who began a series of blues publications with "The Memphis Blues" in 1912. However, A. Maggio's "I Got the Blues" of 1908 has many blues features, which included a 12-bar section with characteristic chord progressions,[12] and Peter van der Merwe has cited an even earlier extant example of a 12-bar blues, "One o' Them Things?" of 1904 by James Chapman.[13] The blues entered the concert repertoire with the second movement of Gershwin's Piano Concerto of 1925. The second movement of Ravel's Violin Sonata of 1927 is also titled "Blues," but it is a blues in which any African-American characteristics have been doused in a heady cocktail of French "art music" techniques. The result, lightly tripping, occasionally sulky, but always clean and never losing sight of decorum, is as remote from the blues as Paris is from the Mississippi Delta. Ravel described his use of jazz idioms in this sonata as "a picturesque adventure," though he had a genuine interest in jazz.[14] His interest, however, was in how "jazz might serve many of us as entertainment"; he was clear that "it has nothing in common with art."[15]

In Europe, as in the United States, jazz appealed to the young, to bo-hemian intellectuals, and to those who felt alienated by or who rejected dominant social values. There was a sense in which this music seemed to promise greater personal freedom.[16] The first jazz recordings were made by the Original Dixieland Jazz Band, an all-white ensemble, for the U.S. Victor Company in 1917. The ODJB visited Britain in 1919, making records and per-forming at various London venues over many months, including at the opening of the Hammersmith Palais de Dance. They were a quintet, which consisted of clarinet, cornet, trombone, piano, and drums, and played the polyphonic small-group jazz of New Orleans that within a few years was ob-scured by the success of commercial big band jazz and, in particular, the "symphonic jazz" of Paul Whiteman, who commissioned Gershwin's *Rhap-sody in Blue* (1924). It was, unsurprisingly, commercial ballroom jazz that became best known in Europe. However, black musicians were in massive demand in the 1920s in restaurants, clubs, and hotels throughout Europe ac-cording to the black entertainer Tom Fletcher.[17] The bands these establish-ments employed were generally four to six strong.

I now propose to single out particular pieces by composers who worked in the European classical tradition, in order to demonstrate some of the dif-ferent ways in which jazz was being used. First, I should explain that here I am using the term "jazz" in what some will feel is an unduly broad sense, for although the 1920s were quickly labeled the "jazz age" in both the United States and Europe, definitions of what was and was not jazz were hotly con-tested even at that time. Charles Hamm has noted that the term was used as a label for three distinct bodies of music in the 1920s: that of the "race records" (understood as being by blacks *for* blacks), that of blacks who were performing for whites within a white cultural milieu, and that performed by whites for whites.[18]

JAZZ AND MODERNISM

Stravinsky said his choice of instruments in *L'Histoire du soldat* (composed in 1918 and published in 1924 after revisions in 1920) was influenced by his discovery of American jazz, and he calls these instruments "jazz legitimates," the bassoon excepted. He chose that as a substitute for the saxophone, an in-strument he thought "turbid and penetrating" and better used in orchestral combinations. He also instances the percussion part as a manifestation of his "enthusiasm for jazz,"[19] though, needless to say, it is not for drum kit. The clarinet and cornet are not typical, either, since he opts for instruments pitched in A rather than B♭. Furthermore, he confesses:

> My knowledge of jazz was derived exclusively from copies of sheet music, and as I had never actually heard any of the music performed, I borrowed its rhythmic style not as played, but as written. I *could* imagine jazz sound, however, or so I liked to think.[20]

Anyone acquainted with the parody of Elvis Presley's rock 'n' roll in Shosta-kovich's *Cheryomushki,* something *that* composer had never actually heard, will be aware of the dangers of this line of thought.

In 1918, also, Stravinsky wrote a piece for eleven instruments titled *Rag-time,* which he arranged for piano in 1920. Roger Scruton has asserted that jazz bequeathed its rhythms to Stravinsky.[21] Yet from the evidence of this and other jazz-influenced pieces, it seems to me that it would be more ac-curate to claim that Stravinsky eliminated vital jazz qualities from those rhythms. It was a consequence of his misunderstanding both jazz swing and the relation between the polyrhythmic dimension of jazz and the steady pulse. Olly Wilson has shown how important the legacy of West African polyrhythm has been to African-American music making.[22] Stravinsky's *Ragtime* is ironically detached, and its satirical gestures assume that the lis-tener finds a such features as tonic-dominant bass movement and Tin Pan Alley type cadential punctuations ridiculously trite—which, of course, they are when found in the "refined" company of classical techniques (see Ex. 8.2).

Everything that defines ragtime as a style is, from Stravinsky's perspec-tive, a cliché with which to have fun. Ragtimes are typically in duple meter; Stravinsky chooses to writes his in common time and makes use of dotted rhythms and shorter note values that are more reminiscent of a fox-trot. He takes the typical ragtime introduction and distorts it melodically (note the

EXAMPLE 8.2.   Stravinsky, *Ragime* (1918), piano version of 1920, opening

displaced octaves in bar 3) and tonally. Ragtime is a strongly tonal style, so he amusingly suggests a tonic-dominant in bar 4, then begins the first section proper in an unrelated key (the musical joke lies in its unexpectedness). Moreover, the bass in bar 4 seems to arrive a beat late (the joke underlined by exaggerating the dynamic level). Once under way, Stravinsky does not swing; he fidgets. There is absolutely no question of the pianist being allowed to indulge in the common practice of stomping his or her left foot while playing this rag, nor is there any sense of that relaxation that André Hodeir claims "plays an essential role in the production of swing."[23] A more pronounced nervous jerkiness is evident in the ragtime in Soldier's Tale, where the genre's functional roots in the march disappear as early as bar 9, presumably because they can serve only to distract the listener from regarding the piece as an autonomous object for aesthetic contemplation. Compare Example 8.2 to an excerpt from J. Reginald MacEachron's "On Easy Street (In Rags)" of 1901 (see Ex. 8.3).[24]

In Example 8.3 we have two independent voices in the treble, as in Stravinsky's *Ragtime*, but here the lower voice is employed as a repetitive motive (or riff), which, in a way characteristic of African-American practice, seems to respond to the other voice. Stravinsky, instead, provides no clear pattern to his semitonal slithering in either part: these voices seem designed mainly to undermine the tonality implied by the tonic-dominant movement in the bass. Nowhere in his prose writings or interviews does he feel the need to explain why he is so careful to avoid the more populist elements of jazz. Henry Pleasants has suggested that "serious" composers constructed their music like this in order to give it "immunity from plebeian emulation."[25] Such a motivation, however, would not be the whole story in Stravinsky's case: he used jazz as an aid in modernist "progress," finding novel directions for his music and achieving compositional coups. He explained that the importance of jazz to his own career was that it meant "a wholly new sound" in his music and remarked that *Histoire* marked his "final break with the Russian orchestral school."[26] Nevertheless, Stravinsky soon tired of jazz features and, by 1930, was under the impression that jazz itself was a passing fashion and "destined to disappear."[27]

EXAMPLE 8.3. J. Reginald MacEachron, "On Easy Street (In Rags)" (1901), beginning of second section

JAZZ AND AFRICA

Most of the carving up of Africa by the great powers of Europe took place between 1870 and 1900: European colonies accounted for barely 10 percent of the continent in 1875 but for 90 percent twenty years later.[28] As a consequence of the Treaty of Berlin of 1885, any European power that occupied fresh African territory was merely called upon to notify the others. Thus, the "scramble for Africa" began in earnest. It was during this time that the French expanded into Tunisia, to the annoyance of Italy. Saint-Saëns's *Africa* compounds the affront by including a Tunisian melody.

Milhaud, having spent two years in Brazil, had not experienced the introduction to jazz that Cocteau and others had enjoyed at the Casino de Paris in 1918. He was, instead, fascinated by hearing jazz for the first time in 1921 at London's Hammersmith Palais, where Billy Arnold's band of white jazz musicians from New York was playing, and went to this dance hall often.[29] Then, in 1922, Milhaud found an opportunity to visit Harlem. He described what he heard there as "authentic music which had its roots in the darkest corners of the Negro soul."[30] It is not surprising that he should think such music highly appropriate for a ballet that concerned the creation of vegetable, animal, and human life by African deities. Lawrence Kramer has reminded us that French exploitation of its Congo colony formed the backdrop to French fantasies of "black Africa as a primitive Eden" in the 1920s. Moreover, Kramer has identified jazz as the "chief medium" for the fantasy.[31] It was ironic that jazz, that music of the city, was to receive one of its most successful classical incarnations as a representation of a nonurban world. In this, Milhaud followed in the footsteps of the "primitivist" movement in art, which was linked to a critique of "technological rationality."[32] The concerns were the ever-increasing impact of the machine, the development of the chemical industries, and the constant new building and disappearing green under black asphalt—in other words, the anxieties that issued from the experience of modernity. Nowhere was the experience of such change greater than in the metropolis.[33]

The term "art nègre" came to be synonymous with "primitive art" in Paris. The label "primitive" is ethnocentric but was not, as an artistic term, intended pejoratively. For the avant-garde, the primitive was something of which they approved, since it allowed them to champion an aesthetic different from that of the official Beaux Arts and salon and to challenge bourgeois values. In art as in music, Orientalist attitudes persisted for a while (for example, in some early work of the Fauves), but change was effected by Picasso and the Cubists (beginning, famously, with *Les Demoiselles d'Avignon* of 1907). Just as jazz was to have little eventual impact on musical modernism, so African tribal art was to cause "no fundamental change in the direction of modern art," with even Picasso admitting that the African sculptures in his studios were more witnesses to his works than models.[34] Indeed, Cézanne's painting may have played a greater role in the development of Cubism. Whatever the case may be, there were certainly as many misreadings of African art by painters and sculptors of this time as there were misconceptions of African-American music by composers.[35]

The setting of *La Création du monde* is Africa, and the use of jazz idioms reveals the common confusion of African and black American in the European mind. It was performed by the Ballet Suédois in 1923, with décor and costumes by Fernand Léger, who would have benefited from seeing the *art nègre* exhibition in Paris in 1919. His décor was originally intended to represent power and darkness through use of African art and divinities, but he "was disappointed at the result, which he never thought terrifying enough."[36] The scenario was by Blaise Cendrars, based on African creation myths drawn from an anthology of African writing he had published in 1921. In the wider social context, the "new birth" trope appealed to the desire for renewal after the First World War. Finally, the choreography was by Jean Börlin, who involved himself in some ethnographic research. The dancers were, of course, white; this "African" ballet was not performed with black dancers until 1939 at the Ballet Theater in New York.[37] Milhaud made conflicting statements about his choice of seventeen solo instruments, claiming to be influenced by Harlem orchestras (presumably the pit bands of theaters), but also admitting to being inspired by a contemporary musical, *Liza* by Maceo Pinkard.[38]

I intend to examine the four-voice jazz fugue that accompanies the opening scene as the gods of creation Nzamé, Médère, and N'kva hold counsel and circle around a formless mass of intertwined bodies. Milhaud enjoyed listening to jazz records, and Gunther Schuller has revealed Milhaud's indebtedness to the ODJB's "Livery Stable Blues"[39] in this fugue, especially with respect to anacrusis figures, alternating major and minor thirds, and syncopations.[40] The fugue subject is at first 6 bars long (though after the initial statement it becomes 5), and shares the use of flattened third and seventh and the subdominant inclinations that are characteristic of the blues.[41] What we have in the end, however, is classical counterpoint with a jazz flavor (see Ex. 8.4).

Example 8.4 shows the fugal exposition, which begins with the entry of the subject, followed by the answer in the supertonic. At the next entry of the subject (in the dominant) we become aware that Milhaud is writing a regular countersubject in the best academic practice. When the answer follows in the tonic, we find that the second countersubject is also designed to be regular. Except for the unusual melodic and rhythmic character of the theme and the unorthodox key scheme, Milhaud is closer to German Baroque practice than New Orleans polyphony. As an example of jazz counterpoint, consider Louis Armstrong's Hot Five recording of "Muskrat Ramble" (Ory).[42] It demonstrates the characteristic three-part counterpoint of the clarinet, cornet, and trombone front line heard in New Orleans bands of the twenties (see Ex. 8.5). On this record, the counterpoint is set against a rhythm section of banjo and piano. The cornet is the melodic lead instrument, but notice the instances of dialogue between parts in this excerpt: the cornet and clarinet taking over from the trombone in the second bar, the

EXAMPLE 8.4. Milhaud, *La Création du monde,* op. 81 (1923), fugue

trombone returning with a response in the third bar, and the clarinet imitating the cornet's rhythmic figure in the fifth bar. There are also two moments that defy conventional notation: the "dirty" intonation on trombone in bar 2 and the cornet downward slide in the last bar (this effect was lost on European composers, though they were fond of a trombone glissando). There is, finally, an example of the chance crudity that is inevitable when players are improvising simultaneously: the momentary textural imbalance caused by the octave doubling between cornet and trombone in bars 4 and 5.

Milhaud also departs from jazz practice in the way he treats the percussion during his fugal exposition. He constructs a 4-bar pattern that he then repeats unchanged five times. Because it cuts across the 5-bar fugal entries, its character is independent and detached; it does not respond to the entries

EXAMPLE 8.5. "Muskrat Ramble" (Ory, Louis Armstrong and His Hot Five, recorded Chicago, 26 Feb. 1926 9538-A), transcribed by Richard Middleton[43]

by engaging in any form of musical dialogue. Thus, as in Stravinsky's Ragtime, we find a crucial African-American musical feature willfully cast aside. Milhaud did not show any further interest in the style he had developed in *La Création* and, his days as a jazz tourist over, was quick to advise others of his reservations about the value of African-American music making to the European classical tradition.[44] In one sense he was right, because jazz had begun its own classical tradition with the recordings of King Oliver's Creole Jazz Band in the same year as *La Création*, an achievement consolidated and enhanced by the first recordings of Louis Armstrong's Hot Five in 1926. Milhaud later claimed he had made "use of the jazz style to convey a purely classical feeling."[45] Léger, too, had no lasting interest in African art and in his collected essays (*Functions of Painting*) barely mentions the African dimension of *La Création*; his enduring interests were in dynamism and spectacle, and the African context of *La Création* gave him an opportunity to develop these.[46]

JAZZ AS SATIRICAL WEAPON

African-American jazz was barely known in Weimar Germany, and what jazz existed tended to be German imitations of white American dance bands. Jazz in Berlin, more so than in Paris, often meant simply American popular music. The reception of jazz had been strongly affected by Germany's postwar isolation and hyperinflation and by the subsequent unwillingness of foreign companies to reestablish business ties. Performers were also reluctant to tour there, given the country's economic problems. Jazz was, if anything, an enthusiasm of the middle class. Records of African-American jazz were extremely difficult to obtain, and radio broadcasts concentrated on German dance bands, ignoring Armstrong and Ellington.[47]

American jazz musicians, however, began touring Germany in the later 1920s, and Paul Whiteman made a big impact with a concert that included Gershwin's *Rhapsody in Blue* at Berlin's Grosses Schauspielhaus in 1926.[48] Jazz-influenced works in the Weimar Republic ranged from Hindemith's *1922* suite for piano to Wilhelm Grosz's *Baby in der Bar* (1928), a musical dance play comprised mainly of fox-trots that called for an onstage jazz band. Grosz later wrote popular songs such as "Red Sails in the Sunset" under the name of Hugh Williams. Some took to jazz and quickly abandoned it. In explaining the transition from his *Zeitoper* (opera of the times) *Jonny spielt auf* (1927) with its bilingual jazz talk ("Oh, ma bell', nicht so schnell") to the Greek-myth-inspired *Das Leben des Orest* two years later, Ernst Krenek does not mention jazz or jazz influence once. He refers to *Jonny* as a "more or less naturalistic contemporary piece."[49] However, this opera became a paradigmatic example of *entartete Musik* (degenerate music) for the Nazis, who adopted as a logo for such music an apelike caricature of a black saxophonist in a tuxedo (with, for good measure, a Star of David on the lapel) called Jonny.[50]

J. Bradford Robinson cites the rhythmic figure that hails Jonny's first entrance (see Ex. 8.6) as a figure "meant to be immediately recognizable as jazz," though today we listen for it in vain in Morton, Oliver, Armstrong, and even Whiteman.[51] This figure, common in German commercial music of 1923–24,[52] was closely associated with the idea of jazz and found in much of the jazz-influenced output of composers during the Weimar period. It appears often in Weill—for example, in the verse accompaniment to "Seeräuber-Jenny" (Pirate Jenny) from *Die Dreigroschenoper* (1928).

The associations of jazz for most composers working in the European classical tradition were probably primarily hedonistic, and no doubt its appeal was considerable in the context of a reaction against social formality that occurred after the First World War, such as the dancing to bands in new halls built for this purpose and in high-class hotels. This music suggested fun, decadence, and "cocking a snook" at outmoded morality. It was not, however, generally thought of as linked to a political agenda or welcomed as part of a desire to signal ideological solidarity with oppressed minorities, whether black or white. Stravinsky, who relished the shock potential of jazz,

EXAMPLE 8.6. The "Jonny" rhythm

did not relish any implication that he held left-wing sympathies. In the blunt words of Robert Craft, "Stravinsky preferred Mussolini's Fascism to British and French democracy," and he took issue with the description of his music as "democratic" in the *Manchester Guardian* (22 Feb. 1934).[53]

For Bertolt Brecht and Kurt Weill, however, jazz was seen as a weapon of subversion. They first collaborated on the *Mahagonny Songspiel* in 1927, and Brecht next suggested a reworking of John Gay's *Beggar's Opera* of 1728. Weill introduces a European decadence into the jazz sound world that is not a typical feature of that style. Consider the harmonies of "Moon of Alabama" for example; it adds a kind of overripe romanticism to the novelty of jazz, producing a knowingly maudlin and meretricious effect. This is what enables Weill to incorporate jazz features into satire in a different way from, for example, William Walton in *Façade* (1923). The jazz features are not "cheeky" in Weill; the tone is ironic; they are "tarty" and "cheap," but the quotation marks that encompass those words are an essential part of the effect. Lambert detected in *Die Dreigroschenoper* "a certain Hogarthian quality, a poetic sordidness,"[54] and Ernst Bloch remarked that "its beggars and rogues are no longer those of the opera buffa . . . but of subverted society in person."[55]

In Brecht's "epic theater," characters are drawn so that they invite comparisons with archetypal persons of a particular society. The aim of the new "epic opera" was "to narrate and report" according to Weill in 1928; the music was for "interrupting the narrative at slack points rather than trying to inflate it with great gusts of extra wind" and should move from the culture of a social elite in the direction of a new audience brought up on "work, sport and technology."[56] Brecht distances the audience from emotional involvement with characters by emphasizing theatrical artificiality. In the opening scene of *Die Dreigroschenoper,* a street singer announces to the audience that they are going to hear a street ballad about the robber Macheath, known as Mackie Messer (Mac the Knife). Macheath's archetype is the violent robber, and Brecht contrasts this socially and culturally produced type with one of nature's killers, the shark:

Und der Haifisch, der hat Zähne
Und die trägt er im Gesicht
Und Macheath, der hat ein Messer
Doch das Messer sieht man nicht.

And the shark, he has teeth
And wears them in his face
And Macheath, he has a knife
But the knife is seen by nobody

We find immediately in this well-known first song of the opera ("Die Moritat von Mackie Messer") an example of what Brecht would call gestic music. Weill does not try to heighten Brecht's text emotionally or to interpret it musically; instead he finds a style and form that increases the impact of the words by contrasting sharply in musical mood (see Ex. 8.7).

Neither Weill nor Brecht ever gave a systematic definition of *gestische Musik* (in his plays, *Gestus* meant for Brecht a stylized presentation of social behavior).[57] In general terms, both were agreed that, as in Example 8.7, the music should function as a medium for communicating the text without trying to add psychological insight into the character singing the song or attempting the musical representation of emotions and deeds within the song. Weill's task is to achieve a musical *Verfremdungseffekt* (a "making strange" or distancing effect) equal to those used by Brecht, such as masks, explanatory posters, and deliberate highlighting of theatrical artificiality by use of an onstage narrator. An alienating effect can be achieved musically by accompanying, for example, harsh words with a sentimental tune. The jarring that results keeps the listener alert, instead of the song becoming a catalyst for melancholy self-indulgence. A sense of irony can also be conveyed by parodies of different styles. Brecht had experimented along these lines in his songs (usually to borrowed tunes) before working with Weill.[58]

In the "Moritat," the music functions in some way as a mask, the style of music contradicting what would be expected from verses about murder, robbery, arson, and rape. The accompaniment is marked to be played in the manner of a barrel organ; the prominent added sixths in the harmony func-

EXAMPLE 8.7. Weill, "Die Moritat von Mackie Messer" (1928)

tion as a sign of popular music vulgarity (the sixth degree—the note A—is present during every bar of Ex. 8.7) and the 2-bar melodic phrasing and tonic-dominant bass as a sign of banality. The tempo is indicated as that of a blues, which at this time referred to an American jazz dance style. In the third verse, Weill changes from harmonium[59] to piano and introduces some mild syncopation in the accompaniment. He also brings in percussion and banjo and doubles the melody on trombone. Later he adds two saxophones and trumpet, which completes the jazz band instrumentation. His final variations to the accompaniment include a parody of Tin Pan Alley sentimental descending chromatics. Weill's music underlines Brecht's satirical purpose, since it conceals the violence as Macheath conceals his knife and covers his bloodstained hands with gloves. The real target of Brecht's satire is, of course, capitalism, and in the larger social context Brecht has in mind the "out of sight" tanks and guns of capitalist society.

Sometimes the *Verfremdung* breaks down: in the kitchen maid's bloodthirsty dream of being Pirate Jenny, Weill's setting of the refrain ("the ship with eight sails") creates a powerful emotional effect. Of course, this song has become very well known and has had many interpreters, and this has taken it far from the original aesthetic intentions. How much colder and more frightening is Lotte Lenya on her early recording of 1930, where she sounds like a childish psychopath, than on that of 1958, where she appears embittered and triumphant crying, "Alle!" as she demands mass executions and "Hoppla!" as the heads roll.[60]

In contrast to the modernists, Weill declared that he sought a new public, rather than new forms or theories.[61] He certainly achieved the rare distinction of having his music adopted by African-American jazz musicians (for example, Louis Armstrong and Ella Fitzgerald for "Mack the Knife," and Nina Simone for "Pirate Jenny"). John Willet contends that Weill was "less easily bored with jazz" than Milhaud, because he was less concerned with "new formal conventions" than with "a shift in the social basis of the arts."[62]

Other satirical uses of jazz styles abound in the music of European composers. One of the earliest was Satie's *Parade* of 1917, in which ragtime (among other popular styles) is co-opted by the avant-garde—not to be confused with Stravinsky's modernism. Satie's ballet displays the historic characteristics of French avant-garde movements in being deliberately confrontational socially (suggesting a mechanized society) as well as aesthetically (with a "sweeping away" attitude to high art, rather than a building upon or an "evolving" of tradition). Jean Cocteau, who famously called for an everyday music in his pamphlet *Le Coq et l'Arlequin* (1918) and devised the scenario of *Parade,* commented that at that time Parisians were unacquainted with jazz bands.[63] It was, of course, wartime (and Stravinsky had fled to Switzerland). Poulenc's *Rapsodie nègre* of 1917 is still reminiscent of the pseudo-Asian style. Poulenc had read some poetry by Makoko Kangourou, who was supposed to be a black Liberian writing in French, though the received opinion now is that this was highly unlikely. Yet the uncertainty that surrounded Kangourou may have been part of the appeal, since Poulenc writes his own text for the third movement using an "ethnic-nonsense" language: "Honoloulou, poti lama! Honoloulou, Honoloulou, Kati moko," and so on. The director of the Paris Conservatoire, unimpressed, described it tersely as "bollocks" (*un couillonerie*). The poem is not unlike those chanted by Richard Huelsenbeck at the Cabaret Voltaire in Zurich in 1916, which all finished with shouts of "umba, umba."[64] In Poulenc's ballet score *Les Biches* of 1923, the "Rag-Mazurka" fails to sound convincing as either a rag or a mazurka, and unlike Wilfrid Mellers, I fail to hear any reminiscence of a tango in the B♭ minor episode.[65] Poulenc's French biographer Henri Hell speaks of its syncopated rhythms,[66] but simply beginning phrases on an off-beat does not produce jazz or ragtime. There is no sense of swing, and the dotted rhythms are clearly not intended to be played with a triplet feel. The dry staccato brass chords and treatment of rhythm in the accompaniment are more typical of Stravinsky. What is more, the avant-garde as represented by Poulenc and the rest of "Les Six" is, at this time, turning into a group whose rebellion is located solely in the aesthetic domain. Jazz was soon to be found an unsuitable comrade in that rebellion. Poulenc is quoted as saying of jazz, "It amuses me while I listen to records of it while taking my bath, but it is frankly distasteful to me in the concert hall."[67]

In the United Kingdom, Walton's use of parody and jazz differed from that of Weill and came closer to Les Six. Sitwell's and Walton's satirical purpose in *Façade* (a work that gradually expanded in size between 1922 and 1928) was to run deliberately counter to high art trends in order to challenge them. In other words, it was a form of aesthetic satire rather than social satire. Walton and Constant Lambert were the most prominent among British composers attracted to jazz. Lambert's *The Rio Grande* of 1927 was reviewed in the *Guardian* with the comment that it "transfigures jazz into poetry."[68] This is the familiar classical notion that jazz is in need of a bit of polish and refinement, which still survives in the writings of Roger Scruton. The "Popular Song" (added in 1928) from Walton's *Façade* is more reminiscent, however, of the latter stages of blackface minstrelsy than jazz. Compare it with, for example, Leslie Stuart's "Lily of Laguna" (1898).

"Sweet jazz" and "light classical"

In the second half of the twenties, jazz and jazz-influenced music had become established as the dominant type of popular music. These years witnessed hundreds of thousands of Americans touring Europe. The records they took with them increased the European interest in jazz, the ground having been laid already by the growing numbers of touring jazz musicians, white and black. This alone explains why some composers were abandoning jazz features, since these now possessed an entertainment value that overrode any shock value. Josephine Baker was among the African-American musicians who made their home in Paris after the First World War. *La Revue nègre,* in which she starred with an all-black troupe, opened in 1925 at the Music-hall des Champs-Élysées, having been brought there from New York by its manager. She became an immediate sensation and was then, as now, regarded as an emblematic figure of the 1920s "jazz age" in Paris (see Fig. 8.1).[69] Her scat singing on "Then I'll Be Happy," recorded in Paris in 1927,[70] comes less than a year after Armstrong's pioneering example on "Heebie Jeebies" and nine months *before* Adelaide Hall's famous vocal on "Creole Love Call." The growling vocal sound is also two months in advance of Bubber Miley's use of a plunger mute to produce a similar effect on trumpet in "East St. Louis Toodle-Oo."

FIGURE 8.1. Josephine Baker Art Deco photo

The reception accorded to *La Revue nègre* created an insatiable appetite for *revues noires*. One of the most celebrated, *Blackbirds,* arrived in 1926 direct from the Cotton Club, Harlem. It was updated as *Blackbirds 1928* and presented at the Moulin Rouge in 1929, starring the aforementioned Adelaide Hall (who was to settle in London). In 1928 George Gershwin, an example of a composer who had moved from the popular show to the concert hall and not the other way round, was in Paris. The time could not have been more tempting for European composers to try their hand at emulating popular music.

Bohuslav Martinů at first seems an unlikely case, since little of his output resembles jazz—hot, sweet, or otherwise. Even *La Revue de cuisine* sounds more like Stravinsky. But *Le Jazz* of 1928 does capture something of the character of a "sweet jazz" dance orchestra. Martinů was living in Paris at the time, and among the sweeter jazz bands playing and recording there in the later twenties were Jazz Oliver and His Boys des Folies Bergères, Jacob's Jazz, and Edmond Mahieux and Le Melodic Jazz du Casino de Paris. Martinů's *Le Jazz,* which shows the influence of Paul Whiteman's "symphonic jazz" as well as, perhaps, the dance band directed in Paris by Martinů's fellow Czech Jaroslav Ježek,[71] was a piece that modernist critics found shocking. The reason, undoubtedly, was because it did not sound like "art music." Paradoxically, they seldom found modernist music shocking, because the shocks were to their taste: it confirmed their expectations of what genuine art music *should* sound like. This was a traitorous intervention in the world of popular music by Martinů, and its "vulgar" excesses could not be read as satire. Cocteau himself was opposed to any attempts to create jazz pastiches.[72] Indeed, Bernard Gendron has argued that jazz was co-opted by Cocteau and his circle to help define and legitimate a new depoliticized avant-garde; it was a music "for artistic slumming and avant-garde play."[73]

In Austria, the popularity of Viennese light music, especially waltzes and operetta, was for some time an effective barricade against jazz. However, in the same year as *Die Dreigroschenoper,* Viennese operetta openly faced the challenge of jazz in Emmerich Kálmán's *Die Herzogin von Chicago* (The Duchess of Chicago), in which the culture class between Austro-Hungarian popular dance music and jazz holds center stage. The reception was enthusiastic, and some songs from the operetta, such as "Ein kleiner Slowfox mit Mary" and "In Chicago," became popular hits. From here on, jazz influence was to be found in other Viennese operettas until the Nazi clampdown on degenerate music that followed the Anschluss in 1938. Needless, to say jazz was no more welcome in Stalin's Russia. Yet before the years of suppression, jazz was heard and composers showed interest. Shostakovich's "Tahiti Trot" (1928) is a skilful and witty arrangement of Vincent Youman's "Tea for Two." Shostakovich heard jazz from visiting musicians in the 1920s. He later wrote two jazz suites (1934 and 1938), the first as part of a move to improve the quality of café musical entertainment. Suite no. 1 falls short of jazz by some distance; the second, for promenade orchestra, is jazz in name only.

Misconceptions of african-american music making

My chapter's title draws attention to African-American music making rather than African-American music, placing an emphasis on African-American performance practice. It is exactly this matter of practice that the classical appropriators of jazz at best misconstrue and at worst neglect altogether in favor of a few melodic, rhythmic, and harmonic mannerisms. In the context of the classical repertoire, jazz is heard as amusing and irreverent because many of its features carry connotations of rudeness and vulgarity—trombone glissandi, clichés at cadences and in bass lines (for example, repetitive tonic to dominant motion). For many French composers, the function of jazz in a classical context was *épater le bourgeois*. At the same time, dabbling in jazz allowed them to demonstrate their imagined superiority in matters of technique and formal control. Thus, jazz was not to prove aesthetically disruptive to modernism and was aesthetically shocking only to a particular social group.

Many of the features a jazz musician would recognize as crucial to jazz performance are absent in classical appropriations of jazz. I shall discuss these here, beginning with what many jazz musicians regard first as the music's most defining characteristic, improvisation—what Stan Hawkins has called "performance and composition fused into one act."[74] Lambert's prophecy that "the next move in the development of jazz will come, almost inevitably, from the sophisticated or highbrow composer" was incorrect[75] and showed his misunderstanding of the importance of the improvising performer in jazz. As a consequence he failed to understand the significance of Louis Armstrong: "It is the greatest mistake to class Louis Armstrong and Duke Ellington together as similar exponents of Negro music—the one is a trumpet player, the other a genuine composer."[76] This is Lambert's own greatest mistake about the nature of jazz, to think it is the creative fruit of "genuine composers," by which he means those who bear comparison with the canonical figures of the European classical tradition. A conventional framework is required for jazz improvisation, yet modernist music had turned in the direction of fewer and fewer conventions, whether structural, rhythmic, or harmonic. Jazz improvisation relied at its most adventurous on the chords found in Tin Pan Alley songs. Indeed, the two patterns of chord changes that were to prove most popular for jazz improvisers were those of the blues and of Gershwin's "I Got Rhythm" (and the last was usually simplified).

Improvisation, for Lambert, has "expressive and formal limitations" that he relates to its need to take place over a simple harmonic and formal structure in order for a jazz band not to fall into chaos; and though acknowledging that Armstrong is an expert improviser, he believes Armstrong relies on a "restricted circle of ideas."[77] Nowhere does Lambert appear to relish the spontaneity of improvisation or suspect for an instant that jazz may be created primarily by performers. In the 1920s, "genuine composers" of the

European classical tradition were, in the main, suspicious of spontaneity. Jack Sullivan has contrasted the painstaking care with which Ravel created his jazz-influenced works with the spontaneity of jazz (Ravel's violin sonata took four years to compose).[78] European composers ignore the crucial importance of improvisation to African-American musical practice and its function in making every performance vital and new. It is not a supplement to an inadequate musical score. Portia Maultsby observes that even when black music genres circulate as scores, as in the case of gospel songs, in interpreting the score "performers must demonstrate their knowledge of the improvisatory devices that characterize black music performances."[79] This points to the problem classical performers have in trying to play jazz from notation only, since, as Eileen Southern explains, "those who would learn to play it do so by *listening* to others playing jazz" (my emphasis).[80]

Almost as important as the ability to improvise is the manner in which the improvisation is played. In particular, European classical composers did not take on board Duke Ellington's warning that "it don't mean a thing if it ain't got that swing." Swing, as Hodeir has noted, is what even Milhaud's *La Création* lacks.[81] While examples can be found of composers adopting what Wilson has called "the heterogeneous sound ideal," a musical texture that combines diverse timbres, they have failed to understand that swing is an essential quality.[82] He also notes the tendency of black musicians to create music in which "call-and-response musical structures abound" and "to incorporate physical body motion as an integral part of the music making process."[83]

Samuel A. Floyd, Jr., too, stresses the relationship between black music and black dance,[84] though his writing is best known for its musical application of Henry Louis Gates, Jr.'s interpretive insights that concern the relation of African-American signifying to African-American literature.[85] As a frame for Floyd's analysis of black music making, he turns to Sterling Stuckey's formulation of the nineteenth-century ring shout,[86] a practice in which Floyd finds "all of the defining elements of black music," such as call and response, offbeat rhythms, and characteristic vocal production.[87] Floyd develops a theoretical framework based on the black cultural practice of signifying (which, written as "signifyin[g]," differentiates it from the word's other meanings). In African-American usage "signifyin(g)" implies a deliberate indirectness in communication. Claudia Mitchell-Kernan explains that labeling a particular utterance "signifyin(g)" involves "the recognition and attribution of some implicit content or function which is potentially obscured by the surface content or function."[88] She gives as one among many examples a wife saying to her husband seeing him leave for work in, unusually, a suit, "You didn't tell me you got a promotion." This is, on the one hand an indirect way of asking why he is wearing a suit, but on the other hand, the purpose of the signifyin(g) is to let him know she thinks he is *not* going to work.[89] A satirical element such as this is often present.

Floyd lists among the musical devices that can be used for signifyin(g) hollers, riffs, licks, and overlapping antiphony. These can all be used to comment on (signify on) performances and different pieces of music, as well as on genres. Floyd argues that "ragtime Signifies on European and early Euro-American dance music, including the march; blues on the ballad; the spiritual on the hymn," but also so does jazz on blues and ragtime, and gospel on the spiritual.[90] Signifyin(g) transforms material by troping it—using it as part of a rhetorical game or figuratively—for example, showing respect by some forms of pastiche or poking fun by parody. The device of call and response is, as its name implies, an imitation of dialogue and thus, for Floyd, a classic example of musical signifyin(g).[91] Floyd maintains that it is through "musical troping and Signifyin(g) that the more profound meanings of black music are expressed and communicated."[92] He even explains that elusive quality of swing as a troping of the time line. The trope of tropes he labels Call-Response—not to indicate the device of call and response but rather the musical principle of "a dialogical musical rhetoric under which are subsumed all the music tropological devices, including call-and-response."[93] If there is a criticism of Floyd's theory of signifyin(g), it is that it transcends class; there is no difference, apparently, between the signifyin(g) of working-class musicians such as Armstrong and middle-class musicians such as Ellington.

Floyd notes that black music making is "self-criticizing and self-validating,"[94] which is why there is often commenting on the music itself (for example, Yellen and Ager's "Crazy Words, Crazy Tune" and Ellington's "It Don't Mean a Thing" already quoted). This was something that puzzled Constant Lambert, who wondered why there were no English folk songs that announced they were in the Dorian mode or $\frac{6}{8}$ time.[95]

Missing from "classical jazz" are the features that are African-derived. Mellonee Burnim, in a study of the black gospel music tradition, has singled out African-derived qualities that relate to style of delivery, sound quality, and mechanics of delivery,[96] and Maultsby has discussed the way that these qualities, which she terms "Africanisms," have impacted upon African-American music making. Maultsby stresses the communal approach to music making by black Americans and gives many examples of how music making is conceptualized as a participatory activity (a legacy, she argues, of African music making). Performers onstage will encourage audience participation—for example, hand clapping—and audiences will encourage performers by shouts or spontaneous applause. All this is designed to generate a sense of group expression.[97]

One of the things that most bedeviled the European composer was the idea that jazz needed to be made "respectable." Usually this involves an invocation of the Western musical canon. Hindemith, for example, claimed, "If Bach were alive today, perhaps he would invent the shimmy or at least take it over into respectable music."[98] Lambert had similar ideas: "I see no reason why a composer should not be able to rid himself as much from the night-club element in jazz as Haydn did from the ballroom element in the minuet, and produce the modern equivalent of those dance suites of Bach."[99]

At the same time, Lambert recognized that "the modern highbrow composer who writes a foxtrot can hardly hope to go one better than Duke Ellington."[100] It is unclear whether or not Lambert considered Ellington a highbrow composer, but he remarked that Ellington's musical skill "is hardly appreciated by any except the highbrow public"[101] and called him "the first jazz composer of distinction."[102] Lambert maintained that nothing more dexterous was to be found in Ravel than the varied solos in the middle of Ellington's "Hot and Bothered" and "nothing in Stravinsky more dynamic than the final section."[103]

THE FEAR OF JAZZ

Why is jazz-influenced classical music so toothless compared to the jazz it supposedly emulates? I would argue that it is because what I believe to be a politically challenging quality in jazz—a quality of physicality aligned to pleasure that offers resistance to ideological norms—is caged in by a variety of devices that reassert the discipline of classical structures and reestablish the ideological importance of mind over body. If the notion of excess as political threat is doubted, consider the following reactionary and racist statement that concerns jazz, which appeared in the *Revue Musicale* in 1920:

> It is entirely excess, and for that reason more than monotone: the monkey is left to his own devices, without morals, without discipline, thrown back to all the groves of instinct, showing his meat still more obscene. These slaves must be subjugated, or there will be no more master.[104]

The last sentence is particularly unfortunate, given African-American history. Lawrence Kramer has identified "the material character, and especially the bodily character, of blues or jazz proper" as just what one does *not* hear in jazz citation.[105] Bodily excess is normally held in check in European concert music or constrained by its context: for example, the love duet in *Tristan* or Salome's dance. Even when constrained within a framing device, however, bodily excess is still prone to be perceived as vulgar, embarrassing, or tasteless. This is not to suggest that jazz itself constantly takes on a physically excessive character but rather to recognize that the body is important to jazz and that this is not something that jazz musicians find uncomfortable or feel a need to apologize about.

There is no doubt that some critics perceived the black body as being different from the white. A Norwegian journalist writing in 1921 of the 5 Jazzing Devils, one of the first American groups to perform in Oslo, comments that the group consisted of "four Negroes and a man."[106] And here is the Austrian scholar Heinrich Eduard Jacob explaining the "Origins and Triumphs of Jazz" in 1940: "The blacks have the secret of innervating their muscles in a different way from the white"; Jacob's evidence is unusually compelling: "If this were not the case," he argues, "they could not carry heavy weights so untiringly."[107] This explains for him the "dangling-shambling dances" that lack poise and their musical counterpart, "in which the autocratic rule of the beat had been challenged by syncopation." Having relieved himself of further absurd racist nonsense, he goes on to reassure the reader that society will not tolerate jazz for long. What Jacob has failed to recognize, though it is crucially important, is that African-Americans make certain *cultural* and not *racial* choices. These musical practices come from living in and absorbing the cultural experience of African-American communities. They are not "in the blood." African Americans who have white relations or a paler skin color do not have their capacity for engaging in these practices genetically reduced. In contrast to Jacob, Henry Raynor sees the triumph of jazz as a "reaction against the negative politeness and lack of vitality" that had befallen contemporary light music in the 1920s.[108]

In the United Kingdom, Constant Lambert writes (in 1934) of

> crusty old colonels, the choleric judges and beer-sodden columnists who imagine they represent the European tradition, murmuring "swamp stuff," "jungle rhythms," "Negro decadence" whenever they hear the innocent and anodyne strains of the average English jazz band.[109]

Lambert was of the opinion, however, that a "barbaric and vital Negro element" existed and that in symphonic jazz it provided the same stimulus in the 1920s as Oriental exoticism did in the 1890s. But black American signifiers in European concert music are intriguingly different in effect from Oriental signifiers, because black music making is historically and culturally much more familiar as a consequence of the African Diaspora. This familiarity is, for many, accompanied by the connotations of pleasure, entertainment, and leisure that spring from their experience of hearing and seeing black musicians perform. The fear that arose for some during the early days of jazz reception in Europe was that the perceived physical quality of black music making would corrupt a refined and disciplined art music tradition. There was then, for some, a fear of the Other that might be compared with Orientalist fears. However, for the majority, this fear did not exist, the reason being that jazz was already a fusion of black and white practices, a cross-fertilization of European and African musics that took place on a third continent, North America.

NOTES

INTRODUCTION

1. V. N. Volosinov, "The Study of Ideologies and Philosophy of Language," in Tony Bennett, Graham Martin, Colin Mercer, and Janet Woollacott, eds., *Culture, Ideology and Social Process: A Reader* (London: Batsford, 1981), 145–52, 146.

2. "If, as is nearly always the case, music appears to express something, this is only an illusion and not a reality. It is simply an additional attribute which, by tacit and inveterate agreement, we have lent it, thrust upon it, as a label, a convention—in short, an aspect unconsciously or by force of habit, we have come to confuse with its essential being" (Igor Stravinsky, *An Autobiography* [London: Calder and Boyars, 1975, orig. pub. Gollancz, 1936], 53–54).

3. Evidence of a paradigm shift that occurred between 1980 and 1990 was noted by Joseph Kerman in "American Musicology in the 1990s," *Journal of Musicology* (1991). However, it was not obvious everywhere and to everyone overnight. For example, in 1989 a conference report from Cheong Wai-Ling in *Music Analysis* 8, no. 3 (p. 355), assumed confidently that Schenkerian theory was unassailable. Yet at the International Music and Gender Conference in London in 1991 the mere mention of Schenker brought forth derisive groans from delegates. An uncompromising critique of what was actually achieved in the last two decades of the twentieth century appears in John Shepherd and Peter Wicke, *Music and Cultural Theory* (Polity Press), 7–94.

4. Reception theory had barely made an impact on musicology before 1980; see Mark Everist, "Reception Theories, Canonic Discourses, and Musical Value," in Nicholas Cook and Mark Everist, eds., *Rethinking Music* (Oxford: Oxford University Press, 1999), 378–402, 381–82. I should, perhaps, note here that my treatment of reception differs from that of Gadamer and Jauss in refusing to idealize the original cultural artifact.

5. See Leo Treitler, "On Historical Criticism," *Musical Quarterly* 53 (1967), 188–205. For his more recent thoughts on how music embodies its historicity, see "The

Historiography of Music," an essay that includes a critique of hermeneutic as well as causal models, in Cook and Everist, *Rethinking Music*, 356–77.

6. The series includes Adam Krims, ed., *Music/Ideology: Resisting the Aesthetic* (Amsterdam: G+B Arts International, 1998).

7. Julia Kristeva, "Revolution in Poetic Language" (1974), trans. Margaret Waller (1984), excerpted in Toril Moi, ed., *The Kristeva Reader* (Oxford: Blackwell, 1986), 89–136, 111.

8. Kristeva coined the term "intertextuality." Graham Allen's *Intertextuality* (London: Routledge, 2000) is a book-length study of its history and meaning in cultural theory.

9. Roland Barthes, *Mythologies*, trans. Annette Lavers (London: Paladin, 1973, orig. pub. 1957).

10. Terry Eagleton, *The Ideology of the Aesthetic* (Oxford: Blackwell, 1990).

11. Rose Rosengard Subotnik, *Developing Variations: Style and Ideology in Western Music* (Minneapolis: University of Minnesota Press, 1991), xxv–xxvi.

12. Ibid., 9.

13. It is not my wish to become unduly complex in this introduction, but perhaps I may be pedantic here and explain here that my "meaning" is shorthand for what Greimas describes more precisely as "meaning effect." See Ronald Schleifer, *A. J. Greimas and the Nature of Meaning: Linguistics, Semiotics and Discourse Theory* (Lincoln: University of Nebraska Press, 1987), 7.

14. Peter Kivy, *Sound and Semblance: Reflections on Musical Representation* (Ithaca, NY: Cornell University Press, 1991, orig. pub. 1984), 175, 203.

15. Ibid., 183, 199, 205.

16. Ibid., 143.

17. Ibid., 203–6.

18. Younger readers may need to know that the Rossini overture was used for the title credits of the TV series *The Lone Ranger*.

19. Eero Tarasti, *A Theory of Musical Semiotics* (Bloomington: Indiana University Press, 1994), 55. Tarasti actually prefers, in his own work, to concentrate on Peirce's sign as it relates to an object (icon, index, and symbol); above all, however, his work is influenced by the structuralist semantics of A. J. Greimas.

20. Donald Davidson, "Radical Interpretation," in *Inquiries into Truth and Interpretation* (Oxford: Clarendon Press, 2001), 125–39, 127. Orig. pub. in *Dialectica*, vol. 27 (1973), 318–28.

21. Kofi Agawu, "The Challenge of Semiotics," in Cook and Everist, *Rethinking Music*, 138–60, 147–53.

22. Gino Stefani, "A Theory of Musical Competence," *Semiotica* 66, no. 1/3 (1987), 7–22, 14, excerpted in Derek B. Scott, *Music, Culture, and Society: A Reader* (Oxford: Oxford University Press, 2000), 50–55, 54.

23. Susan McClary, "Constructions of Subjectivity in Schubert's Music," in Philip Brett, Elizabeth Wood, and Gary C. Thomas, eds., *Queering the Pitch: The New Gay and Lesbian Musicology* (New York: Routledge, 1994), 205–28, 228.

24. A vocal critic of close reading is Gary Tomlinson; see especially his "Musical Pasts and Postmodern Musicologies: A Response to Lawrence Kramer," *Current Musicology* 53 (1993), 18–24, 21–22. However, a call to refigure rather than abandon the practice of close reading in order to develop a postmodern critique of musical poetics is made by Adam Krims in "Introduction: Postmodern Musical Poetics and the Problem of "Close Reading,'" in *Music/Ideology*, 1–14.

CHAPTER 1

1. Simon Frith and Angela McRobbie, "Rock and Sexuality," *Screen Education* 29 (1978), 3–19, reprinted in Simon Frith and Andrew Goodwin, eds., *On Record: Rock, Pop, and the Written Word* (London: Routledge, 1990), 371–89, excerpted in Derek B. Scott, ed., *Music, Culture, and Society: A Reader* (Oxford: Oxford University Press, 2000), 65–70.

2. John Shepherd, "Music and Male Hegemony," in Richard Leppert and Susan McClary, eds., *Music and Society: The Politics of Composition, Performance and Reception* (Cambridge: Cambridge University Press, 1987), 151–72, 172, reprinted in John Shepherd, *Music as Social Text* (Cambridge: Polity Press, 1991), 152–73.

3. Roland Bartles, *Le Grain de la voix*, translated by Stephen Heath as "The Grain of the Voice" in Roland Barthes, *Image-Music-Text* (London: Fontana, 1977, orig. pub. in *Musique en jeu* 9 [1972]), 179–89, reprinted in Frith and Goodwin, *On Record*, 293–300.

4. Jenny Taylor and Dave Laing, "Disco-Pleasure-Discourse: On 'Rock and Sexuality,'" *Screen Education* 31 (1979), 43–48, 46, excerpted in Scott, *Music, Culture, and Society*, 71–76.

5. See Martha Mockus, "Queer Thoughts on Country Music and k. d. lang," in Philip Brett, Elizabeth Wood, and Gary C. Thomas, eds., *Queering the Pitch: The New Gay and Lesbian Musicology* (New York: Routledge, 1994), 257–71, 259.

6. Louis Althusser explains his theory of how ideology interpellates individuals as subjects in his essay "Ideology and the State" in *Lenin and Philosophy and Other Essays*, trans. B. Brewster (London: New Left Books, 1977), 136–69, 152–55.

7. In Julie Kristeva, *Revolution in Poetic Language*, trans. Margaret Waller (New York: Columbia University Press, 1984), excerpts reprinted in Toril Moi, ed., *The Kristeva Reader* (Oxford: Blackwell, 1986, orig. pub. as *La Révolution du langage poétique*, 1974), 90–136.

8. In Barthes, "The Grain of the Voice," 182. Joke Dame has applied Kristeva's concepts of phenotext and genotext to her interpretation of Luciano Berio's *Sequenza III* (1966) in "Voices Within the Voice," in Adam Krims, ed., *Music/Ideology: Resisting the Aesthetic* (Amsterdam: G+B Arts International, 1998), 233–46.

9. Butler's theory of the performativity of sex and gender is expounded in Susan Cusick, *Gender Trouble: Feminism and the Subversion of Identity* (London: Routledge, 1990). Butler's idea that biological sex as well as gender is performed has been the subject of heated debate. In the present context, we might ask: is a bass voice an option for a woman? However, matters are rarely so "straight" forward: Joke Dame reminds us that "crafty examples of gender-disguised singing" can be found in pop, classical, and non-Western music ("Unveiled Voices: Sexual Difference and the Castrato" in Brett, Wood, and Thomas, *Queering the Pitch*, 138–53, 140). To move forward to an idea advanced toward the end of this chapter that a new epoch in representations of sexuality began in the 1960s, it may be noted that Sonny and Cher's "I Got You, Babe" (Bono) of 1965 established what became the common pop practice of the woman singing at the *same* pitch as the man rather than an octave higher.

10. Susan Cusick, "On Musical Performances of Gender and Sex," in Elaine Barkin and Lydia Hamessley, eds., *Audible Traces: Gender, Identity and Music* (Zurich: Carciofoli Verlagshaus, 1999), 25–48, 27–28.

11. Sheila Whiteley, *Women and Popular Music: Sexuality, Identity and Subjectivity* (London: Routledge, 2000), 153.

12. Richard Leppert, *The Sight of Sound: Music, Representation, and the History of the Body* (Berkeley: University of California Press, 1993), xxi.

13. Michel Foucault, *The History of Sexuality,* vol. 1: *An Introduction,* trans. Robert Hurley (Harmondsworth: Penguin, 1981, orig. pub. 1976), 116.

14. See Leonard B. Meyer, *Emotion and Meaning in Music* (Chicago: University of Chicago Press, 1956), 219.

15. Susan McClary, "Constructions of Gender in Monteverdi's Dramatic Music," *Cambridge Opera Journal* 1, no. 3 (1990), 203–23, 223, reprinted in *Feminine Endings: Music, Gender, and Sexuality* (Minneapolis: University of Minnesota Press, 1991), 35–52, 52.

16. Jacques Attali, *Noise: The Political Economy of Music,* trans. Brian Massumi (Minneapolis: University of Minnesota Press, 1985, orig. pub. as *Bruits: Essai sur l'économie politique de la musique* [Paris: Presses Universitaires de France, 1977]), 81.

17. Susan McClary, "Afterword: The Politics of Silence and Sound," in Attali, *Noise,* 149–58, 154.

18. Carl Dahlhaus, *Esthetics of Music,* trans. William Austin (Cambridge: Cambridge University Press, 1982, orig. pub. as *Musikästhetik* [Cologne: Gerig, 1967]), 98.

19. Ambroise Paré, *The Workes of That Famous Chirugian Ambrose Parey,* trans. Thomas Johnson (London: Thomas Cotes, 1634), 889, quoted in Stephen Greenblatt, *Shakespearean Negotiations: The Circulation of Social Energy in Renaissance England* (Oxford: Clarendon Press, 1988), 180.

20. Margaret Murata, "Scylla and Charybdis, or Steering Between Form and Social Context in the Seventeenth Century," in Eugene Narmour and Ruth A. Solie, eds., *Explorations in Music, the Arts, and Ideas: Essays in Honor of Leonard B. Meyer* (Stuyvesant, NY: Pendragon Press, 1988), 67–85.

21. McClary, "Constructions of Gender in Monteverdi's Dramatic Music," 206, and in *Feminine Endings,* 37.

22. Greenblatt, *Shakespearean Negotiations,* 89–90.

23. Lucy Hughes-Hallett, *Cleopatra: Histories, Dreams and Distortions* (London: Bloomsbury, 1990), 209.

24. McClary, "Constructions of Gender in Monteverdi's Dramatic Music," 211–15, and in *Feminine Endings,* 42–44.

25. Foucault, *The History of Sexuality,* vol. 1, 119.

26. Ibid., 116.

27. Notably at her words "Nur sollst du ihr ein scheues Opfer weihn; mit der Liebe Göttin schwelge im Verein!" (No timid homage shall you offer it [love]; with the goddess of love wallow in union!) It is employed even earlier by Haydn as a romantic device (slow movement of Symphony no. 104).

28. Kramer approaches this question by considering amatory relationships of tutelage; however, I have not seen evidence that these were as common in England as among the German philologists that are relevant to his scrutiny of Mendelssohn's Lieder. See Lawrence Kramer, "The Lied as Cultural Practice: Tutelage, Gender, and Desire in Mendelssohn's Goethe Songs," in *Classical Music and Postmodern Knowledge* (Berkeley: University of California Press, 1995), 143–73.

29. See Roy Palmer, *The Sound of History: Songs and Social Comment* (Oxford: Oxford University Press, 1988), 217–18.

30. "Colin and Susan," reprinted in Aline Waites and Robin Hunter, *The Illustrated Victorian Songbook* (London: Michael Joseph, 1984), 65.

31. See Foucault, *The History of Sexuality,* vol. 1, 68.

32. Judith Tick, "Passed Away Is the Piano Girl: Changes in American Musical Life, 1870–1900," in Jane Bowers and Judith Tick, eds., *Women Making Music: The Western Art Tradition, 1150–1950* (London: Macmillan, 1986), 325–48, 336.

33. Stephen Stratton, "Women in Relation to Musical Art," *Proceedings* of the Royal Musical Association 9 (1883), 125–31, 131.

34. J. B. Macdonell, "Classical Music and British Musical Taste," *Macmillan's Magazine*, 1 (1860), 383–89, 384.

35. Cited by Stratton, "Women in Relation to Musical Art," 128.

36. Hugh Haweis, *Music and Morals* (London: Longmans, Green, 1912, orig. pub. Statham, 1871), 102.

37. John Ruskin, *Sesame and Lilies* (London: Allen, 1907, orig. pub. 1865), 98.

38. For Sigmund Freud, repression is a "transformation of affect," so that, for example, the fulfillment of unconscious sexual wishful impulses would generate an affect of disgust rather than pleasure. See *The Interpretation of Dreams* (Harmondsworth: Penguin, 1976, orig. pub. as *Die Traumdeutung,* [Leipzig and Vienna: Deuticke, 1899]), 764. Freud makes repression the main topic of his second lecture in "Five Lectures on Psycho-Analysis," in *Two Short Accounts of Psycho-Analysis,* trans. and ed. James Strachey (Harmonsworth: Penguin, 1962, orig. pub. as *Über Psychoanalyse,* [Vienna: Deuticke, 1910]), 45–54. In challenging Freud's theory, Gilles Deleuze and Félix Guattari ask: "What is 'real' desire, since repression is also desired? How can we tell them apart?" (*Anti-Oedipus: Capitalism and Schizophrenia* [London: Athlone Press, 1984, orig. pub. as *L'Anti-Oedipe* (Paris: Les Editions de Minuit, 1972)], 116).

39. Foucault, *The History of Sexuality,* vol. 1, 122, 128, 129.

40. For example, using Freud's concept of the libido as a force that ebbs and flows without a privileged object, Kramer shows Wagner's *Tristan* to be "a radical work not only in its musical procedures but also in its sexual ideology," in that it represents desire as a fluid force. As an illustration of the ability of the libido to shift from one object to another, Kramer argues that the waves of pleasure that overwhelm Isolde in her *Liebestod* are narcissistic, the product of her ego-libido rather than her libidinal investment in Tristan. It is also possible to reject this psychoanalytical model and interpret the ebbing and surging of desire in *Tristan* through use of the schizoanalytic theory of Deleuze and Guattari. Their model of desiring-production, too, conceptualizes desire in terms of ebbs and flows; they note that "desire proves to have an extraordinary fluidity" (*Anti-Oedipus,* 15). That the music of *Tristan* resonates with later beliefs and feelings about the "real" operations of mind and body does have implications. It means that the music retains its ability to convince as "genuine" or "authentic." One example must suffice: at the end of Baz Luhrmann's film *William Shakespeare's Romeo and Juliet* (1996), which throughout is dominated by a pop music score, Isolde's *Liebestod* accompanies Juliet's death without showing its age (as passé romanticism, sentimentality, or whatever) in the way most nineteenth-century music would.

41. Robert Fink, "Desire, Repression and Brahms's First Symphony," in Krims, *Music/Ideology,* 247–88.

42. Roland Barthes, *The Pleasure of the Text,* trans. Richard Miller (Oxford: Blackwell, 1990, orig. pub. as *Le Plaisir du texte* [Paris: Editions du Seuil, 1973]), 42.

43. Barthes, *The Pleasure of the Text,* 42–43.

44. The songs discussed in this section can be heard on *Classic Years in Digital Stereo: Saucy Songs,* 1989 (BBC ZCF 728).

45. Marybeth Hamilton, *"When I'm Bad, I'm Better": Mae West, Sex and American*

Entertainment" (Berkeley: University of California Press, 1997, orig. pub. New York: HarperCollins, 1996), 151.

46. McClary, "Constructions of Gender in Monteverdi's Dramatic Music," 220, and in *Feminine Endings,* 50.

47. It can be heard as track 1 on the CD *Take It Off! Striptease Classics,* 1997 (Rhino R2 72724).

48. Ernst Krause, Notes, trans. Kenneth Howe, that accompany *The Orchestral Music of Richard Strauss,* vol. 3, (HMV SLS 894), n.p.

49. A eulogy to the sexiness of the waltz is found as late as 1928 in "Das Walzer ist des Lebens schönste Melodie" in act 2 of *Die Herzogin von Chicago* by Emmerich Kálmán.

50. Philip Larkin, "Annus Mirabilis," in *High Windows* (London: ?, 1974), 34.

51. Lester Bangs, "James Taylor Marked for Death" (1971), in *Psychotic Reactions and Carburetor Dung,* ed. Greil Marcus (New York: Vintage Books, 1988), 53–81, 67.

52. Significantly, this was the title Madonna chose for her controversial book of 1992 (London: Secker and Warburg).

53. Hamilton, *"When I'm Bad, I'm Better,"* 55.

54. *New York Daily Mirror,* 31 Dec. 1926, 3, quoted in ibid., 55.

55. Hamilton, *"When I'm Bad, I'm Better,"* 191.

56. Martha Mockus, "Queer Thoughts on Country Music and k. d. lang," in Brett, Wood, and Thomas, *Queering the Pitch,* 260.

57. Ellie Ragland-Sullivan, "The Sexual Masquerade: A Lacanian Theory of Sexual Difference," in Ellie Ragland-Sullivan and Mark Bracher, eds., *Lacan and the Subject of Language* (London: Routledge, 1991), 49–80, 71.

58. There is an irony, however, in the debt Jagger's stage movements had to Tina Turner.

59. Linda Hutcheon, *The Politics of Postmodernism* (London: Routledge, 1989), 106.

60. Jacques Derrida, *Of Grammatology,* trans. Gayatri Chakravorty Spivak (Baltimore: Johns Hopkins University Press, 1974, orig. pub. as *De la Grammatologie* [Paris: Les Editions de Minuit, 1967]), 23.

CHAPTER 2

1. Charles Darwin, *The Descent of Man, and Selection in Relation to Sex* (London: John Murray, 1871); see excerpts in Bojan Bujić, *Music in European Thought 1851–1912* (Cambridge: Cambridge University Press, 1988), 315–19, 319.

2. See Victor J. Seidler, *Rediscovering Masculinity: Reason, Language and Sexuality* (London: Routledge, 1989), 14–21, and Marcia J. Citron, *Gender and the Musical Canon* (Cambridge: Cambridge University Press, 1993), 52–53.

3. I am rehearsing here arguments that have been widely circulated. For an overview of discourses of definition, see Sneja Gunew, ed., *Feminist Knowledge: Critique and Construct* (London: Routledge, 1990), 147–268.

4. Sarah Lewis, *Woman's Mission* (London: John Parker, 1839); see Jane Horowitz Murray, ed., *Strong-Minded Women and Other Lost Voices from Nineteenth-Century England* (Harmondsworth: Penguin, 1984, orig. pub. New York: Pantheon, 1982), 23–24.

5. T. L. Krebs, "Women as Musicians," *Sewanee Review* 2, [Nov. 1893], 76–87, 79.

6. Susan McClary, *Feminine Endings: Music, Gender, and Sexuality* (Minneapolis: University of Minnesota Press, 1991), 18.

7. See Elaine Showalter, *The Female Malady: Women, Madness and English Culture 1830–1980* (London: Virago, 1987), 51–73.

8. George Man Burrows, *Commentaries on the Causes, Forms, Symptoms, & Treatment, Moral & Medical, of Insanity* (London: Underwood, 1828); see Vieda Skultans, *Madness and Morals: Ideas on Insanity in the Nineteenth Century* (London: Routledge, 1975), 224, and Showalter, *The Female Malady*, 56.

9. Henry Maudsley, "Sex in Mind and in Education," *Fortnightly Review* 21 (1874), 466–83, 475.

10. Arthur Schopenhauer, *Die Welt als Wille und Vorstellung* (Leipzig: Brockhaus, 1819), trans. E. F. J. Payne as *The World as Will and Representation*, 2 vols. (Indian Hills, CO: Falcon's Wing Press, 1958), quoted in Terry Eagleton, *The Ideology of the Aesthetic* (Oxford: Blackwell, 1990), 154.

11. See Showalter, *The Female Malady*, 125–26.

12. See Daphne Bennett, *Emily Davies and the Liberation of Women 1830–1921* (London: André Deutsch, 1990), 157. Elizabeth Garrett had passed the examination set by the Society of Apothecaries in 1862 and fought successfully to be put on the Medical Register; therefore, she was able to challenge these ideas as a doctor. Her friend Emily Davies was a pioneer in the cause of women's education and founded Girton, Cambridge's first college for the higher education of women, in 1873.

13. Samuel Smiles, *Life and Labour; or, Characteristics of Men of Industry, Culture and Genius* (London: Routledge, 1997, orig. pub. London: John Murray, 1887), 303.

14. J. F. R., "Women as Musical Critics," *Monthly Musical Record* 25 (1895), 48–50, 50.

15. Elizabeth Stirling was for over twenty years the organist at St. Andrew Undershaft, London, a post she won in open competition.

16. Taken from a selected extract from Thomas Gisbourne, *The Purposes of Ornamental Education* (1797), reproduced in Murray, *Strong-Minded Women*, 198.

17. John Stuart Mill, "The Subjection of Women" (1869) in *Three Essays* (London: Oxford University Press, 1975), 513.

18. Joseph Verey, "Women as Musicians," *Monthly Musical Record* 15 (1885), 196–97, 197.

19. See Elizabeth Wood, "Women in Music," *SIGNS, Journal of Women in Culture and Society*, 6, no. 2 (1980), 295.

20. Mill, "The Subjection of Women," 513.

21. Richard Leppert, "Sexual Identity, Death and the Family Piano in the Nineteenth Century," in *The Sight of Sound: Music, Representation and the History of the Body* (Berkeley: University of California Press, 1993). This book contains much critical discussion of representations of women and music in the visual arts.

22. Anon., *Musical Gazette* 2, no. 17 (25 April 1857), 192–93.

23. These problems are discussed in Citron, *Gender and the Musical Canon*, 80–119.

24. Anon., *Musical Gazette* 2, no. 28 (11 July 1857), 332.

25. Anon., *Musical Gazette* 3, no. 27 (3 July 1858), 313.

26. Anon., *Musical Gazette* 2, no. 30 (25 July 1857), 353.

27. Anon., *Musical Times* 21 (1 Dec. 1880), 600.

28. J. F. R., "Women as Musical Critics," 50.

29. T. L. Krebs, "Women as Musicians," *Sewanee Review* (Tennessee) 2 (1893), 76–87, 81.

30. Ibid., 81.

31. Verey, "Women as Musicians," 196.

32. See Percy A. Scholes, *The Mirror of Music 1844–1944*, vol. 2 (London: Novello and Oxford University Press, 1947), 876.

33. Richard Leppert, *Music and Image: Domesticity, Ideology and Socio-cultural Formation in Eighteenth-Century England* (Cambridge: Cambridge University Press, 1988).

34. Charles Hallé, "The Religion of Music," *Review of Reviews* 12 (1895), 430.

35. See Van Akin Burd, ed., *The Winnington Letters* (London: Allen and Unwin, 1969), 528–29. This incident was cited by Sara M. Dodd in "Ruskin and Women's Education," an unpublished paper given at the Association of Art Historians Conference (April 1988).

36. Burd, *The Winnington Letters,* 528.

37. From the late 1860s onward, however, music began to occupy an increasingly important place in Ruskin's aesthetics. See William J. Gatens, "John Ruskin and Music," in Nicholas Temperley, ed., *The Lost Chord: Essays on Victorian Music* (Bloomington: Indiana University Press, 1989), 68–88.

38. Extract from the Queen's Journal, 4 July 1872, in George Earle Buckle, ed., *The Letters of Queen Victoria* (London: John Murray, 1926), 221.

39. Evidence (Part 1) Before the Commissioners on the Revenues and Management of Certain Colleges and Schools, 1864, in *British Parliamentary Papers: Education General 11* (Shannon: Irish University Press, 1969), 228.

40. Ibid., 153.

41. Ibid., 154.

42. Aristotle, *The Politics,* book 8, trans. Thomas A. Sinclair (Harmondsworth: Penguin, 1962), 311.

43. From an interview article on Walter Macfarren in the *Musical Times,* Jan. 1898, quoted in Scholes, *The Mirror of Music,* vol. 2, 625.

44. See Anon., "The Military School of Music, Kneller Hall," *New Penny Magazine* 1 (1899), 695–98.

45. Krebs, "Women as Musicians," 87.

46. Lawrence Kramer, *Classical Music and Postmodern Knowledge* (Berkeley: University of California Press, 1995), 183. On the same topic, in relation to the same composer, see also Judith Tick, "Charles Ives and Gender Ideology," in Ruth A. Solie, ed., *Musicology and Difference: Gender and Sexuality in Music Scholarship* (Berkeley: University of California Press, 1993), 83–106.

47. Reproduced in Leppert, *The Sight of Sound,* 224. In this work, Leppert spends much time demonstrating that, for the Victorian music equals woman, particularly in the section "Music and the Crisis of the Phallus" in the last chapter, "Aspiring to the Condition of Silence (the Iconicity of Music)," 223–27.

48. Robert Schumann, *Schumann on Music and Musicians,* trans. Paul Rosenfeld, ed. Konrad Wolff (New York: Norton, 1969, orig. pub. Pantheon, 1946), 116–17.

49. Ibid., 117.

50. Frederick Niecks, "Franz Schubert: A Study—the Pianoforte Works," *Monthly Musical Record* 7 (1877), 17–21, 18.

51. Several pioneering books on this subject appeared within the space of a year in the mid-1990s: Philip Brett, Elizabeth Wood, and Gary C. Thomas, eds., *Queering the Pitch: The New Gay and Lesbian Musicology* (New York: Routledge, 1994); John Gill, *Queer Noises: Male and Female Homosexuality in Twentieth-Century Music* (London: Cassell, 1995); and Richard Smith, *Seduced and Abandoned: Essays on Gay Men and Popular Music* (New York: Continuum, 1995).

52. For evidence of Schubert's sexuality, see Maynard Solomon, "Franz Schubert and the Peacocks of Benvenuto Cellini," *19th-Century Music* 12, no. 3 (1989), 193–206. For doubts about this evidence, see Rita Steblin, "The Peacock's Tale: Schubert's Sexuality Reconsidered," *19th Century Music* 17, no. 1 (1993), 5–33.

53. Consider, in this connection, the words of Peter Hawker (responsible for the stage clothes of the pop group Right Said Fred): "It's a very masculine campness. They must never look too feminine," (quoted in Nicola Jeal, "All Het Up in the Male Camp," *Observer,* 16 Aug. 1992, 43).

54. See the remarks on this movement in McClary, *Feminine Endings,* p. 69: "It is the lovely, 'feminine' tune with which we are encouraged to identify and which is brutally, tragically quashed in accordance with the destiny predetermined by the 'disinterested' conventions of the form." For McClary's later thoughts on Schubert and sexuality, see "Constructions of Subjectivity in Schubert's Music," in Brett, Wood, and Thomas, *Queering the Pitch,* 205–28.

55. Maudsley, "Sex in Mind and in Education," 468.

56. Niecks, "Franz Schubert," 19.

57. "Artiste," letter to the *Monthly Musical Record* 7 (1877), 108.

58. Ibid.

59. Fanny Raymond Ritter, "Music, and Woman as a Musician," *Victoria Magazine* 28 (1877), 195–205, 198.

60. Ritter, "Music, and Woman as a Musician," was originally given as a paper for the Centennial Congress of the Association for the Advancement of Women (Philadelphia) and brought out as a pamphlet, *Woman as a Musician: An Art-Historical Study,* in 1876

61. F. Niecks, "Excerpts from the Diary of a Musician in Search of the True and Beautiful," *Monthly Musical Record* 8 (1878), 179–80.

62. The effect that separate spheres ideology had on Victorian men is discussed in John Tosh, "Domesticity and Manliness in the Victorian Middle Class," in Michael Roper and John Tosh, eds., *Manful Assertions: Masculinities in Britain since 1800* (London: Routledge, 1991), 44–73, 65–68.

63. Stephen S. Stratton, "Woman in Relation to Musical Art," *Proceedings of the Musical Association* 9 (1883), 115–32, 131.

64. Ibid., 128.

65. Ferdinand Praeger speaking in the discussion that followed Stratton's paper; see ibid., 134.

66. Eustace J. Breakspear, "The Works of Chopin in Their Relationship to Art," *Monthly Musical Record* 5 (1875), 2–4, 4.

67. James Huneker, *Chopin: The Man and His Music* (New York: Charles Scribner's Sons, 1900, reprinted New York: Dover, 1966), 142, cited in Jeffery Kallberg, *Chopin at the Boundaries: Sex, History, and Musical Genre* (Cambridge, MA: Harvard University Press, 1996), 43.

68. See Showalter, *The Female Malady,* 127–37.

69. Thomas Carlyle, "The Hero as Poet. Dante; Shakespeare" (1840), reprinted in Edmund D. Jones, ed., *English Critical Essays (Nineteenth Century)* (London: Oxford University Press, 1971, orig. pub. London: World Classics, 1916), 254–99, 261.

70. Richard Leppert, "The Piano, Misogyny and 'The Kreuzer Sonata,'" in *The Sight of Sound,* 153–87, 186–87.

71. Terry Eagleton, *The Ideology of the Aesthetic* (Oxford: Blackwell, 1990).

72. Edmund Burke, *A Philosophical Enquiry into the Origin of Our Ideas of the Sub-*

lime and the Beautiful (1757); see excerpts in Peter le Huray and James Day, eds., *Music and Aesthetics in the Eighteenth and Early-Nineteenth Centuries* (Cambridge: Cambridge University Press, 1981), 69–74, 70–71.

73. Ibid., 71.

74. Niecks, "Franz Schubert," 19.

75. See William Crotch, *Substance of Several Courses of Lectures on Music* (London: Longman, 1831); see excerpts in le Huray and Day, *Music and Aesthetics*, 427–42, 429–35.

76. Ibid., 432.

77. Ibid.

78. Ibid.

79. Ibid., 433.

80. Ibid., 434.

81. E. P. [Ebenezer Prout?], "The Beautiful in Music," *Monthly Musical Record* 1 (1871), 87–89, 88.

82. William Weber, "The History of Musical Canon," in Nicholas Cook and Mark Everist, eds., *Rethinking Music* (Oxford: Oxford University Press, 1999), 336–55, 341. This essay gives a brief history of the rise of scholarly, pedagogical, and performing canons.

83. Citron, *Gender and the Musical Canon*, 202.

84. For further information on nineteenth-century women ballad composers, see Derek Hyde, *New Found Voices: Women in Nineteenth Century English Music* (Aldershot: Ashgate, 3d ed. 1998, orig. pub. London: Belvedere Press, 1984); Derek B. Scott, *The Singing Bourgeois: Songs of the Victorian Drawing Room and Parlour* (Aldershot: Ashgate, 2d ed. 2001, orig. pub. Milton Keynes: Open University Press, 1989); and Judith Tick, *American Women Composers Before 1870* (Rochester, NY: University of Rochester Press, 1995, orig. pub. Ann Arbor, MI: University Microfilm Inc. Research Press, 1983).

85. Virginia Gabriel was to some extent an exception, since she sometimes used tonic minor for a verse section and tonic major for a refrain.

86. Crotch, *Substance*, in le Huray and Day, *Music and Aesthetics*, 438.

87. Burke, *A Philosophical Enquiry*, 73.

88. Ibid., 74.

89. Charlotte Alington Barnard, née Pye (1830–69) moved from Louth (Lincolnshire) to London after her marriage, studied for a short time with the piano virtuoso W. H. Holmes, and took singing lessons from some of the finest singers of the day, such as Charlotte Sainton-Dolby (who helped promote her songs). Barnard was the most commercially successful of ballad composers in the 1860s. For further information, see Scott, *The Singing Bourgeois*, 72–77.

90. Little is known of the private life of Miss M. Lindsay, who sometimes adds her married name, Mrs J. Worthington Bliss, in parentheses. She was one of the two most popular composers in the song catalog of Robert Cocks & Co. in the 1860s (the other was the prolific Franz Abt). See ibid., 66–68.

91. Ellen Dickson (1819–78) began to make her reputation as a ballad composer in the 1850s, about the same time as Miss M. Lindsay. Dickson's songs are often characterized by unusual permutations of broken chord patterns and delicate use of grace notes. See ibid., 68–69.

92. Caroline Norton (1808–77) was a granddaughter of the playwright Richard

Sheridan. She endured a stormy relationship with her politician husband, and her career as a poet and songwriter was often interrupted by her campaigning (for example, for the Infant Custody Bill in the late 1830s and the Married Women's Property Bill in the 1850s). See Alice Acland, *Caroline Norton* (London: Constable, 1948), and Scott, *The Singing Bourgeois,* 65–66.

93. Felicia Hemans was an influential figure with her collection of songs titled *Peninsular Melodies* (pub. Goulding & D'Almaine), and it is significant that some of her songs with music composed by her sister, Harriet Browne, were published by Willis in about 1830 "with an accompaniment for the Spanish guitar" by C. M. Sola.

94. See Scott, *The Singing Bourgeois,* 106.

95. Helen Blackwood, née Sheridan (1807–67) moved to Ireland when her husband succeeded his father as Baron Dufferin in 1839. In songs such as "Terence's Farewell" (1848), which make use of traditional airs, she writes words in a quasi-Irish vernacular. She published anonymously at first, but her identity began to be known in the 1850s.

96. "Sons of the Sea" (McGlennon, 1897), "A Bandit's Life Is the Life for Me" (Harper, 1872), and "Yes! Let Me like a Soldier Fall" (Fitzball-Wallace, 1845).

97. "Nancy Lee" (Weatherly-Adams, 1876).

98. A woman who wrote "masculine" music invited, of course, the kind of criticism discussed earlier that was hurled at Alice Mary Smith. She was certain to be labeled a mere musical male impersonator and accused of being untrue to her "nature."

99. Virginia Gabriel (1825–77) studied piano with the distinguished teachers Johann Pixis, Theodor Döhler, and Sigismond Thalberg and studied composition with Bernhard Molique and Saverio Mercadante.

100. Maud Valérie White (1855–1937) studied at the Royal Academy of Music and in 1879 became the first woman to win the Mendelssohn Scholarship. Her output, for the most part, consisted of drawing-room ballads that are distinguished for their lyricism, imaginative harmony, and skillfully crafted accompaniments. See Sophie Fuller, "Unearthing a World of Music: Victorian and Edwardian Women Composers," *Women: A Cultural Review* 3, no. 1 (1992), 16–22.

101. Christian Friedrich Michaelis in the *Berlinische musikalische Zeitung,* 1805; see le Huray and Day, *Music and Aesthetics,* 289.

102. Richard Wagner, "Beethoven," 1870, excerpts trans. Martin Cooper in Bujić, *Music in European Thought,* 65–75, 68.

103. See E. T. A. Hoffmann, "Beethoven's Instrumental Music" (orig. pub. anonymously in the *Zeitung für die elegante Welt,* 1813), in Oliver Strunk, ed., *Source Readings in Music History: From Classical Antiquity to the Romantic Era* (London: Faber, 1952), 775–81, 778.

104. The new woman demanded an active participatory role in society and was prepared to challenge conventional expectations. The *Westminster Review* noted with an air of revelation in 1884: "Wifehood and motherhood are incidental parts, which may or may not enter into the life of each woman" (January 1884), 153.

105. See Eagleton, *The Ideology of the Aesthetic,* 167; le Huray and Day, *Music and Aesthetics,* 324–25; and Stratton, "Woman in Relation to Musical Art," 115–16, 131.

106. On this subject, see Judith Tick, "Passed Away Is the Piano Girl: Changes in American Musical Life, 1870–1900," in Jane Bowers and Judith Tick, eds., *Women Making Music: The Western Art Tradition, 1150–1950* (London: Macmillan, 1986), 325–48, 333–34.

107. George Upton, *Woman in Music: An Essay* (London: Paul and Chicago: Mc-Clurg, 1909, orig. pub. Boston: Osgood, 1880), 23–24. Upton's book is intended to show that where women in music are concerned, "there is a field in which she has accomplished great results; namely her influence upon the production of music" (31). He demonstrates this by reference to canonic composers. Some may be interested to know that whatever the evidence may be to suggest that Handel had same-sex preferences, Upton has no doubts that he was indebted creatively to his "loving mother" (52).

108. Ibid., 23.

109. Ibid., 31.

110. Eduard Hanslick, *Vom musikalisch-Schönen* (Leipzig: Rudolph Weigel, 1854, rev. ed. 1858), excerpts trans. Martin Cooper in Bujić, *Music in European Thought*, 11–39, 16.

111. Immanuel Kant, *Kritic der Urteilskraft* (Berlin: 1790), section 23, excerpts trans. the eds. in le Huray and Day, *Music and Aesthetics*, 214–29, 223.

112. Hanslick, *Vom musikalisch-Schönen,* in Bujić, *Music in European Thought*, 20.

113. Friedrich Nietzsche, *Der Fall Wagner* (1888), excerpts trans. Walter Kaufmann in Bujić, *Music in European Thought*, 103–7, 103.

114. Sigmund Freud, "Five Lectures on Psycho-Analysis," in *Two Short Accounts of Psycho-Analysis,* trans. and ed. James Strachey (Harmonsworth: Penguin, 1962, orig. pub. as *Über Psychoanalyse* [Vienna: Deuticke, 1910]), 85–86. As ever, Deleuze and Guattari take issue with Freud; see *Anti-Oedipus,* 353.

115. Burke, *A Philosophical Enquiry*, 74.

116. Reports from Commissioners (Education*)*, 1872, in *British Parliamentary Papers: Reports, Commissioners,* 1872, vol. 12 (Shannon: Irish University Press, 1977).

117. See M, "Upon the Philosophy of Art," *Quarterly Musical Magazine and Review* 2 (1820), reprinted in le Huray and Day, *Music and Aesthetics,* 331–38, 338.

118. Daniel Webb, *Observations on the Correspondence Between Poetry and Music* (London: 1769), extracts in le Huray and Day, *Music and Aesthetics,* 118–19, 118.

119. Ethel Smyth was the first British woman composer to achieve the kind of musical status normally reserved for men; the performance of her opera *The Wreckers* in Germany in 1906 was of particular importance to her career.

120. George Bernard Shaw, letter to Ethel Smith, in Richard Terry, *On Music's Borders* (London: Fisher Unwin, 1927), 54.

121. Suzanne Raitt speaks of Smyth as being "openly bisexual"; see "The Singers of Sargent: Mabel Batten, Elsie Swinton, Ethel Smyth," *Women: A Cultural Review* 3, no. 1, (1992), 23–29, 23, 27–29. Elizabeth Wood argues that a distinct lesbian voice can sometimes be heard in Smyth's music in "Sapphonics," in Brett, Wood, and Thomas, *Queering the Pitch,* 22–66, 45–55.

122. Fifty years earlier, Haweis had devoted time to illustrating the theory (not new even then) that women were artistic "not in a creative, but in a receptive sense" in section 37, "Women and Music," of *Music and Morals* (London: Longmans, Green, 1912, orig. pub. Straham, 1871), 102.

123. J. Swinburne, "Women and Music," 1920, *Proceedings of the Royal Musical Association* 46 (1919–20), 21–34, 23. See Tick, "Passed Away Is the Piano Girl," for a similar double bind: the small "feminine" forms show inadequate breadth of imagination, but writing in larger forms is a betrayal of sexual identity.

124. Camille Paglia, *Sexual Personae: Art and Decadence from Nefertiti to Emily Dickinson* (New Haven: Yale University Press, 1990), 247.

CHAPTER 3

1. U.S. citizenship was provided by the Snyder Act. Resistance to the idea of the "assimilated Indian" is bound up with the coercive attempts by boarding schools of the late nineteenth and early twentieth centuries to create the English-speaking Christian Indian with short hair and a tie. Needless to say, what these schools produced was the institutionalized Indian rather than the assimilated Indian.

2. Robert F. Berkhofer, *White Man's Indian: Images of the American Indian from Columbus to the Present* (New York: Knopf, 1978), 195.

3. A "generation by models of a real without origin" (Jean Baudrillard, *Simulations*, trans. Paul Foss, Paul Patton, and Philip Beitchman [New York: Semiotext(e), 1983, orig. pub. as *Simulacres et Simulations* Paris: Galilée, 1975], 1).

4. The inaccuracies of Indian costume and custom in Hollywood films are dealt with in Ralph E. Friar and Natasha A. Friar, *The Only Good Indian . . . : The Hollywood Gospel* (New York: Drama Book Specialists, 1972).

5. John E. O'Connor, *The Hollywood Indian: Stereotypes of Native Americans in Films* (Trenton: New Jersey State Museum, 1980), 10.

6. Two early American songs, Sarah Wentworth Morton and Hans Gram's "The Death Song of an Indian Chief" (1791) and Anne Julia Hatton and James Hewitt's "Alknomook, the Death Song of the Cherokee Indian" from *Tammany* (1794), may be found in William Thomas Marrozo and Harold Gleason, eds., *Music in America: An Anthology from the Landing of the Pilgrim Fathers to the Close of the Civil War 1620–1865* (New York: Norton, 1964), 213, 225–26.

7. Miriam K. Whaples, "Early Exoticism Revisited," in Jonathan Bellman, ed., *The Exotic in Western Music* (Boston: Northeastern University Press, 1998), 3–25, 17; Rameau's words "j'ai caracterisé le chant et la danse des sauvages" are quoted in Roger Savage, "Rameau's American Dancers," *Early Music*, 11, no. 4 (1983), 441–52, 446.

8. Stephen Storace, *The Cherokee*, 1794, an opera in three acts, performed at the Theatre Royal, Drury Lane, London. Lest it seem very odd to find such subject matter in an English opera, it should be pointed out that in the eighteenth century some English settlers (those on the wooded frontiers) were living closer to Native American villages than to colonial towns on the Atlantic coast. See James Axtell, *The European and the Indian: Essays in the Ethnohistory of Colonial North America* (New York: Oxford University Press, 1981), 284.

9. See Storace, *The Cherokee*, "Invocation and Chorus," bars 138–80.

10. The *London Stage*, 22 Dec. 1794, quotes an announcement on a playbill at Drury Lane: "The Public are respectfully informed that the War-Whoop Chorus, which was so much honoured with their Approbation, is now removed to the End of the First Act" (cited in Jane Girdham, *English Opera in Late Eighteenth-Century London: Stephen Storace at Drury Lane* [Oxford: Clarendon Press, 1997], 49). The most popular tune in the opera, however, was "A Shepherd Once." It appears as No. 3 of Beethoven's *Original Welsh Airs* (pub. George Thomson), probably because it is sung by Winifred the Welsh maid in *The Cherokee*. It is labeled "Air Ecossais" when it appears as No. 1 of the Op. 105 variations. All the same, it is most probably Storace's own composition. See Girdham, *English Opera in Late Eighteenth-Century London*, 117–18, and Roger Fiske, *English Theatre Music in the Eighteenth Century* (London: Oxford University Press, 1973), 531.

11. William B. Wood, *Personal Recollections of the Stage* (Philadelphia: Baird, 1855), quoted in Victor Fell Yellin, "Two Early American Musical Plays," in the accompany-

ing booklet to the CD recording John Bray, *The Indian Princess,* The Federal Music Society Opera Company conducted by John Baldon, 1996, orig. released 1978 (New World Records 80232–2), 2–11, 7.

12. When *The Indian Princess* work was adapted for Drury Lane, London, in Dec. 1820, it was renamed *Pocahontas,* the original title becoming a subtitle.

13. Bray, *The Indian Princess,* incidental music to act 2, scene 2, "Smith brought in prisoner."

14. Larry's song is titled "Och! Hubbaboo! Gramachree! Hone!"

15. Kate is usually comic, too, as in the song "Katy's Letter" by Lady Dufferin.

16. Samuel Lover continues this Irish style in songs such as "Rory O'More."

17. On the recording, Bray's *The Indian Princess* has been restored by Victor Fell Yellin from a simplified keyboard version that gives occasional indications of instruments.

18. Consider, for example, the case of the Prince and Liù in Puccini's *Turandot* discussed in chapter 7.

19. See Roy Harvey Pearce, *Savagism and Civilization: A Study of the Indian and the American Mind* (Berkeley: University of California Press, rev. ed. 1988, orig. pub. 1953), 173–95, and Berkhofer, *White Man's Indian,* 86–96.

20. Washington Irving, *The Sketch Book,* 2 vols. (London: John Murray, 1821), vol. 2, 151, quoted in Nicholas Tawa, *A Music for the Million: Antebellum Democratic Attitudes and the Birth of American Popular Music* (New York: Pendragon Press, 1984), 26.

21. See Trudy Griffin-Pierce, *Native Americans: Enduring Cultures and Traditions* (New York: Friedman, 1996), 147.

22. Jon W. Finson, *The Voices That Are Gone: Themes in 19th-Century American Popular Song* (New York: Oxford University Press, 1994), 246. An example of the unadaptable Noble Savage is given in the song "The Indian Student" by Mrs L. L. D. J. (1851).

23. Henry Rowe Schoolcraft, *Algic Researches* (New York: Dover, 1999, orig. pub. Harper and Brothers, 1839).

24. Michael Pisani, "I'm an Indian, Too: Creating Native American Identities in Nineteenth- and Early Twentieth-Century Music," in Bellman, *The Exotic in Western Music,* 218–57, 231. Pisani's informative essay is largely concerned with concert music. He presents a summary of "the standard language for the musical depiction of Indians" on pages 229–30.

25. Lester S. Levy, *Grace Notes in American History: Popular Sheet Music from 1820 to 1900* (Norman: University of Oklahoma Press, 1967), 280. An earlier song, however, "The Death Song of the Cherokee Indians," did enjoy much favor in the first half of the nineteenth century. Its origins are obscure. There was an unlikely claim that it was a genuine Cherokee air as recollected by a Mr. Turner, from whom it was taken and adapted by the poet and composer Anne Hunter; see Whaples, "Early Exoticism Revisited," 24–25.

26. See Charles Hamm, *Music in the New World* (New York: Norton, 1983), 189–91.

27. I would like to thank Grahame Shrubsole for bringing this song to my attention and providing me with a copy. He assures me that the two editions held in the New York Public Library have been misdated (1836–37), and that Russell wrote the song on his return to England in the autumn of 1842.

28. The image of the buffalo hunter bedecked in eagle feathers and dwelling in a conical tepee is familiar from old Hollywood films, but this stereotypical image emerged earlier in paintings and novels and is discussed by John C. Ewers in "The Emergence of the Plains Indian as the Symbol of the North American Indian," *An-*

nual Report Smithsonian Institution 1964 (Washington, D.C.). Moreover, the Indian Wars of 1860−90 concerned the Plains tribes, and some of these (mainly Sioux) participated in the enormously influential Buffalo Bill's Wild West Shows that began in 1883 and continued for over thirty years. In 1903, Buffalo Bill brought his show to Manchester, England, for the start of a provincial tour and the organizers told the *Manchester Guardian* (28 April 1903) that they had "done exceedingly well."

29. It should be noted that the term "tribe" is a convenient but not an entirely appropriate way of describing different Native American peoples, since it implies branches of one homogeneous ethnic group rather than of a diversity of ethnic minority groups.

30. See Charles Hamm, *Yesterdays: Popular Song in America* (New York: Norton, 1979), 180−82, and Derek B. Scott, *The Singing Bourgeois: Songs of the Victorian Drawing Room and Parlour* (Aldershot: Ashgate, 2d ed. 2001, orig. pub. 1989), 40−41.

31. Melody line and words given in Levy, *Grace Notes in American History,* 287. Levy seems unaware of this duplication.

32. Melody and words given in ibid., 282.

33. "Colors of the Wind" (Menken-Schwartz), available on CD *Pocahontas,* 1996 (Walt Disney Records WD481424).

34. Melody and words given in Levy, *Grace Notes in American History,* 284−85. Other Noble Savage songs of the 1840s were "The Indian and His Bride" (Morris-Brown), 1844, and "The Indian's Dream" (Farrell-Howard), 1848.

35. The myth of Indians always going around attacking forts or wagon trains is exposed as having little basis in fact by Robert M. Utley and Wilcomb E. Washburn in *The Indian Wars* (New York: American Heritage Publishing, 1977).

36. The songs "Sioux Indians," "Haunted Wood," and "Texas Jack" can be found in Austin E. Fife and Alta S. Fife, eds., *Cowboy and Western Songs: A Comprehensive Anthology* (Ojai, CA: Creative Concepts Publishing, 1969), 122−23, 118−19, and 125−26.

37. See Vine Deloria, Jr., *Custer Died for Your Sins: An Indian Manifesto* (New York: Avon Books, 1969), 14.

38. Henry Clay Work, *Songs,* ed. H. Wiley Hitchcock (New York: Da Capo Press, 1974), 21−5.

39. The idea of the vanishing Indian can be traced back to certain songs that followed the forced removal of large numbers of Native Americans in the 1830s and 1840s, for example, John W. Hutchinson's "The Indian's Lament" (music arranged by E. L. White, 1846) and James G. Clark's "The Indian Mother's Lullaby" (1855). See Finson, *The Voices That Are Gone,* 249−52.

40. Brian W. Dippie, *The Vanishing American: White Attitudes and American Indian Policy in the Nineteenth Century* (Middletown, CT: Wesleyan University Press, 1982), 241.

41. "Arrah Wanna" (Drislane-Morse), 1906.

42. See William H. A. Williams, *'Twas Only an Irishman's Dream: The Image of Ireland and the Irish in American Popular Song Lyrics, 1800−1920* (Urbana: University of Illinois Press, 1996), 193.

43. Quoted in O'Connor, *The Hollywood Indian,* 23. "Navajo" (Williams-Van Alystyne), 1903, is a love song from an African-American man to a Native American woman. When the song became a hit in France, however, it was adapted to French colonial interests and rewritten by Paul Briollet and Léo Lelièvre (1906) as the serenade of a woman to a man from the Congo.

44. "Red Wing" (Chattaway-Mills), 1907.

45. Another "innocent" song that became popular in the following decade was

"By the Waters of Minnetonka" "An Indian Love Song" (Cavanass-Lieurance), 1917. The vocal melody is almost entirely pentatonic throughout and is characterized by the rhythm familiarly known as the "Scotch snap." It was recorded by Nellie Melba in 1921, rereleased on *Love's Old Sweet Song: 25 Great Singers in Popular Ballads,* 1994 (ASV Living Era CD AJA 5130); a jazz version from 1954 is on Charlie Barnet, *Redskin Romp,* 1996 (RCA 74321421292).

46. Woody Guthrie, "Union Maid," 1940; see Mal Collins, Dave Harker, and Geoff White, *The Big Red Songbook,* eds. (London: Pluto Press, enlarged ed. 1981), 60, 86–87.

47. "Indian Love Call," from *Rose Marie* (Frimi-Harbach/Hammerstein), 1924.

48. Gilles Deleuze and Félix Guattari, *A Thousand Plateaus: Capitalism and Schizophrenia,* trans. Brian Massumi (Minneapolis: University of Minnesota Press, 1987, orig. pub. as *Mille Plateaux,* vol. 2 of *Capitalisme et Schizophrénie,* [Paris: Les Editions de Minuit, 1980]), 19.

49. Pisani points out whole tones in "I'm an Indian, Too" (Berlin) in his essay of that title cited earlier.

50. "Indianola," an "instrumental novelty and fox trot" (Henry-Onivas [real name: Domenico Savino]), 1917.

51. It was not long before a crucial sign for the presence of Indians was found— the drum. In Henry Bishop's glee of 1823, "Hark! 'Tis the Indian Drum" (from *Cortez, or The Conquest of Mexico,* a historical play, words by I. R. Planche), it found its first simple representation as four staccato chords per bar. The glee is for four voices, later arranged for three.

52. *Massacre* Pressbook, Performing Arts Collection, New York Public Library at Lincoln Center, cited in O'Connor, *The Hollywood Indian,* 33.

53. The musical example is taken from the duet "Rose der Prairie," act 2 of Emmerich Kálmán's *Die Herzogin von Chicago* (words by Julius Brammer and Alfred Grünwald), 1928.

54. Charlie Barnet and His Orchestra, "Cherokee" (Noble), recorded Hollywood, CA, 6 Dec. 1954, *Redskin Romp,* 1996 (RCA 74321421292).

55. See Nat Shapiro and Nat Hentoff, *Hear Me Talkin' to Ya* (New York: Dover, 1966, orig. pub. 1955), 354–60.

56. The music to the film is available on disc: *Steiner: They Died with Their Boots On,* Moscow Symphony Orchestra, cond. Stromberg, 1999 (Marco Polo 8225079).

57. See Kate Daubney, *The View from the Piano: A Critical Examination and Contextualisation of the Film Scores of Max Steiner 1939–45* (University of Leeds., Ph.D. thesis, 1996), 237.

58. Despite showing some sympathy for Crazy Horse, the film was much criticized for its portrayal of the Sioux. There was nothing especially new about this: as early as 1911 portrayals of Indians in films were being criticized in articles in *Motion Picture World;* see O'Connor, *The Hollywood Indian,* 3.

59. John Fiske, *Understanding Popular Culture* (London: Unwin Hyman, 1989), 25.

60. Hank Williams, "Kaw-Liga" (Williams-Rose), 1953 (MGM 11416), rereleased on Hank Williams, *40 Greatest Hits,* 1978 (MGM Select Double 2683 071), and *The Great Hits of Hank Williams Senior,* n.d. (Pickwick International CN4 2076).

61. Another piece inspired by such figures is Raymond Scott's "War Dance for Wooden Indians." It can be heard performed by the Beau Hunks Sextette on *Celebration on Planet Mars: A Tribute to Raymond Scott,* 1995 (Koch International 379092).

62. Johnny Preston, "Running Bear" (J. Richardson), 1960 (Mercury Records 45-AMT 1079). Richardson, who wrote the song, was better known as the Big Bopper.

63. William Shakespeare, *Romeo and Juliet*, act 1, scene 5. Elsewhere, Shakespeare's words "as patient as the female dove" (*Hamlet*, act 5, scene 1) could not be less suited to the impetuous White Dove of this song.

64. B. Lee Cooper, *A Resource Guide to Themes in Contemporary American Song Lyrics 1950–1985* (New York: Greenwood Press, 1986), 61, 154.

65. For example, the "Fast Sioux War Dance" on the CD *Authentic Native American Music*, 1995 (Laserlight 12 551).

66. On the subject of the Hollywood Indian's grunting and limited linguistic ability, see Deloria, *Custer Died for Your Sins*, 34, and the same author's "We Talk, You Listen" (1970), in Frederick W. Turner III, ed., *The Portable North American Indian Reader* (New York: Viking Press, 1973), 587–96, 588.

67. Walt Disney, *Peter Pan*, animated film 1952, (The Walt Disney Company, Buena Vista Home Video D202452–1). The musical score is by Oliver Wallace, the orchestration by Edward Plumb, and the vocal arrangements by Jud Conlon. A general credit only is given for the songs, so the item in question could have been the work of any of the following: Sammy Fain, Sammy Cahn, Oliver Wallace, Frank Churchill, Erdman Penner, Winston Hibler, and Ted Sears.

68. "*La valse chaloupée*," (arranged by Charles Dubourg, words added by Lucien Boyer and Léo Lelièvre.

69 The Shadows, "Apache" (London), 1960 (Columbia DB4484).

70. Consider the well-known theme music to the MGM film *Hang 'Em High* (Frontiere), 1967.

71. The Shadows, "Geronimo," (Marvin) 1963 (Columbia DB7163).

72. Johnny Cash, "The Ballad of Ira Hayes" (La Farge), *Johnny Cash's Greatest Hits*, vol. 1, 1967 (CBS 40-32565).

73. Alison R. Bernstein, *American Indians and World War II: Toward a New Era in Indian Affairs* (Norman and London: University of Oklahoma Press, 1991), 51. See also Barthes's discussion of the ideological import of the black soldier saluting the French flag in *Mythologies*, trans. Annette Lavers (London: Paladin, 1973, orig. pub. Paris: Editions de Seuil, 1959), 125–26.

74. Cash's once-vaunted Cherokee roots now appear to be fictional; see Colin Larkin, ed., *The Encyclopedia of Popular Music* (New York: MUZE, 3d ed. 1998), vol. 2, 976.

75. See Turner, *The Portable North American Indian Reader*, 10.

76. See Joann W. Kealiinohomoku, "The Would-be Indian," in Charlotte J. Frisbie, ed., *Explorations in Ethnomusicology: Essays in Honor of David P. McAllester*, Detroit Monographs in Musicology 9 (Detroit: Information Coordinators, 1986), 111–26. Concern about preserving Native American culture becomes problematic when, for example, the Makah (of Washington State) decide to return to whaling (1999) or the Lakota reintroduce bison (1990) and kill them for food.

77. Dee Brown, *Bury My Heart at Wounded Knee* (London: Barrie and Jenkins, 1970), xvii.

78. Vine Deloria, Jr., *God Is Red* (Golden, Col: North American Press, 1992, orig. pub. New York: Grosset and Dunlap, 1973).

79. "City of Dreams" (Byrne), Talking Heads, *True Stories*, 1986 (Fame, EMI TC-FA 3231).

80. Iron Maiden's "Run to the Hills" was released as a single in June 1982 (EMI 5263); it is on the album *The Number of the Beast*, 1994 (EMI CDEMS1533), and on the two-CD collection *Best of the Beast*, 1996 (CDEMDS1097). A live performance is

featured on *Live after Death,* 1985 (EMI CDP 7 461862). "Black Elk Speaks" is on Hawkwind's album *Space Bandits,* 1990 (GWR GWCD103), rereleased by Castle Communications, 1992 (CLACD282).

81. A study of the Native American in relation to film music may be found in Claudia Gorbman, "Scoring the Indian: Music in the Liberal Western," in Georgina Born and David Hesmondhalgh, eds., *Western Music and Its Others: Difference, Representation, and Appropriation in Music* (Berkeley: University of California Press, 2000), 234–54.

82. Dan Georgakas, review of *Dances with Wolves, Cineaste* 18, no. 2 (1991), 51.

83. Its best-known theme is for John Dunbar, and the opening gestures made around an E♭ triad have been employed as a heroic sign ever since Beethoven's Third Symphony. The original soundtrack is available on *Dances with Wolves* 1990 (Epic 467591 2).

84. Cited on the back of the soundtrack CD, *Geronimo: An American Legend* 1993 (Columbia CK57760).

85. *Sacred Spirit: Chants and Dances of the Native Americans,* 1994 (Virgin Records CDVX 2753).

86. The photograph is of someone not recognizably Native American in physiognomy and appeals to the Western admiration for youth rather than the Native American admiration for wisdom and age. Regrettably, this is all too reminiscent of the Hollywood practice of using white actors for their "important" Indian roles because they "looked better"; see O'Connor, *The Hollywood Indian,* 10.

87. The arranging, mixing, and production of all tracks are credited to "The Fearsome Brave."

88. *Culture Clash: Sacred Spirit 2,* 1997 (Virgin Records CDV 2827).

89. *Raindance,* Polygram TV, 1996 (529 862–2).

90. As revealed on *Secret History: Natural Born Americans,* produced and directed by David Upshal for Channel 4 Television (UK), 14 Sept. 2000.

91. ITV Yorkshire, late evening, 6 June 1997.

92. Tim McGraw, "Indian Outlaw" (Barnes-Simmons-Loudermilk), 1994.

93. "Indian Reservation" ("The Lament of the Cherokee Reservation Indian") was also a hit for the Raiders in 1971.

94. J. Kay Dowell, quoted by P. Cronin, "'Indian Outlaw' Stirs Up a Controversy: McGraw, Curb Respond to Native Americans' Objections," *Billboard* 106 (19 March 1994), 38.

95. In 1988 the Indian Gaming Regulatory Act was passed, allowing the establishment of casinos provided that they play a role in the economic regeneration of reservations.

96. This music has come to be known as *waila* and can be heard played by the Native American band Southern Scratch on their album *Em-we-hejed* (For all of you) 1994 (Canyon Records CR-8097).

97. An example of Joanne Shenandoah's art is the album *Matriarch: Iroquois Women's Songs* 1997 (Silver Wave Records SD913).

98. Buffy Sainte-Marie, *Up Where We Belong,* 1996 (EMI Music Canada 7243 8 35059 2 0) CD booklet, n.p.

99. However, Saint-Marie's rerecording of "Soldier Blue" on *Up Where We Belong* includes a powwow sample.

100. Sainte-Marie, *Up Where We Belong,* n.p.

101. Luther Standing Bear comments on the beat of the tom-tom: "They are heart-

beats, and once all men danced to its rhythm." "Land of the Spotted Eagle" in Turner, *The Portable North American Indian Reader,* 567–77, 576. See also Tara Browner, *"Heartbeat of the People": Music and Dance of the Northern Pow-wow* (Urbana: University of Illinois Press, forthcoming).

102. "We need the public at large to drop the myths in which it has clothed us for so long" (Deloria, *Custer Died for Your Sins,* 34).

103. I suspect it is as a consequence of the embarrassment now felt at the treatment of Native Americans in pop music that David Marsh excluded huge hits such as "Kaw-Liga" and "Running Bear" from *The Heart of Rock & Soul: The 1001 Greatest Singles Ever Made* (New York: New American Library, 1989).

104. On the subversive challenge of carnivalesque inversions of norms, for example, see Linda Hutcheon, *A Theory of Parody: The Teachings of Twentieth-Century Art Forms* (New York: Methuen, 1985), 72–74.

CHAPTER 4

1. For example, Stuart Robertson's singing on Ronnie Munro and His Dance Orchestra, "Hello, Aloha, How Are You?" (Gilbert-Baer), ? Aug. 1926 (777–2).

2. Henry Hall and the BBC Dance Orchestra, "It's a Sin to Tell a Lie" (Mayhew), 12 Sept. 1936 (matrix unknown). Henry Hall (1898–1989) led the re-formed BBC Dance Orchestra from 1932 to 1937.

3. The BBC asked singers not to adopt American accents and originally tried to ban crooning; see Paddy Scanell and David Cardiff, "Serving the Nation: Public Service Broadcasting Before the War," in Bernard Waites, Tony Bennett, and Graham Martin, eds., *Popular Culture: Past and Present* (London: Croom Helm, 1982), p. 181. Scat singing, too, was frowned upon, yet even the mild-natured Bud Flanagan scats on "Underneath the Arches" (Flanagan-Allen), Henry Hall and the BBC Dance Orchestra, vocal: Flanagan and Allen, 15 July 1932 (matrix unknown).

4. Gracie Fields's recording of "Ave Maria" (Bach-Gounod), 25 Oct. 1934 (2EA 1011–3) was a best-seller.

5. Charles Hamm, *Putting Popular Music in Its Place* (Cambridge: Cambridge University Press, 1995), 379–80.

6. In more recent times, Danny Thompson's album *Whatever,* 1987 (Hannibal HNCD1326) comes to mind.

7. For details of which musicians were playing with which bands, addresses of venues, and other information for which there is no space here, see Sid Colin, *And the Bands Played On* (London: Elm Tree, 1977); Jim Godbolt, *A History of Jazz in Britain 1919–50* (London: Quartet Books, 1984); Albert McCarthy, *The Dance Band Era* (London: November Books, 1971); and Brian Rust, *The Dance Bands* (London: Ian Allan, 1972).

8. Gino Stefani, "A Theory of Musical Competence," *Semiotica,* 66, no. 1/3 (1987), 14, excerpted in Derek B. Scott, ed., *Music, Culture, and Society: A Reader* (Oxford: Oxford University Press, 2000), 50–55, 54.

9. The Squadronaires, a Royal Air Force band formed during the Second World War, contained several ex-members of Ambrose's band who had been called up. It was the most admired of the services' bands and was the closest the United Kingdom got to emulating Glenn Miller's wartime band.

10. "American Patrol" (Meacham), which dates from 1885, was turned into a song titled "We Must Be Vigilant," by E. Leslie in 1943.

11. Several notable jazz musicians, however, had a regimental background; one such was Leslie Thompson (trumpet and trombone), who studied music at Kneller Hall (1919–20) and played with the West India Regiment before leaving Jamaica in 1929.

12. Ted Heath (1900–1969) had a reputation as a trombonist and songwriter before forming his own band in 1945. This was widely acknowledged to be the United Kingdom's finest swing band.

13. Jack Hylton and His Orchestra, vocal: trio, "Happy Days Are Here Again" (Yellen-Ager) 30 Jan. 1930 (Bb 18627). Jack Hylton (1892–1965) led a band from 1921 to 1940. He enjoyed great popularity, which was helped by European tours (in the 1920s), broadcasts to the United States (in the 1930s), and the large number of records he made.

14. Lew Stone and His Band, vocal: trio, "Zing! Went the Strings of My Heart" (Hanly), 4 May 1935 (CAR 3404-1). Lew Stone (1898–1969) was a pianist and admired arranger who led his own band (partly inherited from Roy Fox) at the Monseigneur Restaurant, London, from 1932.

15. The Savoy Orpheans, vocal: duet, "Baby Face" (Davis-Akst), 13 Oct. 1926 (matrix unknown). The Savoy Orpheans were associated with London's Savoy Hotel in the 1920s.

16. Peter Wicke, *Rock Music: Culture, Aesthetics and Sociology* (Cambridge: Cambridge University Press, 1990), 52.

17. Bert Ambrose (1897–1973), though English-born, had the enviable experience of having been a bandleader in New York before he took over the band at the Embassy Club in London. In 1927 eyebrows were raised when he was offered the enormous salary of £10,000 a year to lead the band at the Mayfair Club. In the 1930s, Ambrose's band was the most highly rated of all dance bands in the United Kingdom.

18. Richard Caroll Gibbons (1903–54), an American, took over the Savoy Orpheans in 1927. Soon after, he was appointed head of light music at HMV Records.

19. Jack Smith and Ambrose's Whispering Orchestra, "My Blue Heaven" (Whiting-Donaldson), 10 Jan. 1928 (Bb 12338).

20. Billy Cotton and His Band, vocal: Alan Breeze, "I've Got Sixpence" (Box-Cox-Hall), 22 April 1941 (5603-1). Billy Cotton (1899–1969) led a band from 1925. He was in great demand at major dance halls and nightclubs, but in the second half of the 1930s he turned his band into a show band for variety theater work. He later became a radio and TV celebrity.

21. Henry Hall and the BBC Dance Orchestra, vocal: ?, "Rusty and Dusty" (Kennedy-Carr), 29 Nov. 1936 (matrix unknown).

22. Ken Barry, for example, covered a range of hits in the 1950s and 1960s, which included songs as disparate as Roy Orbison's "In Dreams" and Bob Dylan's "Subterranean Homesick Blues," for Woolworth's Embassy label.

23. Ambrose and His Orchestra at the Mayfair Hotel, vocal: Elsie Carlisle, "The Clouds Will Soon Roll By" (Woods-Dixon), 22 July 1932 (OY-2376-2).

24. See Paul Oliver, (ed., *Black Music in Britain: Essays on the Afro-Asian Contribution to Popular Music* (Milton Keynes and Philadelphia: Open University Press, 1990).

25. The Versatile Four, "After You've Gone" (Creamer-Layton), ? Sept. 1919 (6399).

26. See Michael Pickering, "White Skin, Black Masks," in Jacqueline Bratton, (ed., *Music Hall: Performance and Style* (Milton Keynes and Philadelphia: Open University Press, 1986), and Derek B. Scott, *The Singing Bourgeois: Songs of the Victorian Drawing Room and Parlour* (Aldershot: Ashgate, 2d ed. 2001, orig. pub. 1989), 81–92.

27. David Brackett, *Interpreting Popular Music* (Cambridge: Cambridge University Press, 1995), 56.

28. Rose Rosengard Subotnik "Towards a Deconstruction of Structural Listening," in E. Narmour and Ruth Solie, ed., *Explorations in Music, the Arts, and Ideas* (New York: Pendragon Press, 1988), 104.

29. In this connection such enthusiasts might cite the jazz attractions of Nat Gonella's improvised trumpet obbligato in Ray Noble and His Orchestra, vocal: Dorothy Carless, "Oh, You Nasty Man" (Yellen-Caesar-Henderson), 28 June 1934 (OB-7431-2), or Bert Read's piano in Ambrose and His Orchestra, vocal: Sam Browne, "Bye Bye Blues" (Hamm-Bennett-Lown-Gray), 13 Oct. 1930 (Bb-20237-3). Ray Noble (1907–78) succeeded Caroll Gibbons as head of light music at HMV Records. Noble made a string of successful records with the New Mayfair Orchestra (HMV's house band) that featured Al Bowlly as vocalist before moving to the United States in 1934.

30. For a fuller discussion of the reception of jazz in the United Kingdom than that given here, see Derek B. Scott, "The 'Jazz Age,'" in *The Blackwell History of Music in Britain* vol. 6: *The Twentieth Century,* ed. Stephen Banfield (Oxford: Blackwell, 1995), 57–78.

31. Godbolt, *A History of Jazz in Britain,* 42.

32. Bert Firman and the Rhythmic Eight, "Painting the Clouds with Sunshine" (Dubin-Burke), 27 Nov. 1929 (matrix unknown).

33. Since there is little room here for detail concerning personnel on records, the reader is referred to Rust, *The Dance Bands,* and Brian Rust and Sandy Forbes, *British Dance Bands on Record 1911–1945* (Harrow: General Gramophone Publications, 1989, orig. pub. 1987).

34. André Hodeir, *Jazz: Its Evolution and Essence,* trans. David Noakes (New York: Grove Press, 1956), 144.

35. Fred Elizalde and His Music, vocal: Al Bowlly, "Misery Farm" (Wallis), ? Dec. 1928 (BB 170-3).

36. Colin, *And the Bands Played On,* 45.

37. Spike Hughes and His Decca-Dents, vocal: Val Rosing, "It's Unanimous Now" (Stept-Green), 12 March 1930 (De F-1690); it has Sylvester Ahola on trumpet.

38. Godbolt, *A History of Jazz in Britain,* 111.

39. *Melody Maker,* 13 May 1939, 9.

40. Jack Hylton, "Jazz! The Music of the People," in *The Jack Hylton Song Book,* supplement to *Woman's World,* 7 Oct. 1934, ii.

41. Godbolt, *A History of Jazz in Britain,* 150.

42. Constant Lambert, *Music Ho! A Study of Music in Decline* (London: Faber, 1966, orig. pub. 1934), 198.

43. Fred Elizalde, "Jazz—What of the Future?" *Gramophone,* Feb. 1929, 392–93, 393.

44. Victor Silvester was first driven to making records as a consequence of the unsuitability of many existing records for dance practice. He coined the expression "strict tempo" for his dance records.

45. See Ian Whitcomb, *After the Ball* (New York: Limelight Editions, 1986, orig. pub. 1972), 171.

46. Jack Payne (1899–1969) led the BBC Dance Orchestra from 1928 to 1932 and took the band with him when he left to play the variety theaters.

47. Show bands could, for example, perform numbers in flexible tempo, such as "My Old Dutch" (Chevalier-Ingle).

48. Henry Hall and the BBC Dance Orchestra, vocal: George Pizzey, "The Teddy Bears' Picnic" (Kennedy-Bratton), 1932 (matrix unknown), and Henry Hall and the BBC Dance Orchestra, vocal: Dan Donovan, "I Like Bananas (Because They Have No Bones)" (Yacich), 2 June 1936 (matrix unknown).

49. Jack Hylton and His Orchestra, vocal: Eve Becke, "It's the Talk of the Town" (Symes-Neiburg-Levinson), 6 Oct. 1933 (matrix unknown), and Roy Fox and His Band, vocal: Denny Dennis, "I've Got an Invitation to a Dance" (Symes-Neiburg-Levinson), 4 Jan. 1935 (matrix unknown).

50. Henry Hall and the BBC Dance Orchestra, vocal: Les Allen, "In a Little Second Hand Store" (Pease-Dreyer-Nelson), 8 July 1933 (matrix unknown).

51. Jack Harris and His Orchestra, vocal: Sam Browne, "On Linger Longer Island" (Kennedy-Carr), 8 Jan. 1938 (OEA 5160-1).

52. The Moonlight Revellers, "Misty Islands of the Highlands" (Kennedy-Carr), 12 Nov. 1935 (CAR 3719-1).

53. Billy Cotton and His Band, vocal: Alan Breeze, "Did Your Mother Come from Ireland?" (Kennedy-Carr), 27 Oct. 1936 (CAR 4255-1).

54. For example, "Kathleen Mavourneen" (Crawford-Crouch, c. 1838), "The Rose of Tralee" (Spencer-Glover, 1847), and "Come Back to Erin" (Claribel, 1866).

55. Henry Hall and the BBC Dance Orchestra, vocal: Flanagan and Allen, "That's Another Scottish Story" (Flanagan), 13 Nov. 1933 (matrix unknown).

56. Joe Loss and His Band, vocal: Chick Henderson, "The General's Fast Asleep" (Kennedy-Carr), 22 Oct. 1935 (OEA 2000-1), and Jack Hylton and His Orchestra, vocal: George Baker? And Doreen Stephens, "The Handsome Territorial" (Kennedy-Carr), 25 May 1939 (OEA 7816-1).

57. Henry Hall and His Orchestra, vocal: Bob Malin, "South of the Border" (Kennedy-Carr), 25 May 1939 (CA 17467-1).

58. Ambrose and His Orchestra, "The Sunset Trail" (Kennedy-Carr), ? April 1936 (matrix unknown), and Jack Jackson and His Orchestra, vocal: Fred Latham, "Ole Faithful" (Kennedy-Carr), 12 Oct. 1934 (matrix unknown).

59. Roland Barthes Mythologies, trans. Annette Lavers (London: Paladin, 1973, orig. pub. 1957), 123.

60. Ambrose and His Orchestra, vocal: Sam Browne, "Ho Hum" (Suesse-Heyman), 9 June 1931 (OB-972−2).

61. See also Charles Hamm's discussion of the use of this tune in Irving Berlin's "That Mesmerizing Mendelssohn Tune" (1909), in Putting Popular Music in Its Place, 376.

62. A classic account of subcultural bricolage can be found in Dick Hebdige, Subculture: The Meaning of Style (London: Methuen, 1979), 102−6.

63. Jack Hylton and His Orchestra, vocal: Jack Hylton, "Meadow Lark" (Fiorito), 13 Jan. 1927 (Bb 9814).

64. Jack Hylton and His Orchestra, vocal: trio, "Speaking of Kentucky Days" (Gilbert), 17 Jan. 1930 (Bb 18573).

65. Lew Stone and His Band, vocal: Nat Gonella, "My Old Dog" (Sarony), 25 Feb. 1935 (CAR 3244−1).

66. Roy Fox and His Band, vocal: Bobby Joy, "Calling Me Home" (Wilfred), 12 June 1936 (matrix unknown). Roy Fox (1901−82), having made a reputation as a cornetist and bandleader in Hollywood, was invited to play at the Café de Paris, in London with a small American band. He formed a British band in 1931, which was

largely taken over by Lew Stone when Fox fell ill later that year. In 1932 he formed another band, and he played in clubs and theaters until ill health struck again in 1938.

67. Richard Middleton, *Studying Popular Music* (Milton Keynes and Philadelphia: Open University Press, 1990), 275–79.

68. Philip Tagg, *Kojak—50 Seconds of Television Music: Towards the Analysis of Affekt in Popular Music* (Gothenburg: Gothenburg University, 1979), 71.

69. Jack Hylton and His Orchestra, vocal: Jack Hylton, "Yes Sir, That's My Baby" (Kahn-Donaldson), 30 June 1925 (matrix unknown).

70. The Savoy Orpheans, "Charleston" (Mack-Johnson), 7 July 1925 (matrix unknown).

71. This rhythm is featured, for example, in the introduction and elsewhere in "Peg o' My Heart" (Bryan-Fisher) of 1913.

72. See Gunther Schuller, *Early Jazz* (New York: Oxford University Press, 1968), 273–74.

73. Cf. Jack Hylton and His Orchestra, vocal: Jack Hylton and Chappie d'Amato, "Under the Ukelele [*sic*] Tree" (Henderson), 11 June 1926 (Bb 8525).

74. The Original Dixieland Jazz Band, "I'm Forever Blowing Bubbles" (Kenbrovin-Kellette), 10 Jan. 1920 (76754), and "Alice Blue Gown" (Tierney), 14 May 1920 (74104).

75. See Leonard Feather, *The Jazz Years: Earwitness to an Era* (1986; London: Pan, 1988). He has also written a "Twelve Tone Blues."

76. Lew Stone and His Band, "Garden of Weed" (Foresyth), 24 April 1934 (TB-1207-2).

77. Ambrose and His Orchestra, vocal: Elsie Carlisle, Sam Browne, "Let's Put Out the Lights" (Hupfeld), 26 Oct. 1932 (OB-3474-2).

78. The Savoy Havana Band, vocal: Cyril Ramon Newton, "Valencia" (Valentine-Padilla), 16 Feb. 1926 (Bb-7903–2).

79. Raymond Williams, *The Long Revolution* (Harmondsworth: Penguin, 1965, orig. pub. 1961), 291.

80. There is no homogeneous classical style, of course, but this was not widely recognized in the 1920s and 1930s.

81. Adorno refers to this book in a footnote to his article "On Popular Music" *Studies in Philosophy and Social Science,* vol. 9 (1941), 17–48. See Antony Easthope and Kate McGowan, *A Critical and Cultural Theory Reader* (Buckingham and Philadelphia: Open University Press, 1992), 222.

CHAPTER 5

1. Received opinion is summed up by Paul Driver's remark, "It is perfectly abstract music," in "Master Builders of Symphonic Form," *Sunday Times,* "The Culture," section 9, 7 April 1996, 27.

2. See Benjamin M. Korstvedt, "'Return to the Pure Sources': The Ideology and Text-Critical Legacy of the First Bruckner *Gesamtausgabe,*" in Timothy L. Jackson and Paul Hawkshaw, eds., *Bruckner Studies* (Cambridge: Cambridge University Press, 1997), 91–109, especially 101–3, and Morten Solvik, "The International Bruckner Society and the N.S.D.A.P.: A Case Study of Robert Haas and the Critical Edition," *Musical Quarterly* 82, no. 2 (1998), 362–82.

3. Max Auer's phrase used when addressing the International Bruckner Society in 1946; see Bryan Gilliam, "The Annexation of Anton Bruckner: Nazi Revisionism

and the Politics of Appropriation," in Jackson and Hawkshaw, *Bruckner Studies*, 72–90, especially 79–80 and 88–89. Gilliam also scrutinizes the portrayal of Bruckner as victim of Jewish criticism (81). The politicizing of Bruckner's life and music is dealt with extensively in Christa Brüstle's book-length study *Anton Bruckner und die Nachwelt. Zur Rezeptions-geschichte des Komponisten in der ersten Hälfte des 20. Jahrhunderts* (Stuttgart: Metzler Verlag, 1998).

4. Constantin Floros, *Brahms und Bruckner. Studien zur musikalischen Exegetik* (Wiesbaden: Breitkopf and Härtel, 1980), part 3.

5. Dika Newlin, *Bruckner-Mahler-Schoenberg* (London: Marion Boyars, rev. ed., 1979, orig. pub. 1947), 3.

6. Derek Watson, *Bruckner* (Oxford: Oxford University Press, rev. ed. 1996, orig. pub. London: Dent, 1975), 1.

7. Newlin, *Bruckner-Mahler-Schoenberg*, 3.

8. Ibid., 21. For more information on Bruckner's formative social and musical experiences, see A. Crawford Howie, "Traditional and Novel Elements in Bruckner's Sacred Music," *Musical Quarterly* 67 (1981), 544–67, 544–50.

9. Hans Hubert Schönzeler, *Bruckner* (London: Calder and Boyars, 1970), 124; the exceptions were a book on the Mexican war and one on an Austrian expedition to the North Pole. Bruckner's lack of intellectual curiosity is attested to by his ex-pupil Friedrich Klose in *Meine Lehrjahre bei Bruckner* (Regensburg: 1927), 96–98, excerpted in Stephen Johnson, *Bruckner Remembered* (London: Faber, 1998), 31–32.

10. Robert Simpson, *The Essence of Bruckner* (London: Victor Gollancz, rev. ed., 1992, orig. pub. 1967), 74.

11. Deryck Cooke, "Bruckner," in *The New Grove Late Romantic Masters* (London: Macmillan, 1985), 41.

12. On the influence of Haydn, Beethoven, and Schubert's Masses, see Howie, "Traditional and Novel Elements in Bruckner's Sacred Music," 563–67; on the influence of earlier sacred music, see 556–60.

13. Schönzeler, *Bruckner*, 167.

14. Cooke, "Bruckner," 42. Cooke cites as examples the chorale in the Finale of the Fifth and the second theme of the second group in the Adagio of the Eighth.

15. "The choir of angels was a very common image in eighteenth-century writings about church music" (Alexander H. Shapiro, "'Drama of an Infinitely Superior Nature': Handel's Early English Oratorios and the Religious Sublime," *Music and Letters* 74, no. 2 [1993], 215–45, 230).

16. Schönzeler, *Bruckner*, 48.

17. Howie, "Traditional and Novel Elements in Bruckner's Sacred Music," 551.

18. Cooke, "Bruckner," 45.

19. Newlin, *Bruckner-Mahler-Schoenberg*, 81. On the sacred character of Bruckner's music, see R. W. S. Mendl, *The Divine Quest in Music* (London: Rockliff, 1957), 136–38.

20. In 1862 Bruckner studied *Tannhäuser* with Otto Kitzler, who gave its first performance in Linz that year.

21. Ernst Kurth describes the "sleep motive" from *Walküre* as symbolizing "a dreamlike suspension of the senses" (*Romantische Harmonik und ihre Krise in Wagners "Tristan"* [Berne: Haupt, 1920], 225, in *Ernst Kurth: Selected Writings*, ed. and trans. Lee A. Rothfarb [Cambridge: Cambridge University Press, 1991], 133; this work contains extracts from Kurth's *Bruckner*, 2 vols. [Berlin: Hesse, 1925]).

22. Theodor Adorno uses the term "phantasmagoria" in his Wagner criticism to

describe what he sees as a magic delusion related to commodity fetishism. He interprets the last 60 bars of *Walküre* as a trope for magic fire (for him, the dominant phantasmagoria of the *Ring*). See Theodor W. Adorno, *In Search of Wagner*, trans. Rodney Livingstone (London: Verso, 1991, orig. pub. as *Versuch über Wagner* [Frankfurt am Main: Suhrkamp Verlag, 1952]), 89. The ending of Bruckner's Seventh has certain resemblances to these bars from *Walküre*, such as the almost-added sixth to the E-major triad; but notice how here, too, Bruckner has no interest in Wagner's six harps, glockenspiel, and two piccolos.

    23. See Hans F. Redlich Foreword, *Bruckner Symphony No. 9* (London: Eulenburg, 1963), i–xxiii, xviii–xx.

    24. Walter Wiora argues that the religious element in Bruckner's symphonies is greater than that in those of any other composer; see Walter Wiora, ed., *Religiöse Musik in nicht-liturgischen Werken von Beethoven bis Reger* (Regensburg: Bosse, 1978), 157–84.

    25. Deryck Cooke, *The Language of Music* (Oxford: Oxford University Press, 1959), 108.

    26. Vulgate, St. John 8:12.

    27. Psalms 27:1.

    28. Jude 6.

    29. St. John 3:19.

    30. See Watson, *Bruckner*, 115.

    31. Here it is interesting to note the connection in Bruckner's mind between dissonance and the unclean. Alma Mahler records an incident (probably recounted by Gustav Mahler) in which Bruckner took out a dirty handkerchief in front of his pupils and exclaimed, "That's disgusting, eh? That's a dirty chord—a discord" (*Gustave Mahler: Erinnerungen und Briefe* [Amsterdam: Allert de Lange, 1940]), excerpted in Johnson, *Bruckner Remembered*, 85.

    32. St. John 8:12.

    33. Job 10:21: "The land of darkness and the shadow of death"; Isaiah 9:2: "The people that walked in darkness have seen a great light: they that dwell in the land of the shadow of death, upon them hath the light shined"; and St. Luke 1:79: "To give light to them that sit in darkness and in the shadow of death, to guide our feet into the way of peace."

    34. Simpson, *The Essence of Bruckner*, 158.

    35. Quoted in Schönzeler, *Bruckner*, 80. The whole Adagio was written in anticipation of Wagner's death; see Edwin Doernberg, *The Life and Symphonies of Anton Bruckner* (London: Barrie and Rockliff, 1960), 90.

    36. Timothy Jackson refers to C major as "traditionally a symbol for divine glory" in "Reply to Parkany 1988" *Nineteenth Century Music* 13 (1989), 74–75, 74. Bruckner's Te Deum and *Psalm 150* offer further confirmation of this convention.

    37. Genesis 1:2, 1:4.

    38. Max Auer, *Anton Bruckner, sein Leben und Werk* (2d ed., Vienna: Brünn, 1934), 424, quoted in Newlin, *Bruckner-Mahler-Schoenberg*, 83.

    39. August Halm, *Die Symphonie Anton Bruckners* (Munich: 1914), 43, quoted in Newlin, *Bruckner-Mahler-Schoenberg*, 83.

    40. Watson, *Bruckner*, 67.

    41. Auer, *Anton Bruckner, sein Leben und Werk,* 424, quoted in Newlin, *Bruckner-Mahler-Schoenberg*, 83.

    42. Simpson, *The Essence of Bruckner*, 210, discussing the coda to Symphony no. 8.

43. That the pairing of themes originated in Bruckner's reaction to a body lying in state amid the sounds of a grand ball from an adjacent mansion is well known; see, for example, Doernberg, *The Life and Symphonies of Anton Bruckner,* 145–46; Newlin, *Bruckner-Mahler-Schoenberg*, 89; Simpson, *The Essence of Bruckner,* 79; and Watson, *Bruckner,* 89. The anecdote is from August Göllerich's biography *Anton Bruckner,* ed. Max Auer, 4 vols. (Regensburg: Bosse, 1922–37).

44. "Media vita morte sumus" is from an antiphon circa A.D. 911 attributed to Saint Notker Balbulus of the monastery of St. Gall, Switzerland, and appears in the Book of Common Prayer ("Burial of the Dead") as "in the midst of life we are in death."

45. St. John 1:5.

46. In the same way as writing is understood as an absence of the voice, but the voice is not an absence of writing; see Jacques Derrida, *Of Grammatology,* trans. Gayatri Chakravorty Spivak (Baltimore: John Hopkins University Press, 1976, orig. pub. as *De la Grammatologie,* [Paris: Les Editions de Minuit, 1967]), 144, 295.

47. Derrida, *Of Grammatology,* and *Writing and Difference,* trans. Alan Bass (London: RKP, 1978).

48. See H. T. Andrews, "Apocalyptic Literature," in *A Commentary on the Bible,* ed. Arthur S. Peake (London: T. C. and E. C. Jack, 1919), 431–35.

49. Simpson, *The Essence of Bruckner,* 204. The metaphor of the cathedral was common in the critical reception of Bruckner in the 1920s.

50. Henry George Liddell and Robert Scott, *Greek-English Lexicon* (Oxford: Clarendon Press, 1996, orig. pub. Oxford University Press, 1843).

51. Simpson, *The Essence of Bruckner,* 232; a reference to the Eighth Symphony follows.

52. Ernst Bloch, *Essays on the Philosophy of Music,* trans. Peter Palmer (Cambridge: Cambridge University Press, 1985, orig. pub. as *Zur Philosophie der Musik* [Frankfurt am Main: Suhrkamp Verlag, 1974]), 41.

53. Rose Rosengard Subotnik, *Developing Variations: Style and Ideology in Western Music* (Minneapolis: University of Minnesota Press, 1991), 21. She is explaining ideas from Adorno based on her own translation of passages from his *Einleitung in der Musiksoziologie* (Reinbeck bei Hamburg: Rowohlt 1968), 223–25, 232, and *Moments Musicaux* (Frankfurt: Suhrkamp Verlag 1964), 182–83, and from Anne G. Mitchell and Wesley G. Blomster's translation of Adorno's *Philosophy of Modern Music* (London: Sheen and Ward, 1973 orig. pub. as *Philosophie der Neuen Musik* Tübingen: Mohr 1949), 55–56.

54. Bloch, *Essays on the Philosophy of Music,* 41.

55. Ibid., 41–42; however, Bloch thinks it does stem from a composer such as Beethoven's "ultimate experience."

56. Ibid., 42; this, Bloch claims, is a goal rarely achieved and "more wont to occur in the adagio than in the finale with its fancifully epic structure."

57. Consider Christopher Norris's words: "Any analysis of musical form based on notions of organic unity or self-contained thematic development will be closed to whatever potential the work possesses for renewing our perceptions through repeated acts of creative listening" ("Utopian Deconstruction: Ernst Bloch, Paul de Man and the Politics of Music," in Norris, ed., *Music and the Politics of Culture* [London: Lawrence and Wishart, 1989], 305–47, 327). For more recent accounts of the challenges to ideas of deep structure and organicism in music, see Robert Fink, "Going Flat: Post-Hierarchical Music Theory and the Musical Surface," in Nicholas

Cook and Mark Everist, eds., *Rethinking Music* (Oxford: Oxford University Press, 1999), 102–37, especially 132–37, and Alan Street, "Superior Myths, Dogmatic Allegories: The Resistance to Musical Unity," in Adam Krims, ed., *Music/Ideology: Resisting the Aesthetic* (Amsterdam: G+B Arts, 1998), 57–112, especially 87–89. See also Steve Sweeney-Turner, *The Sonorous Body: Music, Enlightenment & Deconstruction* (Ph.D. thesis, University of Edinburgh, 1995).

58. Subotnik, *Developing Variations,* 23. The reference is to Adorno's *Einleitung,* 225.

59. Subotnik, *Developing Variations,* 217. The reference this time is to Adorno, *Philosophy of Modern Music,* 40–41.

60. See Subotnik, *Developing Variations,* 218–19, which refers to Adorno, *Philosophy of Modern Music,* 56, 60, 190.

61. See Watson, *Bruckner,* 93–95.

62. Simpson, *The Essence of Bruckner,* 172.

63. Susan McClary, *Feminine Endings: Music, Gender, and Sexuality* (Minneapolis: University of Minnesota Press, 1991), 15.

64. Ibid., 114.

65. See Max von Oberleithner, *Meine Erinnerungen an Anton Bruckner* (Regensburg: Bosse, 1933), excerpted in Johnson, *Bruckner Remembered,* 99–100, 100.

66. Constantin Floros, "Bruckner Propositions (II)," *Bruckner Journal* 1, no. 2 (1997), 8–9, 9. Floros's "Propositions" were originally published in Heinz-Klaus Metzger and Rainer Riehn, eds., *Musik-Konzepte 23/24: Anton Bruckner* (Munich: Text und Kritik, 1982).

67. See Derrick Puffett, "Bruckner's Way: The Adagio of the Ninth Symphony," *Music Analysis* 18, no. 1 (1999), 5–99, 13–14.

68. Howie, "Traditional and Novel Elements in Bruckner's Sacred Music," 554.

69. Doernberg, *The Life and Symphonies of Anton Bruckner,* 109.

70. In Karl Grunsky, ed., *Bruckners Sinfonien,* Meisterführer 4 (Berlin: Lienau, 1907), 165, cited in Korstvedt, *Bruckner Symphony No. 8,* 54.

71. This is not the only way in which Bruckner changes his motives, but it is the way that is relevant to my argument. Another type of change to motives has been interpreted as mutation by Werner Korte in *Bruckner und Brahms: Die spätromantische Lösung der autonomen Konzeption* (Tutzing: Schneider, 1963).

72. Beethoven's minor *Egmont* Overture ends triumphantly in the major, but with a new theme (not an option in a Beethoven minor symphonic movement).

73. This would not be the only occasion on which Bruckner was influenced by *Der Fliegende Holländer.* Constantin Floros maintains that Bruckner's inspiration for the first movement of the Eighth Symphony was the Flying Dutchman's C-minor aria from Act 1 ("Bruckner Propositions [III]," *Bruckner Journal* 1, no. 3 [1997], 10–11, 11).

74. Carl Dahlhaus, *Nineteenth-Century Music,* trans. J. Bradford Robinson (Berkeley: University of California Press, 1989, orig. pub. as *Die Musik des 19. Jahrhunderts* [Wiesbaden: Akademische Verlagsgesellschaft Athenaion, 1980]), 272.

75. Ibid.

76. Simpson, *The Essence of Bruckner,* 151.

77. Ibid., 156.

78. Watson, *Bruckner,* 109.

79. Ibid.

80. St. Matthew 17:2.

81. Linda Murray, *The High Renaissance and Mannerism: Italy, the North and Spain 1500–1600* (London: Thames and Hudson, 1977, orig. pub. as 2 vols., 1967), 68–

70, monochrome illustration, 69. For a color illustration, see Marco Albertario, *Raphael* (Milan: Electa, 1996), 55.

82. Doernberg, *The Life and Symphonies of Anton Bruckner,* 194.

83. Watson, *Bruckner,* 115.

84. I am indebted to Stan and Carmen Hawkins for providing me with this information.

85. This figure reappears prominently in *Psalm 150.*

86. Hugo Wolf, letter to Emil Kauffmann, 23 Dec. 1892, quoted in Leopold Nowak, Preface, *Anton Bruckner, Sämtliche Werke, VIII Symphonie C-Moll, Fassung von 1890* (Vienna: Musikwissenschaftlicher Verlag, 1955), n.p. The performance referred to was given under Hans Richter, Grosser Musikvereinssaal, Vienna, 18 Dec. 1892.

87. Simpson, *The Essence of Bruckner,* 220.

88. Bruckner's own description; see Redlich, Foreword, xv.

89. A. E. Brooke, "John," in Peake, *A Commentary on the Bible,* 746.

90. Martin Kettle, "The Bumpkin Who Became a Holy Fool," *Guardian,* Saturday, 27 Jan. 1996, 27.

91. Watson, *Bruckner,* 111.

92. Ibid., 118.

93. Simpson, *The Essence of Bruckner,* 131.

94. For example, the Adagio of the Eighth, 1890 version, bars 125–28.

95. Eero Tarasti, *Myth and Music: A Semiotic Approach to the Aesthetics of Myth in Music* (The Hague: Mouton, 1979), 92.

96. Note, incidentally, that Mendelssohn was content to begin a symphony in the major and end in the minor (the *Italian*).

97. Tarasti, *Myth and Music,* 91.

98. See ibid., 108.

99. Martin Pulbrook, "'Death, Release and Resolve': An Analysis of Anton Bruckner's Seventh Symphony," *Maynooth Review* 9 (1983), 93, footnote 4.

100. Simpson, *The Essence of Bruckner,* 103.

101. Cooke, "Bruckner," 53.

102. Seeking evidence in performance for the ideas presented here, I would cite Sergiu Celibidache's later interpretations of Bruckner with the Münchner Philharmoniker.

103. Ibid., 50.

104. Gregory Bateson, *Steps to an Ecology of Mind* (New York: Ballantine, 1972), 113.

105. Gilles Deleuze and Félix Guattari, *A Thousand Plateaus: Capitalism and Schizophrenia,* trans. Brian Massumi (Minneapolis: University of Minnesota Press, 1987, orig. pub. as *Mille Plateaux,* vol. 2 of *Capitalisme et Shizophrénie* [Paris: Les Editions de Minuit, 1980]), 22.

106. Ibid.

107. Evidence for this claim is provided by the work of German critical scholarship in the nineteenth century; see Rowland Williams, "Bunsen's Biblical Researches," in Frederick Temple, Rowland Williams, Benjamin Jowett, et al., *Essays and Reviews* (London: Parker, 1860).

108. Quoted in Benjamin Korstvedt, *Bruckner Symphony No. 8* (Cambridge: Cambridge University Press, 2000), 7. This statement originally appeared in "Anton Bruckner," *Die Zeit* 7 (1896), and is reprinted in *Heinrich Schenker als Essayist und Kritiker: Gesammelte Aufsätze Rezensionen und kleinere Berichte aus den Jahren 1891–1901,* ed. Hellmut Federhofer (Hildesheim: Olms, 1990), 200–201.

109. Puffett, "Bruckner's Way," 9, 33. Furthermore, it is a reversed recapitulation (the second theme arriving first).

110. Deleuze and Guattari, *A Thousand Plateaus*, 22; a rhizome is an underground stem with a mixture of roots and shoots.

111. Simpson, *The Essence of Bruckner*, 232.

112. Newlin, *Bruckner-Mahler-Schoenberg* , 96.

113. Simpson, *The Essence of Bruckner*, 164.

114. Ibid., 167–68.

115. Kurth, *Ernst Kurth: Selected Writings*, 203.

116. Doernberg, *The Life and Symphonies of Anton Bruckner*, 136.

117. Bryan Gilliam, "The Two Versions of Bruckner's Eighth Symphony," *Nineteenth Century Music* 16 (1992), 59–69, 66.

118. Ibid.

119. Ibid., footnote 22.

120. The original coda of this work was revised; see Arthur D. Walker, Foreword, *Overture in G Minor by Anton Bruckner* (London: Eulenburg, 1971), iii–iv.

121. Deleuze and Guattari, *A Thousand Plateaus*, 12.

122. Doernberg, *The Life and Symphonies of Anton Bruckner*, 220.

123. Deleuze and Guattari, *A Thousand Plateaus*, 9.

124. Robert S. Hatten provides an informative study of disjunction in "The Expressive Role of Disjunction: A Semiotic Approach to Form and Meaning in the Fourth and Fifth Symphonies," in Crawford Howie, Paul Hawkshaw, and Timothy Jackson, eds., *Perspectives on Anton Bruckner* (Aldershot: Ashgate, 2001), 145–84.

125. Floros, "Bruckner Propositions (II)," 9.

126. Newlin, *Bruckner-Mahler-Schoenberg* , 92.

127. Ludwig Finscher, "Zur Stellung der 'Nullten' Symphonie in Bruckners Werk," in *Anton Bruckner: Studien zu Werk und Wirkung:Walter Wiora zum 30. Dezember 1986 / herausgegeben von Christoph-Helmut Mahling, Mainzer Studien zur Musikwissenschaft*, vol. 20 (Tutzing: Schneider, 1988), 63–79, 69–79. I am grateful to John Williamson for bringing this to my attention.

128. Schönzeler, *Bruckner*, 155.

129. Cited by Peter Palmer in "Ludwig Wittgenstein's Remarks on Bruckner," *Perspectives on Anton Bruckner*, 353–62, 356; the remarks are in Ludwig Wittgenstein, *Vermischte Bemerkungen*, ed. Georg Henrik von Wright (Frankfurt am Main: Suhrkamp Verlag, 1977).

130. Reproduced in Dahlhaus, *Nineteenth-Century Music*, 275.

131. Carl Hruby, *Meine Erinnerungen an Anton Bruckner* (Vienna: 1901), in Johnson, *Bruckner Remembered*, 33.

132. See Elisabeth Maier, "A Hidden Personality: Access to an 'Inner Biography' of Anton Bruckner," in Jackson and Hawkshaw, *Bruckner Studies*, 32–53, 51.

133. Newlin, *Bruckner-Mahler-Schoenberg*, 81.

134. Cooke, "Bruckner," 20.

CHAPTER 6

1. Franz Liszt and Carolyne von Sayn-Wittgenstein, "Berlioz and His 'Harold' Symphony," orig. pub. as "Berlioz und seine Haroldsymphonie," in *Neue Zeitschrift für Musik* 43 (1855), excerpted and trans. Oliver Strunk in Ruth Solie, ed., *Strunk's Source Readings in Music History*, vol. 6: *The Nineteenth Century* (New York: Norton, rev. ed., Leo Treitler, general ed., 1998, orig. pub. 1950), 116–32, 126.

2. Liszt and Sayn-Wittgenstein, "Berlioz and his 'Harold' Symphony," 130.

3. Letter to Carolyn von Sayn-Wittgenstein dated 29 Jan. 1848 in Franz Liszt, *Correspondance, lettres choisies, présentées et annotées par Pierre-Antoine Huré et Claude Knepper* (Paris: Éditions Jean-Claude Lattès, 1987), 207. Liszt may have been influenced in this view by Goethe's *Faust,* to which Berlioz had introduced him.

4. See Robert Donington, *The Interpretation of Early Music* (London: Faber, rev. ed. 1989, orig. pub. 1963), 124, 138.

5. Franz Liszt, letter of 9 Oct. 1860 to Emilie Merian-Genast, cited in Serge Gut, *Franz Liszt: Les Élements du Language Musical* (Saverdun: Éditions Klincksieck, 1975), 312.

6. Gut, *Franz Liszt,* 97. See also W. A. Everett, "Chernomor, the Astrologer, and Associtates: Aspects of Shadow and Evil in *Ruslan and Lyndmila* and *The Golden Cockerel,"* Opera Quarterly 12 (1995–96), 23–34.

7. See pages 268–69 of the Eulenburg score.

8. Played by Bukkene Bruse on an album of the same name, 1993 (Grappa GRCD 4053).

9. Alan Walker, *Franz Liszt,* vol. 2: *The Weimar Years 1848–1861* (London: Faber, 1989), 154, footnote 49.

10. See Walker's discussion of the Raff case in particular, in ibid., 202–6 and, more generally, Peter Raabe, *Franz Liszt: Leben und Schaffen,* 2 vols. (Tutzing: Schneider, rev. ed. 1968, orig. pub. Stuttgart: Cotta, 1931), 71–79.

11. Hector Berlioz, *Treatise on Instrumentation* (New York: Kalmus, 1948, orig. pub. as *Grand traité d'instrumentation et d'orchestration modernes,* Paris: Schonenberger, 1843), 118.

12. Ibid., 305.

13. Ibid., 395.

14. Ibid., 187.

15. Ibid., 236.

16. "Diese ganze stelle als ein lästerndes Hohngelächter aufgefaßt, sehr scharf markirt in den beiden Clarinetten und den Violen."

17. Berlioz, *Treatise,* 206.

18. Liszt took the first part of his title, "Après une lecture du Dante: Fantaisie quasi Sonata" (1837–49) from a poem in Victor Hugo's *Les Voix intérieures,* after the work was complete. See Sharon Winklhofer, "Liszt, Marie d'Agoult, and the 'Dante' Sonata," *19th Century Music* 1, no. 1 (1977), 15–32, 29–32.

19. Translation by John D. Sinclair in Dante Alighieri, *The Divine Comedy: Inferno* (London: Oxford University Press, 1971, orig. pub. Oxford: Bodley Head, 1939), 47, 49.

20. See Alan Walker, *Franz Liszt,* vol. 1: *The Virtuoso Years, 1811–1847* (London: Faber, rev. ed. 1989, orig. pub. 1983), 277–28.

21. Karl Tausenau, 25 Feb. 1840, in Dezsö Legány, ed., *Franz Liszt: Unbekannte Presse und Briefe aus Wien 1822–1886* (Budapest: Corvina Kiadó, 1984), 73. The piece was titled *Fragment nach Dante* at the time.

22. Walker, *Franz Liszt,* vol. 2, 336.

23. Ibid., 412.

24. Franz Schubert, no. 4 of *12 Songs by Schubert,* 1838. For its reception, see Walker, *Franz Liszt,* vol. 1, 257.

25. Walker, *Franz Liszt,* vol. 1, 365.

26. Leonard B. Meyer, *Style and Music: Theory, History, and Ideology* (Chicago: University of Chicago Press, 1996, orig. pub. Philadelphia: University of Pennsylvania Press, 1989), 216.

27. Humphrey Searle, *The Music of Liszt* (New York: Dover, 2d ed. 1966, orig. pub. London: Williams and Northgate, 1954), 115.

28. Sacheverell Sitwell, *Liszt* (New York: Dover, 1967, orig. pub. London: Cassell, 1995), xi.

29. For a study of medieval iconography in relation to the devil in music, see Reinhold Hammerstein, *Diabolus in Musica* (Bern: Francke Verlag, 1974).

30. See James Hall, *Dictionary of Subjects and Symbols in Art* (London: John Murray, 1974), 94.

31. See John White, *Art and Architecture in Italy: 1250–1400* (New Haven: Yale University Press, 1993, orig. pub. Harmondsworth: Penguin, 1966), 552–56; an illustration of the fresco (almost entirely destroyed by a bomb in 1944) is given on page 554.

32. See Winklhofer, "Liszt, Marie d'Agoult, and the 'Dante' Sonata," 28. Holbein's woodcuts are discussed in Siglind Bruhn, *Musical Ekphrasis: Composers Responding to Poetry and Painting* (Hillsdale, NY: Pendragon Press, 2000), 394–99.

33. Robert Samuels, *Mahler's Sixth Symphony: A Study in Musical Semiotics* (Cambridge: Cambridge University Press, 1995), 123; the dance of death is discussed on pages 119–31.

34. Liszt transcribed Berlioz's *Symphonie fantastique* for piano in 1833.

35. Ben Arnold, "Liszt and the Music of Revolution and War," in Michael Saffle and James Deaville eds., *New Light on Liszt and His Music: Essays in Honor of Alan Walker's 65th Birthday* (Stuyvesant, NY: Pendragon Press, 1997), 225–38, 238.

36. Sitwell, *Liszt*, 167.

37. Adrian Williams, *Portrait of Liszt by Himself and His Contemporaries* (Oxford: Clarendon Press, 1990), 329, footnote.

38. See Humphrey Searle, "The Orchestral Works," in Alan Walker, ed., *Franz Liszt: The Man and His Music* (London: Barrie and Jenkins, 1970), 279–317, 310.

39. Walker, *Franz Liszt*, vol. 2, 50.

40. Lawrence Kramer, *Music as Cultural Practice, 1800–1900* (Berkeley: University of California Press, 1990), 89–90.

41. Amy Fay, letter of 21 May 1873, excerpted in Adrian Williams, *Portrait of Liszt by Himself and His Contemporaries* (Oxford: Clarendon Press, 1990), 489–90, 490.

42. Sitwell, *Liszt*, 163.

43. Walker, *Franz Liszt*, vol. 2, 326.

44. See Eric Frederick Jensen, "Liszt, Nerval, and *Faust*," *19th Century Music* 6, no. 2 (1982), 151–58, 152.

45. Gut, *Franz Liszt*, 466.

46. Walter Beckett, *Liszt* (London: Dent, rev. ed. 1963, orig. pub. 1956), 10.

47. Quoted in Humphrey Searle, "Franz Liszt," in Stanley Sadie, ed., *The New Grove Dictionary of Music and Musicians*, vol. 11 (London: Macmillan, 1980), 33.

48. Johann Wolfgang Goethe, *Faust: Eine Tragödie, erste Teil* (Leipzig: Münster Presse, 1924), 45 (*Vor dem Tor*).

49. Johann Wolfgang Goethe, *Faust*, part 1, trans. Philip Wayne (Harmondsworth: Penguin, 1949), 67.

50. *Faust: Eine Tragödie*, 53.

51. Alan P. Cottrell, *Goethe's View of Evil and the Search for a New Image of Man in Our Time* (Edinburgh: Floros Books, 1982), 63.

52. Ibid., 75.

53. Søren Kierkegaard, *The Concept of Anxiety,* trans. Walter Lowrie (Princeton: Princeton University Press, 2d ed. 1957, orig. pub. as *Begrebet Angest* by Vigilius Haufniensis [pseud.], ed. S. Kierkegaard, [1844]), 109. See Gregor Malantschuk, *Kierkegaard's Thought,* ed. and trans. Howard V. Hong and Edna H. Hong (Princeton: Princeton University Press, 1971, orig. pub. as *Dialektik og Elksistens hos Søren Kierkegaard* [Copenhagen: Reitzel, 1968], 271.

54. George Pattison, *Kierkegaard: The Aesthetic and the Religious: From the Magic Theatre to the Crucifixion of the Image* (London: Macmillan, 1992), 97.

55. See Eudo C. Mason, *Goethe's* Faust *Its Genesis and Purport* (Berkeley: University of California Press, 1967), 160.

56. See John Douglas Mullen, *Kierkegaard's Philosophy: Self-Deception and Cowardice in the Present Age* (Lanham, MD: University Press of America, 1955), 74.

57. Søren Kierkegaard, *Enten-Eller* (Copenhagen: Bianco Luno Press, 1843); it was originally advertised as edited by Victor Eremita [pseud.].

58. Søren Kierkegaard, "The Immediate Stage of the Erotic, or The Musical Erotic," in *Either/Or,* vol. 1, trans. David F. Swenson and Lillian M. Swenson (London: Oxford University Press, 1944), 35–110, 59.

59. See Malantschuk, *Kierkegaard's Thought,* 39, 221.

60. See Pattison, *Kierkegaard,* 98.

61. Søren Kierkegaard, *Either/Or,* part 2, ed. and trans. Howard V. Hong and Edna H. Hong (Princeton: Princeton University Press, 1987), 164.

62. Søren Kierkegaard, *Journals and Papers,* vol. 1: *A–E,* ed. and trans. Howard V. Hong and Edna H. Hong (Bloomington: Indiana University Press, 1967), 341.

63. See Søren Kierkegaard, *Fear and Trembling,* ed. and trans. Howard V. Hong and Edna H. Hong (Princeton: Princeton University Press, 1983, orig. pub. as *Fryg og Bœven: Dialektist Lyrik* by Johannes de Silentio [pseud.] [Copenhagen: Bianco Luno Press, 1843]), 94–99.

64. Kierkegaard, *Fear and Trembling,* 106.

65. See Malantschuk, *Kierkegaard's Thought,* 240.

66. Note that the love scenes in Liszt's symphonies resemble one another in this restlessness: that between Faust and Gretchen (Affettuoso, poco andante, two bars after Letter Dd, first movement) is an alternating $\frac{3}{4}$ and $\frac{4}{4}$; the love scene between Paulo and Francesca (Andante amoroso) is $\frac{7}{4}$ (but divided $\frac{3}{4}$, $\frac{4}{4}$).

67. See James Collins, *The Mind of Kierkegaard* (Princeton: Princeton University Press, 1983, orig. pub. 1953), 59. For a feminist reading of Kierkegaard's ideas of the demonic, see Birgit Bertung, "Yes, a Woman Can Exist," in Céline Léon and Sylvia Walsh, eds., *Feminist Interpretations of Søren Kierkegaard* (Philadelphia: University of Pennsylvania Press, 1997), 51–66, especially 59–66. A study of the female demoniac in opera might begin with the Queen of the Night in *Die Zauberflöte* and her absorption in the idea of revenge.

68. Geoffrey Clive, "The Demonic in Mozart," *Music and Letters* 37, no. 1 (1956), 1–13, 2, reprinted in Lewis A. Lawson, ed., *Kierkegaard's Presence in Contemporary American Life: Essays from Various Disciplines* (Metuchen, NJ: Scarecrow Press, 1970), 162–76.

69. Ronald Taylor, *Franz Liszt: The Man and the Musician* (London: Grafton Books, 1986), 146.

70. John D. White, "Liszt and Schenker," in Michael Saffle, ed., *Liszt and His World* (Stuyvesant, NY: Pendragon Press, 1998), 353–64, 353.

71. Sitwell, *Liszt*, 165.

72. Lawrence Kramer, "Liszt, Goethe, and the Discourse of Gender," in *Music as Cultural Practice, 1800–1900*, 102–34, 129.

73. Paul Merrick, *Revolution and Religion in the Music of Liszt* (Cambridge: Cambridge University Press, 1987), 274.

74. Ibid., 301.

75. Tibor Szász, "Liszt's Symbols for the Divine and Diabolical: Their Revelation of a Programme in the B Minor Sonata," *Journal of the American Liszt Society* 15 (1984), 39–95.

76. See Kenneth Hamilton, *Liszt: Sonata in B Minor* (Cambridge: Cambridge University Press, 1996), 29–31.

77. Vera Micznik, "The Absolute Limitations of Programme Music: The Case of Liszt's 'Die Ideale,'" *Music and Letters* 80 (1999), 207–40, 217.

78. David Wilde, "Liszt's Sonata: Some Jungian Reflections," in Saffle and Deaville, *New Light on Liszt and His Music*, 197–224, 201.

79. Ibid., 206.

80. Ibid., 215.

81. Louis Kentner, "Solo Piano Music (1827–61)," in Walker, *Franz Liszt: The Man and His Music*, 90.

82. See Hamilton, *Liszt*, 56.

83. Bence Szabolcsi, *The Twilight of Ferenc Liszt*, trans. András Deák (Budapest: Hungarian Academy of Sciences, 1959, orig. pub. as *Liszt Ferenc Estéje*, [Zenemükiadó Vállalat Budapest, 1956]), 40.

84. Szabolcsi, *The Twilight of Ferenc Liszt*, 52–54.

85. Huré and Knepper suggest it may be a reference to the comet in the sky at Liszt's birth; if so, the piece would seem to indicate profound depression about his life's achievement on Liszt's part. See Liszt, *Correspondance*, 48, footnote 1.

86. Allan Forte, "Liszt's Experimental Idiom and Music of the Early Twentieth Century," *19th Century Music* 10, no. 3 (1987), 209–28, 221.

87. Ibid., 221.

88. Searle, "Franz Liszt," 49.

89. Forte, "Liszt's Experimental Idiom," 227.

90. Liszt and Sayn-Wittgenstein, "Berlioz and His 'Harold' Symphony," 126.

91. See Klara Hamburger, *Franz Liszt*, trans. into German by herself (Budapest: Corvina Verlag, 1973, orig. pub. as *Liszt Ferenc* [Gondolat Kiadó, 1966]), 278.

92. Szabolcsi, *The Twilight of Ferenc Liszt*, 73.

93. Cited by Gerald Abraham in his foreword to the Eulenburg score (n.d.), ii.

94. Samples can be heard on tracks 4 and 10 of *Horror!*, Westminster Philharmonic Orchestra, cond. Kenneth Alwyn, 1996 (Silva Screen Records FILMCD 175). *Night of the Demon* (Columbia, dir. Jacques Tourneur) and *The Devil Rides Out* (Hammer, dir. Terence Fisher) were released in the United States as *Curse of the Demon* and *The Devil's Bride*, respectively.

CHAPTER 7

1. "A myth derives its significance not from contemporary or archaic institutions of which it is a reflection, but from its relation to other myths within a transforma-

tion group" (Claude Lévi-Strauss, *The Raw and the Cooked: Introduction to a Science of Mythology,* trans. John and Doreen Weightman [Harmondsworth: Penguin, 1986, orig. pub. as *Le Cru et le cuit,* Paris: Plon, 1964], 51, footnote 5).

2. Edward W. Said, *Orientalism: Western Conceptions of the Orient* (Harmondsworth: Penguin, 1985, orig. pub. London: Routledge and Kegan Paul, 1978), 71–72. It would be wrong to give the impression that this book represents Said's final thoughts on this subject; for the further development of his arguments, see *Culture and Imperialism* (London: Chatto and Windus, 1993).

3. J. A. Westrup, *Purcell* (Oxford: Oxford University Press, 1995, orig. pub. London: Dent, 1937), 142.

4. Carolyn Abbate, *Unsung Voices: Opera and Musical Narrative in the Nineteenth Cenutury* (Princeton: Princeton University Press, 1991), 4.

5. Jonathan Bellman, *The* Style Hongrois *in the Music of Western Europe* (Boston: Northeastern University Press, 1993), 13–14; see also 31–32. Bence Szabolcsi, in "Exoticisms in Mozart," *Music and Letters* 37 (1956), 323–32, is concerned with tracing ethnographic sources for Mozart's exoticisms and rebutting the accusation of "light-hearted toying" on Mozart's part. To rescue Mozart from this charge, Szabolcsi attempts to convey a sense of Mozart dignifying folk music by raising it to the level of art. The question "What are the ideological implications of revoicing these "foreign" elements through the Viennese style?" is not asked. His theoretical model is not of Self and Other but of Art and Folk; he thinks, therefore, in terms of elevation rather than mediation.

6. Ibid., 14.

7. For fuller discussion, see Miriam Karpilow Whaples, *Exoticism in Dramatic Music, 1600–1800* (Ph.D. dissertation, Indiana University, 1958; Ann Arbor: University Microfilms International, 1981); Thomas Bauman, *W. A. Mozart: Die Entführung aus dem Serail* (Cambridge: Cambridge University Press, 1987); and Bellman, *The* Style Hongrois *in the Music of Western Europe,* 33–42.

8. Alfred Einstein, *Essays on Music* (London: Faber, rev. ed., 1958, orig. pub. 1956), 211.

9. Bellman, *The* Style Hongrois *in the Music of Western Europe,* 14.

10. Franz Liszt, *The Gipsy in Music,* trans. Edwin Evans (London: William Reeves, 1960, orig. pub. as *Des Bohémiens et de leur Musique en Hongrie,* [1859]), 301.

11. Ralph P. Locke, "Constructing the Oriental 'Other': Saint-Saëns's *Samson et Dalila,*" *Cambridge Opera Journal* 3, no. 3 (1991), 267. The work cited is Francis Affergan, *Exotisme et altérité: Essai sur les fondements d'une critique de l'anthropologie* (Paris: Presses universitaires de France, 1987), 103–4.

12. "I'll Sing Thee Songs of Araby" (Wills-Clay), 1877 (from the cantata *Lalla Rookh*).

13. "A Son of the Desert Am I" (Wilson-Phillips), 1898 (published in New York).

14. "The Arab's Farewell to His Favourite Steed" (Norton-Blockley), c. 1865.

15. No. 2 of Caroline Norton's *Sabbath Lays* of 1853. The words of this song reflect upon a biblical text, Revelation 21:1, 4. For details of this tune's dissemination in France, see Ralph P. Locke, "Cutthroats and Casbah Dancers, Muezzins and Timeless Sands: Musical Images of the Middle East," in Jonathan Bellman, ed., *The Exotic in Western Music* (Boston: Northeastern University Press, 1998), 104–36, 116.

16. Supposedly composed by New York congressman Sol Bloom for an Egyptian dance at the Chicago World's Columbian Exposition in 1893; see Derek B. Scott, *The Singing Bourgeois: Songs of the Victorian Drawing Room and Parlour* (Aldershot: Ashgate, 2d ed. 2001, orig. pub. Milton Keynes: Open University Press, 1989), 106.

17. Whole-tone scales on trombones accompany the act 3 chorus of followers of the evil magician.

18. See Said, *Orientalism*, 191.

19. Richard Taruskin, "'Entoiling the Falconet': Russian Musical Orientalism in Context," *Cambridge Opera Journal* 4, no. 3 (1992), 253–80, 255, republished in Bellman, *The Exotic in Western Music*, 194–217).

20. Alexander Korda, *The Thief of Bagdad,* London Films, UK, 1940.

21. Roy M. Prendergast, *Film Music: A Neglected Art* (New York: Norton, 2d ed., 1992, orig. pub. 1977), 69.

22. Ibid., 126.

23. Pius Alexander Wolff's play *Preciosa* was based on Cervantes's tale "La Gitanella."

24. See Bellman, *The* Style Hongrois, 144. John Warrack refers to a Dresden librarian's recollection of Weber's studying a collection of Spanish national tunes and even turning up examples of "genuine Gipsy music" but adds that Weber's "own knowledge of Spain was negligible, being based chiefly on his overhearing of a few Spanish songs in the company of Spohr from Spanish soldiers garrisoned near Gotha" (*Carl Maria von Weber* [Cambridge: Cambridge University Press, 2d ed., 1976, orig. pub. London: Hamish Hamilton, 1968]), 241–42.

25. "Mother, O! Sing Me to Rest" (words by Felicia Hemans, music anon.), 1830.

26. "The Bandolero" (Stuart), 1894.

27. It has often been remarked that Bizet was influenced by Spanish music in *Carmen:* for example, that his Habañera is based on Sebastián Yradier's *El Arreglito* and the entr'acte to act 4 on an arrangement by Manuel García of a Spanish *polo* and that other tunes are taken from a Paris edition of Spanish songs. For a discussion of Spanish music in *Carmen,* the extent to which it was already mediated before Bizet appropriated it, and how far he altered it to suit his own purpose, see Susan McClary, *Georges Bizet: Carmen* (Cambridge: Cambridge University Press, 1992), 51–58. Bizet's Orientalism, however, is evident in this music's treatment (especially in his harmony and orchestration) and the decisions he makes as to who sings in this style—for example, Don José is Spanish, but musically he is French (on this subject, see James Parakilas, "The Soldier and the Exotic: Operatic Variations on a Theme of Racial Encounter," *Opera Quarterly* 10, no. 2, 33–56 and no. 3 [1994], 43–69).

28. Interestingly, Italians almost become the cultural Other in Tchaikovsky's *Capriccio Italien* (1880), so that some people find the piece suggests Spain rather than Italy.

29. Sullivan treats Scottish music in a similar way in *Haddon Hall* (at the same time showing informed knowledge of Highland bagpipe ornamentation).

30. However, "Abdulmajid" from Glass's *Heroes* Symphony does adopt an Orientalist manner.

31. Donald J. Grout, *A Short History of Opera* (New York: Columbia University Press, 2d ed., 1965, orig. pub. 1947), 321–22, 328. For the influence of Félicien David's "Oriental" works, see ibid., 328, and Locke, "Constructing the Oriental 'Other,'" 265–6.

32. This change suggests that Berlioz was not merely trying to be "ancient" by using modal melody in the previous section (although to some extent, of course, Berlioz wished the whole of *L'Enfance du Christ* to sound "ancient"). An unmistakable exotic moment, earlier in the work, is the cabalistic dance of the soothsayers.

33. Said, *Orientalism*, 51.

34. "Kashmiri Song" from *Four Indian Love Lyrics* (Hope–Woodforde-Finden), 1902.

35. Rudolph Valentino, "Kashmiri Song," n.d., *The Great Screen Lovers Collection*, 1987 (Deja Vu Records DVMC 2117), item 2, side 2.

36. "The Mousmee; Or, His Sweetheart in Japan" (Sladen-Hedgcock), 1893.

37. As a further illustration of this ideology at work, note how in *Les Troyens* Berlioz characterizes όι πολλοι with drone fifths, exotic percussion (antique cymbals), and clashing grace notes but not, say, Aeneas or Cassandra.

38. "The Sheik of Araby" (Smith and Wheeler–Snyder), 1921.

39. See "The Story of Ali Baba, and the Forty Thieves Destroyed by a Slave," in Robert L. Mack, ed., *Arabian Nights' Entertainments* (Oxford: Oxford University Press, 1995), 764–87.

40. Rexton S. Bunnett, *Chu Chin Chow*, CD booklet, 1984 (EMI 0777 7 899392 6), 6.

41. Said, *Orientalism*, 188–90, 309. When, for example, a seedy nightclub advertises "Exotic Dancers," the meaning is clear. As Said says, "The association between the Orient and sex is remarkably persistent" (*Orientalism*, 309). Russians, too, associated the Orient with sex; see Taruskin, "'Entoiling the Falconet,'" 259–61.

42. Oscar Asche, Foreword to *Chu Chin Chow*, reprinted in CD booklet; see note 40.

43. Here I am, of course, referring to the music and not to the show's "book" or to such things as casting policy.

44. Program, *Miss Saigon*, Theatre Royal, London, 1993, n.p.

45. Ambrose (Fields-McHugh), "A Japanese Dream" (Bb-19329-3), 1930.

46. Prendergast, *Film Music: A Neglected Art*, 214.

47. Victor Hugo, in the preface to his volume of verse *Les Orientales* of 1829, states: "Spain is still the Orient; Spain is half African, Africa is half Asian" (quoted in McClary, *Georges Bizet* 30).

48. It is not my contention that such devices are employed in an *utterly* indiscriminate manner: for example, pentatonic melody and gongs are not likely to be used to evoke Spain.

49. For example, Rimsky-Korsakov's *Scheherazade*, bars 8–13.

50. Eero Tarasti, *Myth and Music: A Semiotic Approach to the Aesthetics of Myth in Music* (The Hague: Mouton, 1979). See Tarasti, p. 77; *Scheherazade*, 3d movement, bars 162–64 provides an example.

51. Said, *Orientalism*, 177.

52. For a well-balanced account of these positive and negative factors, see Locke, "Cutthroats and Casbah Dancers," especially 105–8.

53. J. J. Clarke, *Oriental Enlightenment: The Encounter Between Asian and Western Thought* (London: Routledge, 1997), 28.

54. In this case, musical Orientalism operates as a sort of "musical fancy dress." Consider the following comment on Oriental masquerade: "Stereotypical and inaccurate though they often were, exotic costumes marked out a kind of symbolic interpenetration with difference—an almost erotic commingling with the alien" (Terry Castle, *Masquerade and Civilisation: The Carnivalesque in Eighteenth-Century English Culture and Fiction* [London: Methuen, 1986], 61–62). I am grateful to Marian Gilbert Read for drawing my attention to this point and the passage quoted. Sometimes Oriental fancy dress moves to the mainstream: Leon Bakst's "Oriental" designs for the Ballet Russes transformed Paris fashions in the second decade of the

twentieth century; see Colin McDowell, "Choreographer of Change," *Sunday Times*, "The Culture," 28 Jan. 1996, p. 14.

55. For Bakhtin's theory of the carnivalesque, see Mikhail Bakhtin, *Rabelais and His World*, trans. Helene Iswolsky (Bloomington, IN: Indiana University Press, 1984). For a study that links Mozart's Turkish music and the carnivalesque, see Matthew Head, *Orientalism, Masquerade and Mozart's Turkish Music*, Royal Musical Association Monographs 9 (London: Royal Musical Association, 2000), espec. 87–88, 101–3.

56. Remark attributed to Alan Clark, former British government minister for defence, in an Amnesty International advertisement (*Guardian*, Saturday, 16 March 1996, p. 13).

57. Said, *Orientalism*, 108.

58. See Bill Ashcroft, Gareth Griffiths, and Helen Tiffin, eds., *The Post-Colonial Studies Reader* (London: Routledge, 1995), 85.

59. Ibid., 240.

60. Herbert Spencer, *Principles of Biology* (London: Williams and Norgate, 1864), part 6, chapter 12, section 363.

61. See Christine Bolt, "Race and the Victorians," in C. C. Eldridge, ed., *British Imperialism in the Nineteenth Century* (London: Macmillan, 1984), 126–47, 133. Bolt cites D. A. Lorimer, *Colour, Class and the Victorians* (Leicester: Leicester University Press, 1978), chapter 7.

62. Said, *Orientalim*, 19.

63. See ibid., 40.

64. Ibid., 306.

65. J. E. Ritchie, *The Night Side of London* (London: William Tweedie, 2d ed., 1858), 207. The term "costermonger" originally described a person who sold fruit from a market barrow (a costard was a type of large apple), but about this time it began to be used for any street seller and tended to conjure up the image of a "typical" working-class Cockney.

66. See Scott, *The Singing Bourgeois*, 99 and 101.

67. See Bellman, *The Style Hongrois*, 144–48, 153–54.

68. Ibid., 162–73.

69. Consider Ernest Gold's music for *Exodus* (1960), Miklos Rozsa's music for *King of Kings* (1961), or Alfred Newman's score for *The Greatest Story Ever Told* (1965).

70. Archibald T. Davison and Willi Apel, *Historical Anthology of Music*, vol. 1 (Cambridge, MA: Harvard University Press, 1946), 227. The piece may be found on page 108.

71. Denis Stevens pointed out that it "becomes intelligible when the upper string of the lute is tuned a semitone higher according to instructions" (*Musicology: A Practical Guide* [London: Macdonald, 1980], 175). The instruction to tune the chanterelle a semitone higher is given above the tablature.

72. Klingor's poem *Asie*, mentioned earlier during the discussion of Ravel's *Shéhérazade* of 1903.

73. Hugh Macdonald, "Something Borrowed, Something New," in *Pelléas & Mélisande, Opera Guide 9* (London: John Calder, 1982), p. 7.

74. Donald F. Tovey is reminded of the "Homeric seas" in the coda to this movement; see *Essays in Musical Analysis*, vol. 2: *Symphonies (ii)* (London: Oxford University Press, 1966, orig. pub. 1935), 81.

75. Eric Blom, comp., *Everyman's Dictionary of Music*, ed. Jack Westrup (London: Dent, 5th ed., 1971), 720.

CHAPTER 8

1. This is given as the reason the French looked to jazz and things American in Edmund Wilson, "The Aesthetic Upheaval in France: The Influence of Jazz in Paris and Americanization of French Literature and Art," *Vanity Fair* 17 (Feb. 1922), 49, cited in Nancy Perloff, *Art and the Everyday: Popular Entertainment and the Circle of Erik Satie* (Oxford: Clarendon Press, 1991), 45.

2. Krenek's opinion is cited without source in Ronald Taylor, *Kurt Weill: Composer in a Divided World* (London: Simon and Schuster, 1991), 85–86.

3. Lionel Carley, *Delius: A Life in Letters,* vol. 1, 1862–1908 (Cambridge, MA: Harvard University Press, 1983), 5.

4. For information on the Jubilee Singers of Fisk University, Nashville, and their tours, see J. B. T. Marsh, *The Story of the Jubilee Singers* (London: Hodder and Stoughton, new ed. 1899).

5. See Geoffrey Self, *The Hiawatha Man: The Life and Work of Samuel Coleridge-Taylor* (Aldershot: Scolar Press, 1995), 214. The same tune was used by Louis Moreau Gottschalk in his piano piece *Bamboula,* op. 2 (1844–45).

6. *Daily Telegraph,* 1899, reporting on *The Death of Minnehaha,* a cantata produced at the North Staffordshire Music Festival on 26 Oct. 1899. The report is quoted at length on the back cover of Novello's contemporaneous publication of Hubert Parry's choral setting of *Blest Pair of Sirens* (Milton).

7. For the impact of the cakewalk in Paris, 1900–1903, see Perloff, *Art and the Everyday,* 47–50.

8. Marie Lloyd, "The Piccadilly Trot" (David-Arthurs) (Zonophone 980 y16045e), 19 Nov. 1912.

9. George Formby, "John Willie's Ragtime Band" (Murphy) (AK17531e), 1913.

10. "Hitchy-Koo," (Gilbert–Abrahams and Muir), 1911.

11. See Ronald Pearsall, *Edwardian Popular Music* (Newton Abbot: David and Charles, 1975), 185.

12. "I Got the Blues" was published in New Orleans and is reprinted in Trebor Jay Tichenor, *Ragtime Rediscoveries: 64 Works from the Golden Age of Rag* (New York: Dover, 1979), 171–73.

13. Peter van der Merwe, "The Italian Blue Third," in Tarja Hautamäki and Tarja Rautiainen, eds., *Popular Music Studies in Seven Acts* (Tampere, Finland: University of Tampere, 1996), 55–66, 65.

14. Arbie Orenstein, *A Ravel Reader* (New York: Columbia University Press, 1990), 390.

15. Ravel in 1929, quoted in Orenstein, *A Ravel Reader,* 466.

16. See Lawrence W. Levine, *Black Culture and Black Consciousness: Afro-American Folk Thought from Slavery to Freedom* (New York: Oxford University Press, 1977), 294.

17. Tom Fletcher, *100 Years of the Negro in Show Business* (New York: Da Capo, 1984, reprint of ed. orig. pub. Burdge, 1954), 205–6.

18. Charles Hamm, *Putting Popular Music in Its Place* (Cambridge: Cambridge University Press, 1995), 310.

19. Igor Stravinsky and Robert Craft, *Expositions and Developments* (London: Faber, 1962), 91.

20. Ibid., 92.

21. Roger Scruton, *The Aesthetics of Music* (Oxford: Clarendon Press, 1997), 500.

22. Olly Wilson, "The Significance of the Relationship Between Afro-American Music and West African Music," *Black Perspective on Music* 2 (1974), 3–22.

23. André Hodeir, *Jazz: Its Evolution and Essence,* trans. David Noakes (New York: Grove, 1956, a rev. and expanded version of *Hommes et Problèmes du Jazz*), 206. It is only fair to note, however, that Hodeir has suggested charitably that, in places, this *Ragtime* contains formulas of "a rhythmic flexibility that makes them resemble the riffs of jazzmen" (258). Surprisingly, perhaps, Hodeir is not inclined to be so kind about Milhaud.

24. J. Reginald MacEachron, *On Easy Street (In Rags)* (1901), reprinted in Tichenor, *Ragtime Rediscoveries,* 166–70.

25. Henry Pleasants, *Serious Music—and All That Jazz! An Adventure in Music Criticism* (London: Gollancz, 1969), 18.

26. Stravinsky and Craft, *Expositions and Developments,* 92.

27. Vera Stravinsky and Robert Craft, *Stravinsky in Pictures and Documents* (New York: Simon and Schuster, 1978), 203.

28. David Thomson, *Europe since Napoleon* (London: Longmans Green, 1957), 464.

29. Darius Milhaud, *Ma Vie heureuse* (Paris: Belfond, 1973), 99–100.

30. Darius Milhaud, *Notes Without Music,* trans. Donald Evans (New York: Knopf, 1953), 137.

31. Lawrence Kramer, "Powers of Blackness: Africanist Discourse in Modern Concert Music," *Black Music Research Journal* 16, no. 1 (1996), 53–70, 61–62.

32. Michael Newman, "'Primitivism' and Modern Art," *Art Monthly* 86 (May 1985), 6–9, 8.

33. As Georg Simmel detailed in *Die Grosstädte und das Geistesleben* (The Metropolis and mental life, 1903); see Kurt H. Wolff, ed., *The Sociology of Georg Simmel* (London: Macmillan, 1964).

34. William Rubin, ed., *"Primitivism" in 20th Century Art: Affinity of the Tribal and the Modern,* 2 vols. (New York: Museum of Modern Art, 1984), 17.

35. For a discussion of misreadings, see ibid., 35–41. For example, "the sometimes rigid, frontal, symmetrical, and often awkward poses of many African figures" were often misread as examples of Expressionism, as indicating the psychological angst of people living in a fearful environment (35). A frontal pose that signifies "community" in Africa could be read as signifying "social anxiety" in Europe.

36. James Harding, *The Ox on the Roof: Scenes from Musical Life in Paris in the Twenties* (London: Macdonald, 1972), 133.

37. Deborah Mawer, *Darius Milhaud: Modality and Structure in Music of the 1920s* (Aldershot: Scolar Press, 1997), 145.

38. See ibid., 145.

39. "Livery Stable Blues" (Lopez-Nunez-Lee) was the first jazz record by the ODJB, made on 26 Feb. 1917 (B19331). It can be heard on *Finest Vintage Jazz 1917–1941* (ASV Living Era, AJA 5117), 1993, track 1.

40. Gunther Schuller, "Jazz and Musical Exoticism," in Jonathan Bellman, ed., *The Exotic in Western Music* (Boston: Northeastern University Press, 1998), 281–91, 288. Schuller also points to the influence elsewhere in the piece of "Aunt Hagar's Blues" by W. C. Handy's Orchestra.

41. Hodeir praises Milhaud for understanding the importance of tonic-subdominant interplay to the blues (*Jazz: Its Evolution and Essence,* 254).

42. Louis Armstrong and His Hot Five, "Muskrat Ramble" (Ory) recorded Chicago, 26 Feb. 1926 (9538-A). The musicians on this recording are Louis Armstrong

(cornet), Kid Ory (trombone), Johnny Dodds (clarinet), Lil Armstrong (piano), and Johnny St. Cyr (banjo). As a jazz classic, it has been rereleased many times and may be found (as well as elsewhere) on *Louis Armstrong: The 25 Greatest Hot Fives & Hot Sevens,* 1995 (ASV Living Era, CD AJA 5171).

43. Richard Middleton, *Scores 8, The Rise of Modernism in Music 1890–1935* (Milton Keynes: Open University, Course A308), 3–5.

44. Darius Milhaud, "L'évolution du jazz-band et la musique des nègres de l'Amérique du Nord," *Le Courrier musical* 35, no. 9 (1923), 163–64.

45. Milhaud, *Notes Without Music,* 149.

46. Laura Rosenstock, "Léger: 'The Creation of the World,'" in Rubin, *"Primitivism" in 20th Century Art,* vol. 2, 475–85, 482. Léger's contribution to *La Création* is covered in detail in this essay.

47. For a detailed discussion of jazz reception in Weimar Germany, upon which this paragraph leans heavily, see J. Bradford Robinson, "Jazz Reception in Weimar Germany: In Search of a Shimmy Figure," in Bryan Gilliam, ed., *Music and Performance During the Weimar Republic* (Cambridge: Cambridge University Press, 1994), 107–34, 113–17.

48. Ronald Taylor, *Kurt Weill: Composer in a Divided World* (London: Simon and Schuster, 1991), 84.

49. Ernst Krenek, "From *Jonny* to Orest," in *Exploring Music: Essays by Ernst Krenek,* trans. Margaret Shenfeld and Geoffrey Skelton (London: Calder and Boyars, 1966, orig. pub. in *Leipziger Neueste Nachrichten,* Jan. 1930), 23–25, 24.

50. He appears on the cover of the brochure of an Entartete Musik exhibition reproduced in Jack Sullivan, *New World Symphonies: How American Culture Changed European Music* (New Haven: Yale University Press, 1999), 217; it is not clear whether this is the 1937 Munich exhibition or the 1938 Düsseldorf exhibition.

51. Robinson, "Jazz Reception in Weimar Germany," 108–9.

52. Ibid., 122.

53. Igor Stravinsky, *Selected Correspondence,* vol. 3, ed. Robert Craft (London: Faber, 1985), 219, footnote 3.

54. *Music Ho!* Constant Lambert, *A Study of Music in Decline* (Hammondsworth: Penguin, 1948, orig. pub. London: Faber, 1934), 164.

55. Ernst Bloch, "The Threepenny Opera" (1935), trans. by the editor in Stephen Hinton, ed., *Kurt Weill: The Threepenny Opera* (Cambridge: Cambridge University Press, 1990), 135–37, 136.

56. Cited without source in John Willet, *The New Sobriety 1917–1933: Art and Politics in the Weimar Period* (London: Thames and Hudson, 1978), 167.

57. See Michael Morley, "'Suiting the Action to the Word': Some Observations on *Gestus* and *gestische Musik,*" in Kim H. Kowalke, ed., *A New Orpheus: Essays on Kurt Weill* (New Haven: Yale University Press, 1986), 183–201.

58. For example, "Erinnerung an die Marie A." (c. 1905). It can be heard in English on *Robyn Archer Sings Brecht,* vol. 2, 1984 (EMI Records, EL 27 00491), track 9.

59. The harmonium is not generally thought of as a jazz instrument, but it does appear (played by Fred Longshaw) on the famous Bessie Smith and Louis Armstrong recording of "St. Louis Blues" of 14 Jan. 1925 (140241).

60. *Aus der 3-Groschen-Oper,* 7 Dec. 1930 (Telefunken Gesellschaft A752–755), rereleased on CD by Teldec Classics International, 1990 (9031–72025–2), and *Die Dreigroschenoper* conducted by Wilhelm Brückner-Rüggeberg, 1958 (CBS Records MK 42637, rereleased on CD in 1982).

61. "Ich suche weder neue Formen noch neue Theorien, ich suche ein neues Publikum" (quoted without source in Michel Pérez, "Die Dreigroschenoper," CD booklet essay that accompanies CBS recording MK 42637, 1958, rereleased on CD in 1982, 11–17, 12.

62. Willet, *The New Sobriety 1917–1933*, 110.

63. According to Jacques-Charles, the revue *Laisse-les tomber* at the Casino de Paris in 1917 intoduced Parisians to jazz (the music was played by an American band directed by black drummer Louis Mitchell) (*Cent ans de music-hall: Histoire générale du music-hall de ses origines à nos jours* [Geneva: Éditions Jeheber, 1956], 186, cited in Perloff, *Art and the Everyday*, 53).

64. See Rosenstock, "Léger," 475.

65. Wilfrid Mellers, *Francis Poulenc* (Oxford: Oxford University Press, 1993), 22.

66. Henri Hell, *Francis Poulenc: Musicien Français* (Paris: Fayard, 1978, orig. pub. 1958), 69–70.

67. Sullivan, *New World Symphonies* (1999), 191; a footnote explains that this remark is cited in Keith W. Daniel, *Francis Poulenc* (Ann Arbor, MI: UMI Research Press, 1980), 24.

68. Attributed to Neville Cardus in Trevor Hold's CD notes to *Walton-Lambert-Bliss-Warlock-Berners*, 1997 (Symposium Records 1203).

69. See Elaine Brody, *Paris: The Musical Kaleidoscope 1870–1925* (London: Robson Books, 1988), 242–43.

70. Josephine Baker with Jacob's Jazz, "Then I'll Be Happy" (Friend-Clare-Brown), recorded Jan. 1927 (matrix unknown), rereleased on *Joséphine Baker, Star of Les Folies-Bergères: Twenty-Four Hits 1926–1944*, 1997 (ASV Living Era CD AJA 5239).

71. See Brian Large, *Martinu* (London: Duckworth, 1975), 42.

72. Jean Cocteau, "Jazz-Band," *Le Rappel à l'ordre* (Paris: Delamain, 1948), 141.

73. Bernard Gendron, "Jamming at Le Boeuf: Jazz and the Paris Avant-Garde," *Discourse* 12, no. 1 (Fall–Winter 1989–90), 3–27, 23–24.

74. Stan Hawkins, "Eurogrooves," paper delivered at the Black American Music Conference, University of Utrecht, May 1998.

75. Lambert, *Music Ho!*, 166.

76. Ibid., 154.

77. Ibid., 154–55.

78. Sullivan, *New World Symphonies*, 201.

79. Portia Maultsby, "Africanisms in African-American Music," in Joseph E. Holloway, ed., *Africanisms in American Culture* (Bloomington: Indiana University Press, 1990), 202.

80. Eileen Southern, *The Music of Black Americans: A History* (New York: Norton, 2d ed. 1983, orig. pub. 1971), 363.

81. Hodeir, *Jazz: Its Evolution and Essence*, 258. Elsewhere, Hodeir explains that swing "is not simply a question of *time values;* the succession of *attacks* and *intensities* is also an important part of it" (196, footnote 3).

82. Olly Wilson, "The Heterogeneous Sound Ideal in African-American Music," in Gena Dagel Caponi, ed., *Signifyin(g), Sanctifyin', and Slam Dunking: A Reader in African American Expressive Culture* (Amherst: University of Massachusetts Press, 1999, orig. pub. in New Perspectives on Music: Essays in Honor of Eileen Southern, Jessie Ann Owens and Anthony M. Cummings, eds., [Warren, MI: Harmonie Park Press, 1992], 327–38), 157–71, 158–60.

83. Wilson, "The Heterogeneous Sound Ideal," 159.

84. Samuel A. Floyd, Jr., "Ring Shout! Literary Studies, Historical Studies, and Black Music Inquiry," in Caponi, *Signifyin(g), Sanctifyin' and Slam Dunking* (reprinted from *Black Music Research Journal* 11, no. 2 [1991], 265–88), 135–56, 138–39, 154.

85. Henry Louis Gates, Jr., *The Signifying Monkey: A Theory of African-American Literary Criticism* (New York: Oxford University Press, 1987). Gates sees the Signifying Monkey (familiar from his exploits with the lion) as an African-American incarnation of a pan-African mythological figure (known as Esu-Elegbara in Nigeria), a master of rhetoric and trickery.

86. Sterling Stuckey, *Slave Culture: Nationalist Theory and the Foundations of Black America* (New York: Oxford University Press, 1987).

87. Floyd, "Ring Shout!," 138.

88. Claudia Mitchell-Kernan, "Signifying, Loud-Talking and Marking" (1972), in Caponi, *Signifyin(g), Sanctifyin', and Slam Dunking,* 309–30, 312.

89. Ibid., 315–16.

90. Floyd, "Ring Shout!," 141.

91. Ibid., 142.

92. Ibid., 142–3.

93. Ibid., 155. An example of how Floyd's ideas may inform the analysis of black performance can be found in David Brackett, *Interpreting Popular Music* (Cambridge: Cambridge University Press, 1995), 108–56.

94. Floyd, "Ring Shout!," 145.

95. Lambert, *Music Ho!,* 152.

96. Mellonee Burim, "The Black Gospel Music Tradition: A Complex of Ideology, Aesthetic, and Behaviour," in Irene V. Jackson, ed., *More than Dancing* (Westport, CT: Greenwood Press, 1985), 154.

97. Maultsby, "Africanisms in African-American Music," 188; also in Derek B. Scott, *Music, Culture, and Society: A Reader* (Oxford: Oxford University Press, 2000), 92.

98. Quoted in Sullivan, *New World Symphonies,* 212.

99. Lambert, *Music Ho!,* 166.

100. Ibid., 150.

101. Ibid., 166.

102. Ibid., 155.

103. Ibid., 156.

104. *Revue Musicale,* 1920, quoted in Philippe Carles and Jean-Louis Comolli, *Free Jazz et Black Power* (Paris: Champ Libre, 1974), 65–66, and in Jacques Attali, *Noise: The Political Economy of Music,* trans. Brian Massumi (Minneapolis: University of Minnesota Press, 1985, orig. pub. as *Bruits: Essai sur l'économie politique de la musique* [Paris: Presses universitaires de France, 1977]), 104.

105. Kramer, "Powers of Blackness," 65.

106. "Dandin," *Dagbladet,* 29 Jan. 1921, cited in James Dickenson, *Green Landscape Tinted Blue: A Study of the Effects of Norwegian Folk Music on Norwegian Jazz, 1945–1995* (unpub. Ph.D. thesis, University of Salford).

107. Heinrich Eduard Jacob, *Johann Strauss: A Century of Light Music,* trans. Marguerite Wolff (London: Hutchinson, 1940), 333.

108. Henry Raynor, *Music and Society since 1815* (London: Barrie and Jenkins, 1976), 157.

109. Lambert, *Music Ho!,* 146.

*I*NDEX

Abbate, Carolyn, 157
Adams, Stephen (real name: Michael
    Maybrick)
  "The Holy City," 88
  "Nirvana," 171–72
Adorno, Theodor W., 99, 114, 226–
    27 n.22
Affergan, Francis, 160
Africa, 13, 167–68, 179–80, 184, 201
  and jazz, 186–89, 199
African-American music making,
    13–14, 86–87
  its appeal, 180–83
  misconceptions of, 197–200
Agawu, Kofi, 10
Alison, Archibald, 56
Allitsen, Frances, "England, My
    England," 51
Althusser, Louis, 19
Ambrose, Bert, 83, 85, 97, 222 n.17
  "The Clouds Will Soon Roll By," 86
  "Ho Hum," 95
  "A Japanese Dream," 174
  "Let's Put Out the Lights," 99
"American Patrol," 83
American Ragtime Octette,
    "Hitchy-Koo," 182
Apel, Willi, 177

"Arab's Farewell To His Favourite Steed,
    The," 161
Argentina, 174
Aristotle, 38
Arizona, 75, 78
Armstrong, Louis, 81, 89, 94, 190, 197,
    199
  "Heebie Jeebies," 195
  "Mack the Knife," 193
  "Muskrat Ramble," 187–89
  "St. Louis Blues," 242 n.59
Arnold, Billy, 186
Arnold, Edwin, 171
"Arrah Wanna," 67
art nègre, 179, 186–87
Asian Subcontinent, 168–70
Attali, Jacques, 20
Auer, Max, 109
Australia, 72
avant-garde, 193, 196

Bach, J. S., 199
  Peasant Cantata, 107
  The Well-Tempered Clavier, 9, 87, 179
Bache, Walter, 137
Baker, Josephine, 194
  La Revue nègre, 195–96
  "Then I'll Be Happy," 195

Bakhtin, Mikhail, 79, 175, 239 n.55
Bakst, Leon, 238–39 n.54
Balakirev, Mily, 12, 137
   Tamara, 151
Bali, 125, 178
"Bandit's Life Is the Life for Me, A," 51
Bangs, Lester, 30
Barnet, Charles, "Cherokee," 70
Barry, John, 76
Barry, Ken, 222 n.22
Barthes, Roland, 7, 18–19, 28, 95, 219
   n.73
Bartók, Béla, Allegro barbaro, 150
   and Magyar music, 180
Bassey, Shirley, 6
Bateson, Gregory, 125
Bausch, Andy, 78
Baudrillard, Jean, 61, 94
Beatles, The, 30, 83
Beckett, Walter, 140
Beethoven, Ludwig van, 6, 12, 38–39, 41,
      45, 104, 112–15, 123, 135, 178
   "Alla Ingharese," 158
   Eroica Symphony, 124
   Fidelio, 107, 163, 166
   Leonora Overture no. 3, 95
   Missa Solemnis, 108
   Original Welsh Airs, 215 n.10
   Piano Sonata in E, op. 109, 36
   String Quartet in E-flat Major, op. 74,
      138
   Fifth Symphony, 53, 56
   Ninth Symphony, 106, 116–17, 122,
      131, 138
Bellman, Jonathan, 158, 177
Bellow, Saul, 4
Benson, Ivy, 37
Berkhofer, Robert F., 61
Berlin, 190
Berlin, Irving, 180
   "Alexander's Ragtime Band," 97–98
   "Puttin' on the Ritz," 99
Berlioz, Hector, 12, 128
   La Damnation de Faust, 137, 140
   L'Enfance du Christ, 160, 168
   Grande traite d'instrumentation et
      d'orchestration modernes, 133–35
   Roméo et Juliette, 138

Symphonie fantastique, 130, 134, 139,
      144
   Les Troyens, 7
Bernard, James, The Devil Rides Out,
      151
Bernstein, Leonard, West Side Story, 167,
      178
Bertung, Birgit, 234 n.67
"Big Chief 'Swing It,'" 68–70
binary oppositions, 12, 43, 142
Bishop, Henry, "Hark! 'Tis the Indian
      Drum," 218 n.51
Bizet, Georges, Carmen, 166
Black, Ben, "Moonlight and Roses," 83
Blackbirds, 196
Blackbirds 1928, 196
blackface minstrelsy, 13, 81, 86, 94,
      181–82, 194
Blackwood, Helen (Lady Dufferin),
      213 n.95
   "The Charming Woman," 49–51
Bloch, Ernst, 112, 114, 124, 191
bluegrass, 18
blues, 182, 197, 199–200
Bock, Jerry, Fiddler on the Roof, 177
Börlin, Jean, 187
Borodin, Alexander, Prince Igor, 161
bossa nova, 13
Boston, 67
Boubil, Alain, 173
Bowie, David, "China Girl," 174
Bowlly, Al, 83–84
   "Misery Farm," 88
Brackett, David, 87
Brahms, Johannes, 27, 68, 119
brass band, 39, 182
Bray, John, The Indian Princess, 62–63
Breakspear, Eustace J., 42
Brecht, Bertholt, 191–93
British national anthem, 10
Brooke, A. E., 122
Brooks, Shirley, 65
"Brother, Can You Spare a Dime?," 93
Brown, Dee, 75
Browning, Robert, 51
Bruce, Robert, 99
Bruckner, Anton, 11–12, 103–4
   apocalyptic vision, 112–16

Masses, 105–6, 108, 114–15, 117, 125
"Mein Herz und deine Stimme," 127
Missa Solemnis, 104, 107
motets, 105
G-minor Overture, 117–18, 126
plateaus of intensity, 122–26
Psalm 150, 105, 115, 123
Requiem, 107–8
sacred character of compositions,
    104–7
signifiers for darkness and light,
    107–10
Steiermärker, 127
structure and meaning, 110–12
First Symphony, 107, 127
Second Symphony, 105–6, 125–26
    Die Nullte, 106, 127
Third Symphony, 104–6, 110–11,
    113–14, 118, 126
Fourth Symphony, 107, 109–10, 124
Fifth Symphony, 106, 123–26
Sixth Symphony, 109, 119–20, 125–26,
    178
Seventh Symphony, 106, 109–10,
    112–13, 115–17, 120, 123–24, 127,
    227 n.22
Eighth Symphony, 105–7, 109, 112,
    116–17, 122–24, 126
Ninth Symphony, 105–7, 109–10, 115,
    117, 122, 125–26
Te Deum, 105, 107, 109
transfiguration of themes, 117–22
Brussells, 140
Brüstle, Christa, 226 n.3
Buffalo Bill, 217 n.28
Burch, Sharon, 78
Burke, Edmund, 43–45, 55–56
Burma, 170–71
Burnim, Mellonee, 199
Burning Sky, 78
Bush, Kate, "Wuthering Heights," 32
Butler, Josephine, 19–20, 205 n.9
Butt, Clara, 18
Byrd, William
    Mass for four voices, 109
    "Though Amaryllis Dance in Green,"
        178
Byrne, David, "City of Dreams," 75

Caddo, 75
Cage, John, *4′33″*, 6
Cajun, 78
cakewalk, 181–82
California, 66
California Ramblers, 88
camp, 28–29, 31, 40
Canada, 68
canon, musical, 5, 45, 199
Cantor, Eddie, 87
Caribbean, 13, 82
Carlyle, Thomas, 42
Carr, Michael, 93–94 (*see also* Kennedy,
    Jimmy)
    "Did Your Mother Come from
        Ireland?," 94
    "The General's Fast Asleep," 94
    "The Handsome Territorial," 94
    "Misty Islands of the Highlands," 93
    "Ole Faithful," 94
    "On Linger Longer Island," 93
    "South of the Border," 94
    "Sunset Trail," 94
Cash, Johnny, "The Ballad of Ira
    Hayes," 74–75
Castle, Terry, 238 n.54
Celibidache, Sergiu, 230 n.102
Cendrars, Blaise, 187
Cézanne, Paul, 186
Chapman, James, "One o' Them
    Things," 182
Cherokee, 62–63, 75, 77–78
Cheyenne, 77
Chief Thundercloud, 61
China, 170–74
Chopin, Fryderyk, 42
Citron, Marcia, 36, 45
Claribel (Charlotte Alington Barnard),
    212 n.89
    "Children's Voices," 45–46
    "Come Back to Erin," 94
    "Won't You Tell Me Why, Robin?"
        22–24, 27
Clarke, Edward, 34
Clarke, J. J., 175
class, 39, 50–51, 199
Clayton, Ellen, 35
Clive, Franklin, "The Mousmee," 170

Clive, Geoffrey, 143
Cocteau, Jean, 186, 196
  Le Coq et l'Arlequin, 193
Coleridge-Taylor, Samuel
  African Suite, 182
  "La Bamboula," 181
  The Death of Minnehaha, 240 n.6
  Hiawatha's Wedding Feast, 181
"Colin and Susan," 23
"Come into the Garden, Maud," 27
Conradi, Johann, 133
Cooder, Ry, *Geronimo: An American Legend*, 76
Cook, Eliza, 64–65
Cooke, Deryck, 105, 107, 124–25
Cooper, James Fenimore, 63
Cooper, Lee, 72
Cornelius, Peter, 133
Cotton, Billy, 91, 222 n.20
  "Did Your Mother Come from Ireland?," 94
  "I've Got Sixpence," 84
Cottrell, Alan P., 141
Craft, Robert, 191
Crazy Horse, 72
"Crazy Words, Crazy Tune," 199
Cree, 75, 77
Creole music making, 181
Crimean War, 39
critical musicology, 4–5, 103
crooning, 83–84
Crosby, Bing, 87
Crotch, William, 44–45
Cusick, Susan, 19–20
Custer, General, 71, 75

Dahlhaus, Carl, 20, 119
Dame, Joke, 205 n.8
dance bands
  incongruous mix of styles, 81–84
  predictability, 84–99
  sociocultural context, 84–86
Dances with Wolves (film), 75, 77
Dante Alighieri, *Divina Commedia*, 136–37, 140
Darwin, Charles, 33
David, Félicien, *La Perle du Brésil*, 168
Davidson, Donald, 9
Davies, Emily, 34, 209 n.12

Davison, Archibald T., 177
Dearly, Max, 74
Dean, Dora, 181
Debussy, Claude
  Children's Corner Suite, 182
  "Clair de Lune," 83
  La Mer, 178
  Pelléas et Mélisande, 150
  Prélude à l'après-midi d'un faune, 178
  Préludes, 182
  "La Soirée dans Grenade," 166
  "Voiles," 178
deconstruction, 7, 12, 18, 104, 110, 114
Deleuze, Gilles, 10, 12, 68, 125–26, 176, 207 n.40
Delibes, Léo, *Lakmé*, 157–58
Delius, Frederick, 180
  Florida Suite, 181
Deloria Jr., Vine, 75, 79
Derrida, Jacques, 12, 39, 61, 104, 110
  différance, 32, 110
diabolus in musica, 109, 130
dialogism, 20
Dibdin, Charles, 177
Dietrich, Marlene, 28
Dippie, Brian W., 67
Disney, Walt
  Peter Pan, 73
  Pocohontas, 62, 65
Dodd, Sara M., 210 n.35
Doernberg, Edwin, 117, 122, 126
Dolores (Ellen Dickson), 212 n.91
  "Clear and Cool," 47–48
Dowell, Jo Kay, 77
Dvořák, Ann, 68
Dvořák, Antonin, 12, 137
  The Noonday Witch, 150–1
  The Water Goblin, 150–1

Eagleton, Terry, 7, 43
Edwards, Cliff, "Come Up and See Me Sometime," 28, 31
Egypt, 167–68
Einstein, Alfred, 158
Elgar, Edward, 81
  "Land of Hope and Glory," 6
Eliot, George, 40
Elizalde, Fred, 88–90
  "Misery Farm," 88

Ellington, Edward Kennedy 'Duke', 4, 29, 89, 94, 181, 190, 197, 199–200
"Black and Tan Fantasy," 88
"East St. Louis Toodle-Oo," 195
"Hot and Bothered," 90, 200
"It Don't Mean a Thing If It Ain't Got That Swing," 198–99
Elliot, G. H., 86
entartete Musik, 190, 196
epic opera, 191
eroticism, 17–20
in the baroque era, 20–22
in the 19th century, 22–27
in the 20th century, 27–32
Eton, 38–39
Everist, Mark, 203 n.4
Ewers, John C., 216 n.28
Exodus (film), 74

fandango, 163
Fardon, Don, "Indian Reservation," 77
"Fascinating Rhythm," 96
Fay, Amy, 140
Feather, Leonard, 82
"Bass Reflex," 97
Fenby, Eric, 181
Fields, Gracie, 82
"Sing as We Go," 93
Fink, Robert, 27, 228–29 n.57
Finscher, Ludwig, 127
Finson, Jon W., 64
Firman, Bert, "Painting the Clouds with Sunshine," 88
First World War, 57, 85–86, 179–80, 187, 190
Fiske, John, 72
Fitzgerald, Ella, "Mack the Knife," 193
Flanagan and Allen, "That's Another Scottish Story," 94
Flash Gordon Conquers the Universe, 124
Fletcher, Tom, 183
Floros, Constantin, 103–4, 116, 126, 229 n.73
Floyd, Jr., Samuel A., 198–99
Foresyth, Reginald, "Garden of Weed," 97
Formby, Sr., George, "John Willie's Ragtime Band," 182

Forte, Allen, 149–50
Foster, Stephen, "My Old Kentucky Home," 95
Foucault, Michel, 20, 27, 176
Fox, Roy, 224–25 n.66; "Calling Me Home," 96
Franck, César, 137; *Le Chasseur maudit*, 150
Freud, Sigmund, 10, 27, 54, 207 nn.38, 40
Friml, Rudolf, *Rose Marie*, 67–68
Frith, Simon, 18
Fuller, Sophie, 213 n.100

Gabriel, Virginia, 213 n.99
"Only," 24–26
"When Sparrows Build," 51–53
Garciá, Manuel, 237 n.27
Garrett, Elizabeth, 34, 209 n.12
Gates, Jr., Henry Louis, 198, 244 n.85
Gatty, Alfred Scott, *Plantation Songs*, 86
Gay, John, *The Beggar's Opera*, 191
gay/lesbian, 4, 18–20, 28, 31, 40, 56–57, 210 n.51
gender, 11, 31, 33–35, 51
music and femininity, 38–40
women and composition, 41–43
women as musicians, 35–37
Gendron, Bernard, 196
Genelli, Bonaventura, 140
genosong and phenosong, 19
genotext and phenotext, 19
Georgakas, Dan, 76
Geronimo (film, 1939), 61
Gershwin, George, 96, 180, 196
"I Got Rhythm," 197
Piano Concerto, 182
Rhapsody in Blue, 183, 190
gestische Musik, 192
Gibbons, Richard Caroll, 83, 222 n.18
Gilbert, William S. (*see* Sullivan, Arthur)
Gilliam, Bryan, 126, 225–26 n.3
Gisbourne, Thomas, 35
Glass, Philip
Akhnaten, 168
Heroes Symphony, 237 n.30
Glinka, Mikhail, *Ruslan and Lyudmila*, 130, 161

Gluck, Christoph
  Alceste, 134
  Don Juan, 163, 167
  Iphigénie en Tauride, 134
  Orfeo ed Euridice, 133–34
Godard, Susan, 36
Goddard, Arabella, 36
Goethe, Johann Wolfgang, 13, 140–42
Gonella, Nat, 95, 223 n.29
Gorbman, Claudia, 220 n.81
gospel, 198–99
Gottschalk, Louis Morea, 240 n.5
Greenblatt, Stephen, 21
Gregorovius, Ferdinand, 141
Greimas, A. J., 204 n.13
Grey, Zane, 67
Grieg, Edvard, 181
  Pier Gynt, 95
Griffith, Nanci, 6
Grosz, Wilhelm, *Baby in der Bar;* 190
  (*see also* Williams, Hugh)
Guattari, Félix, 10, 12, 68, 125–26,
  207 n.40
guitar, 47–48
Gut, Serge, 130, 137, 140
Guthrie, Woody, 67

Hague, Sam, 86
Hall, Adelaide, 196
  "Creole Love Call," 195
Hall, Henry, 99
  "I Like Bananas," 92
  "It's a Sin To Tell a Lie," 81
  "Rusty and Dusty," 84, 91–92
  "The Teddy Bears' Picnic," 91–92
Hallé, Charles, 38
Halm, August, 110
Hamilton, Marybeth, 28, 30–31
Hamm, Charles, 82, 183
Handel, George F.
  Giulio Cesare in Egitto, 22
  Israel in Egypt, 107, 168
  Judas Maccabeus, 177
  Messiah, 107
  Samson, 107
Handy, W. C., "The Memphis Blues," 182
Hanslick, Eduard, 54, 104, 127
Harper, E., "A Bandit's Life Is the Life
  for Me!," 163, 165

Harris, Jack, "On Linger Longer Island,"
  93
Harrow, 39
Hatten, Robert S., 231 n.124
"Haunted Wood," 66
Haweis, Hugh, 25–26, 214 n.122
Hawkins, Stan, 197
  and Carmen Hawkins, 230 n.84
Hawkwind, "Black Elk Speaks," 75
Hawtrey, Stephen, 38
Haydn, Joseph, 45, 90, 199
  The Creation, 104, 107
  folksong arrangements, 6
  Nelson Mass, 108
  Piano Trio in G Major, Hob. XV: 25,
  158
  Seven Last Words, 105
Hayes, Ira, 74–75
Heath, Ted, 83, 222 n.12
Head, Matthew, 239 n.55
Hebrides, 76, 93
Hegel, Georg W. F., 104, 110, 112–13,
  142
hegemony, 86
Hell, Henri, 194
"Hello! Ma Baby," 182
Hemans, Felicia, 213 n.93
  "Mother, O! Sing Me to Rest," 163–64
Henley, William, 51
hermeneutics, 6, 103
Hindemith, Paul, 199
  1922 Suite, 190
  "Ragtime," 179
Hodeir, André, 88, 185, 198, 241 nn.23,
  41, 81
Holbein, Hans, *Der Todtentanz*, 139
Holiday, Billie, "Don't Explain," 18
Holst, Gustav, 81
Hood, Basil, 176
"Hootchy-Kootchy Dance," 161
Howie, A. Crawford, 105, 117
Hruby, Carl, 127
Huelsenbeck, Richard, 194
Hughes, Patrick, "It's Unanimous Now,"
  89
Hugo, Victor, 238 n.47
Humperdinck, Englebert, *Hänsel und
  Gretel*, 150
Hutcheon, Linda, 32, 221 n.104

Hylton, Jack, 89, 222 n.13
  "Happy Days Are Here Again," 83
  "He Played His Ukulele As the Ship
      Went Down," 91
  "Meadow Lark," 95
  "Speaking of Kentucky Days," 95
  "Yes Sir, That's My Baby," 96

"I Am the Bandolero," 163
ideology, 3, 7–8, 10, 42–43, 51, 166
"If You Want To Touch an Irish Heart,"
  94
"I'll Sing Thee Songs of Araby," 161
impressionism, 177–78, 181
improvisation, 87–89, 197–98
"In a Little Second Hand Store," 92
"Indianola," 68–70
Ingelow, Jean, 51
intertextuality, 4–5
Iron Maiden, "Run to the Hills," 75
Iroquois, 78
"It's the Talk of the Town," 92
"I've Got an Invitation to a Dance," 92
Ives, Charles, 39
Iwo Jima, 74

Jackson, Edgar, 88–90
Jackson, Timothy, 227 n.36
Jacob, Heinrich Eduard, 200–201
Jagger, Mick, 19
  "Let's Spend the Night Together," 31
Japan, 170–71, 174, 177
Jarre, Maurice, Lawrence of Arabia,
  178
Java, 178
jazz, 4, 14, 80, 82, 87–90, 97, 179–80,
  182–83
  and Africa, 186–89
  fear of, 200–201
  and modernism, 183–85
  as satirical weapon, 190–94
  "sweet," 194–96
Jessel, Léon, "The Parade of the Tin
  Soldiers," 82
Jews
  interest in jazz, 180
  represented in music, 177
Ježek, Jaroslav, 196
Joachim, Joseph, 36

Johnson, Charles E., The Creole Show,
  181
Johnson, William, 38
Jolson, Al, 86
  The Jazz Singer, 87
Jones, Sidney
  The Geisha, 170
  San Toy, 170
jouissance, 19
Jung, Carl G., 147

Kähler, Willibald, 117
Kalevala, 64
Kallberg, Jeffrey, 42
Kálmán, Emmerich, Die Herzogin von
  Chicago, 70–71, 196
Kane, Helen, "Is There Anything Wrong
  in That?," 28
Kangourou, Makoko, 193–94
Kant, Immanuel, 51, 54
Kern, Jerome, 180
Kettle, Martin, 122
Kennedy, Jimmy, 93–94 (see also Carr,
  Michael)
Kennedy-Fraser, Marjory, Songs of the
  Hebrides, 76, 93
Kentner, Louis, 148
Kern, Jerome, Show Boat, 95
Ketèlbey, Albert, In a Chinese Temple
  Garden, 171
Kierkegaard, Søren, 13, 142–43
King, Bertie, 82
Kingsley, Charles, 47
Kipling, Rudyard, 170
Kivy, Peter, 8–9
Klingsor, Tristan (real name: Léon
  Leclère), 161–62, 178
Korstvedt, Benjamin M., 225 n.2
Korte, Werner, 229 n.71
Kotzwara, Franz, The Battle of Prague,
  51
Kramer, Lawrence, 10, 23, 27, 39, 140,
  145–46, 186, 200, 206 n.28,
  207 n.40
Krause, Ernst, 29
Krebs, T. L., 34, 39
Krenek, Ernst, 180
  Jonny spielt auf, 190
  Das Leben des Orest, 190

Krim, Adam, 204 n.24
Kristeva, Julia, 4, 17, 19, 204 n.8
Kurth, Ernst, 126

Lacan, Jacques, 31, 176
Laing, Dave, 18
Lambert, Constant, 90, 191, 197, 199–201
    The Rio Grande, 194
lang, k. d., 20
Larkin, Philip, "Annus Mirabilis," 30
"Leave Abie Alone," 92–93
Léger, Fernand, 187, 189
Legion of Decency, 31
Lehár, Franz, *Die lustige Witwe*, 181
Leighton, Frederick, 39
Lemare, Edwin H., Andantino, 83
Lennox, Annie, "I Need a Man," 31
Lenau, Nikolaus, 138
Lenya, Lotte, "Seeräuberjenny," 193
Leppert, Richard, 10, 20, 35, 38, 42–43,
    209 n.21, 210 n.47
Lévi-Strauss, Claude, 155, 235–36 n.1
Lewis, Sarah, 34
Lindsay, Miss M., 212 n.90
    "Queen Mary's Prayer," 46–47
    "When Sparrows Build," 53
Liszt, Franz
    "Bagatelle ohne Tonart," 129, 138
    Chasse-Neige, 143–44
    "Csárdás macabre," 131–32, 150
    and the demonic in Mozart and
        Weber, 128–29
    "Gypsy Scale," 159–60, 166
    Dante Sonata, 130–31, 136–37
    Dante Symphony, 131–32, 134–37,
        139–40, 143, 150
    demonic genres, 137–40
    demonic legacy, 150–51
    demonic negation, 129–30
    demonic typology, 130–37
    Études d'exécution transcendante,
        137–38
    Faust Symphony, 130–31, 133, 135, 137,
        139–42, 144–48
    Hungaria, 159–60
    Hunnenschlacht, 140, 147
    interpreting the demonic, 140–48
    Les Préludes, 123–24

Malédiction Concerto, 132–33, 139,
    146
Mazeppa, 12
Mephisto Polka, 138
First Mephisto Waltz, 131–32, 137
Second Mephisto Waltz, 138
Third Mephisto Waltz, 132–33, 138
Fourth Mephisto Waltz, 129, 138
Missa Solemnis, 105
Pensée des morts, 130
Sonata in B minor, 12, 137, 147–48
St. Elizabeth, 130
Tasso, 118, 123–24
Totentanz, 130–31, 139, 149
Der Traurige Mönch, 130
Two Episodes from Lenau's *Faust*,
    138
Unstern! 12, 130, 137, 139, 148–49
Von der Wiege bis zum Grabe, 130
Zwei Konzertetüden, 138
Little Big Man (film), 75
Lloyd, Marie, 27–28
    "The Piccadilly Trot," 182
Locke, Ralph P., 160, 236 n.15
London, 158, 196
    Hammersmith Palais, 186
    Hanover Square Rooms, 36
    Hippodrome, 90
    London Academy, 34
    Mayfair Hotel, 85–86
    St. Andrew Undershaft (EC3), 209
        n.15
Longfellow, Henry W., 64, 67, 181
Longinus, 43
Loudin, Fred, 181
Luhrmann, Baz, *William Shakespeare's
    Romeo and Juliet*, 207 n.40
Luigini, Alexandre, *Ballet égyptien*,
    167–68

Macdonald, Hugh, 178
MacDowell, Edward, 64
Maceachron, J. Reginald, "On Easy
    Street (In Rags)," 185
Madonna, 32, 208 n.52
Mae, Vanessa, 175
Maggio, A., "I Got the Blues," 182
Mahler, Alma, 227 n.31

Mahler, Gustav, 123
First Symphony, 110, 150
Second, Fifth, and Seventh
Symphonies, 127
Sixth Symphony, 112, 150
Ninth Symphony, 6
Mankiller, Wilma, 78
Mardrus, J. C., 161
Martenot, Maurice, 163
Martinů, Bohuslav
Le Jazz, 196
La Revue de cuisine, 196
Marxism, 3, 43
Mason, Jack, 97
Massacre (film), 68
Maudsley, Henry, 34, 40
Maultsby, Portia, 198–99
McClary, Susan, 10–11, 20–22, 28, 34,
40, 116, 211 n.54, 237 n.27
McGraw, Tim, "Indian Outlaw," 77
McRobbie, Angela, 18
Means, Russell, 63
Mellers, Wilfrid, 194
Melody Maker, 88–89
Mendelssohn, Felix, 12
Sommernachtstraum, 138
"Spring Song," 95
Third Symphony (Scottish), 124
Fourth Symphony (Italian), 230 n.96
Merrick, Paul, 146
Merwe, Peter van der, 182
Messiaen, Olivier, Turangalila-
symphonie, 163
Meyer, Leonard B., 138
Meyerbeer, Giacomo
L'Africaine, 168
Les Huguenots, 135
Robert le Diable, 138
Mexico, 78, 174, 218 n.51
Michaelis, Christian F., 51
Micznik, Vera, 147
Middle East, 160–63
Middleton, Richard, 96
Miley, Bubber, 29, 88
"East St. Louis Toodle-Oo," 195
Milhaud, Darius, 180, 186, 192
La Création du monde, 187–89, 198,
241 n.41

military bands, 82–83
Military School of Music, 39
Mill, John Stuart, 35
Miller, Bill, 78
Milton, John, 129
Mistinguett, danse apache, 74
Mitchell-Kernan, Claudia, 198
Mockus, Martha, 31
modernism, 14, 180, 183–85, 193
modernity, 13, 180, 186
Monteverdi, Claudio
L'incoronazione di Poppea, 21
Orfeo, 22, 28
Mooney, James, 67
Morét, Neil, "Moonlight and Roses," 83
Morison, Duncan, Ceol Mara, 93
Morris, George Pope, 64
Morton, Ferdinand 'Jelly Roll', 190
Mozart, Wolfgang A., 12, 45, 57, 104, 135,
142, 167
Die Entführung aus dem Serail, 158–59
Don Giovanni, 128, 130, 143
The Marriage of Figaro, 163
Violin Concerto in A Major, K. 219,
158
Die Zauberflöte, 158
Murata, Margaret, 21
Murray, Linda, 120
Musical Association (later, Royal), 42,
57
Mussolini, Benito, 86, 191
Mussorgsky, Modest, 12, 137
A Night on the Bare Mountain,
150–51

Nakai, R. Carlos, 78
"Nancy Lee," 51
Nanton, Joe, 29
Nashville, 72
"Navajo," 217 n.43
Nazis, 11, 103, 190, 196
negotiation, 18
Nelson, Stanley, 89
Néruda, Wilhelmine, 37
Netherlands motet, 20
Neusiedler, Hans, "Der Juden Tanz," 177
new musicology, 5, 103
New Orleans, 4, 88, 181, 183, 187

New York, 28, 182, 186
  Ballet Theater, 187
  Cotton Club, Harlem, 13, 29, 94, 196
Newlin, Dika, 106, 125, 127
Nicholls, Horatio (real name: Lawrence
     Wright), "We're All Good Pals at
     Last," 92
Niecks, Frederick, 40–42, 44
Nietzsche, Friedrich, 28, 54
Noble, Ray, 70, 223 n.29
Noble Savage, 63–66
Norris, Christopher, 228 n.57
Norton, Caroline, 212–13 n.92
  "Juanita," 47, 49
  "No More Sea," 161–62
  "The Officer's Funeral," 51
Norton, Frederic, *Chu Chin Chow*,
     172–73
Norway
  "Fanitullen," 132
  and jazz, 181, 200

Offenbach, Jacques, *Le Papillon*, 74
Oklahoma, 64, 77
Oliver, Joe 'King', 87, 189–90
"On the Road to Mandalay," 81, 170–71
Orcagna, Andrea, 139
Orientalism, 13, 71, 153–74, 201
  and ethnicity, 167
  and its meanings, 175–78
  as representation, 174–75
Original Dixieland Jazz Band, 90, 183
  "Alice Blue Gown," 97
  "I'm Forever Blowing Bubbles," 97
  "Livery Stable Blues," 187

Paganini, Nicolò, 131, 140
Paglia, Camille, 57
Parakilas, James, 237 n.27
Paré, Ambroise, 21
Paris, 62, 161, 168, 179, 187, 196
  Casino de Paris, 186, 243 n.63
  Conservatoire, 194
  Moulin Rouge, 74, 196
  Music-hall des Champs-Élysées,
     195
  Notre Dame, 131
Parker, Charlie, 70
Parker, Clifton, *Night of the Demon*, 151

Pater, Walter, 54
Patti, Adelina, 38
Pattison, George, 142
Paul, Walter, 97
Pawnee, 77
Payne, Jack, 223 n.46
  "Choo Choo," 91
Peirce, Charles, 9
Perloff, Nancy, 240 n.7
Petrarch (Francesco Petrarca), 139
Phillips, Sid, 97
piano, 35–36, 168–69
Picasso, Pablo, 179
  Les Demoiselles d'Avignon, 186
Pima, 74–75
Pinkard, Maceo, *Liza*, 187
Pisa, 139
Pisani, Michael V., 64, 70, 216 n.24
Pleasants, Henry, 185
Pogues, The, "Turkish Song of the
     Damned," 178
"Poor Robin," 23
Pop, Iggy, 174
Porter, Cole, "True Love," 23
postdisciplinarity, 4–5
postmodernism, 3–4, 11, 32, 114
poststructuralism, 3, 5, 7, 14, 114
Potter, Dennis, *Pennies from Heaven*, 90
Poulenc, Francis
  Les Biches, 194
  Rapsodie nègre, 193–94
Prendergast, Roy, 174
Presley, Elvis, 184
Preston, Johnny, "Running Bear,"
     72–73, 75
Previn, Charles, 151
Price, Uvedale, 44
Pridham, John, *The Battle March of
     Delhi*, 168–69
Primo Scala, 86
Prout, Ebenezer, 100
psychiatry, 34
psychoanalysis, 27, 31
Public Schools Commission (1862),
     38–39
Puccini, Giacomo
  La Fanciulla del West, 166
  Madama Butterfly, 170–71
  Turandot, 170–71

Puffett, Derrick, 125
Pulbrook, Martin, 124
Purcell, Henry
   Dido and Aeneas, 107
   The Fairy Queen, 107
   The Indian Queen, 107, 156–57, 176

Quinn, Anthony, 72

Raabe, Peter, 133
race, 176, 201
Raff, Joachim, 133
Ragland-Sullivan, Ellie, 31
ragtime, 181–82, 199
Raindance (album), 77
Raitt, Suzanne, 214 n.121
Rameau, Jean-Philippe
   Les Indes Galantes, 155
   Nouvelles Suites de Pièces de Clavecin,
      167
   Les Sauvages, 62
Raphael (Raffaello Sanzio), *Trans-*
      figuration, 120–21
Ravel, Maurice, 200
   Boléro, 166, 174
   L'Enfant et les Sortilèges, 172
   Rapsodie espagnole, 167
   Shéhérazade Overture, 161, 163
   Shéhérazade songs, 161–62
   Violin Sonata, 182, 198
Raynor, Henry, 201
Red Nichols and His Five Pennies, 88
"Red Wing," 67
Redbone, 78
repression, 27
Rimsky-Korsakov, Nicolay, 150, 161, 174
   Capriccio espagnol, 163, 166, 175
   Scheherazade, 160–62
Ritchie, J. E., 176
Ritter, Fanny Raymond, 41
Robinson, Bradford J., 190, 242 n.47
Rolling Stones, 31
Rose, David, "The Stripper," 11, 29–30
Rossini, Gioachino, *William Tell*
      Overture, 9
Rousseau, Jean-Jacques, 63
Rowlandson, Charles, 139
Roy, Harry, 91
Royal Academy of Music, 34, 44

Royal College of Music, 34
Rozsa, Miklos
   Ben-Hur, 163
   The Thief of Bagdad, 163
Rubin, William, 241 n.35
Ruskin, John, 26, 38
Russell, Henry
   "The Chieftain's Daughter," 65
   "The Indian Hunter," 64–65, 79
   "A Life on the Ocean Wave," 64–65
   "Woodman, Spare That Tree!" 64–65
Russia, 161, 196

Sacred Spirit (album), 76–77
Said, Edward W., 155, 168, 175, 236 n.2,
      238 n.41
Saint-Saëns, Camille, 12, 137
   Africa, 180, 186
   Danse macabre, 150
   Samson et Dalila, 160–61
Sainte-Marie, Buffy, 78
   "Bury My Heart at Wounded Knee,"
      79
   "Darling Don't Cry," 79
   "Now That the Buffalo's Gone," 79
   "Soldier Blue," 79
   "Starwalker," 79
Sainton-Dolby, Charlotte, 212 n.89
Salford, Greater Manchester, 5
Salter, Hans J., 151
Samuels, Robert, 139
San Francisco, 78
Satie, Erik
   Parade, 193
   Le Picadilly, 182
Saussure, Ferdinand de, 9
Savoy Orpheans, 222 n.15
   "Baby Face," 83
   "Charleston," 96–97
   "Valencia," 99
Sayn-Wittgenstein, Carolyne von, 137,
      140
Schenker, Heinrich, 125, 143–44,
      203 n.3
Schoolcraft, Henry Rowe, 64
Schönberg, Claude-Michel, *Miss*
      Saigon, 172–74
Schönzeler, Hans-Hubert, 105
Schopenhauer, Arthur, 34, 53

Schubert, Franz, 12, 39–41, 44, 56, 177, 211 n.52
  "Der Doppelgänger," 131
  "Erlkönig," 137
  Mass in A-flat, 108
  Unfinished Symphony, 40
Schuller, Gunther, 187, 241 n.40
Schumann, Clara, 36
Schumann, Robert, 39
  "Ich grolle nicht," 51
  Scenes from Faust, 140
scientia sexualis, 22, 25, 33
Scott, Raymond, "War Dance for Wooden Indians," 218 n.61
Scruton, Roger, 184, 194
Searle, Humphrey, 138, 149
Second World War, 85, 103
semantics, 6, 9, 204 n.13
semiotics, 3, 8–11, 72, 74, 93–6, 104, 107–8, 115, 120, 129–30, 147, 155, 166, 168, 201
separate spheres, 26, 33, 42
sexuality, 10–11, 17–18, 22–27, 31, 40
Shadows, The
  "Apache," 74
  "Geronimo," 74
Shakespeare, William, 21, 72
Shapiro, Alexander H., 226 n.15
Shaw, Bernard, 56
Shenandoah, Joanne, 78
Shepherd, John, 18, 203 n.3
Shinner, Emily, 37
Shostakovich, Dmitry
  Cheryomushki, 184
  jazz suites, 196
  "Tahiti Trot," 196
Showalter, Elaine, 34
Shrubsole, Grahame, 216 n.27
Simone, Nina, "Pirate Jenny," 193
Sibelius, Johan (Jean)
  Lemminkäinen in Tuonela, 151
  Tapiola, 150–51
signifiance, 19
signifyin[g], 198–99
Silver, Abner, 99
Silvester, Victor, 223 n.44
Simpson, Robert, 104–5, 110, 112, 115, 119, 123–25
simulacra, 61, 66, 94

Sinatra, Frank, 81
Sioux, 75–77, 79, 218 n.58
"Sioux Indians," 66, 72
Sitwell, Edith, 194
Sitwell, Sacheverel, 140, 144
Skinner, Frank, 151
Smiles, Samuel, 34
Smith, Alice, *The Passions*, 25, 42
Smith, Bessie, 87
  "St. Louis Blues," 242 n.59
Smith, Jack, "My Blue Heaven," 83–84, 90
Smyth, Ethel, 56, 214 n.119
Snyder, Ted, "The Sheik of Araby," 171–72
"Son of the Desert Am I, A," 161
Sonny and Cher, "I Got You, Babe," 205 n.9
"Sons of the Sea," 51
Sousa, John P., 181–82
  "The Stars and Stripes Forever," 181
South America, 13, 174
Southern, Eileen, 198
Spain, 47, 163–66, 174
Spencer, Herbert, 176
Springsteen, Bruce, "Born in the USA," 6
Squadronaires, 83, 221 n.9
Stalin, Josef, 196
standardization, 81, 100
Standing Bear, Luther, 220–21 n.101
Stefani, Gino, 11, 82
Steiner, Max, *They Died with Their Boots On*, 71–72
stereotypes, 25, 27, 61, 66, 70, 75, 79
Stevens, Denis, 239 n.71
stile rappresentativo, 20
Stirling, Elizabeth, 35, 209 n.15
Stone, Lew, 84, 222 n.14
  "Garden of Weed," 97
  "My Old Dog," 95–96
  "Zing! Went the Strings of My Heart," 83
Storace, Stephen, *The Cherokee*, 62–63, 215 n.10
Stratton, Stephen S., 42
Strauss II, Johann
  "Lucifer," 138
  "Mephistos Höllenrufe," 138

Strauss, Richard, "Dance of the Seven Veils" (*Salome*), 11, 29–30, 200
Stravinsky, Igor, 190–91, 193–94, 196, 200
  The Firebird, 150
  L'Histoire du soldat, 183, 185
  Ragtime, 184–85, 189
  Le Sacre du printemps, 179
Street, Alan, 229 n.57
Stuart, Leslie, "Lily of Laguna," 194
Stuckey, Sterling, 198
style hongrois, 68, 158–59, 163, 177
sublime and the beautiful, 11, 33, 43–56
Subotnik, Rose Rosengard, 7, 87, 112, 114
Sullivan, Arthur
  The Gondoliers, 166
  Haddon Hall, 237 n.29
  "If Doughty Deeds My Lady Please," 51
  Ivanhoe, 177
  The Mikado, 175
  The Rose of Persia, 176
  and W. S. Gilbert, 96
Sullivan, Jack, 198
Suter, Ann, "Pu-leeze! Mister Hemingway," 29
Sweden, 166
  Ballet Suédois, 187
Szabolsci, Bence, 148, 150, 236 n.5
Szász, Tibor, 147

Tagg, Philip, 96
Tarasti, Eero, 9–10, 123–24, 204 n.19
Tartini, Giuseppe, *Devil's Trill* Sonata, 132
Taruskin, Richard, 161, 238 n.41
Taylor, Jenny, 18
Taylor, Ronald, 143
Tchaikovsky, Pyotr, 123, 181
  Capriccio Italien, 237 n.28
  Fifth Symphony, 124
Te Kanawa, Kiri, 6
"Texas Jack," 67
Thalberg, Sigismond, variations on "Home, Sweet Home," 38
Thompson, Leslie, 222 n.11
Tick, Judith, 25, 214 n.123
Tiki music, 13
"To Anthea," 51

Tohono O'odham, 78
Tomlinson, Gary, 204 n.24
topoi, 9, 12, 175
Tosh, John, 211 n.62
Tovey, Donald F., 178
Traini, Francesco, *Trionfo della morte*, 139
Treitler, Leo, 203 n.5
Troggs, "Wild Thing," 30
Tuke, Daniel Hack, 34
Tunisia, 186
Turkish Style, 62, 158–59, 176, 178

University of Cambridge, 35
University of Oxford, 35, 44
Upton, George, 53–54, 214 n.107

Valentino, Rudolph, 169–70
Vallee, Rudy, 83
Vaughan, H. Halford, 38
Vaughan Williams, Ralph, 81
  Fantasia on a Theme by Thomas Tallis, 177
  Job, 150
  Partita, 99
Verdi, Giuseppe
  Aida, 166, 168
  Un Ballo in Maschera, 166
  Nabucco, 166
Verfremdungseffekt, 192–93
Versatile Four, "After You've Gone," 86
Victoria, Queen, 38
Vienna, 30, 108, 127, 158, 196
Vietnam, 75, 173–74
violinists, female, 37
Vodery, Will, *Ziegfeld Follies*, 181
Volosinov, V. N., 3
Vonholf, Madame, 36

Wagner, Richard, 21, 53–54, 124, 143
  Faust Ouvertüre, 140
  Der Fliegende Holländer, 118–19
  Parsifal, 179
  Tannhäuser, 23, 106
  Tristan und Isolde, 109, 182, 200, 207 n.40
  Die Walküre, 106, 227 n.22
waila, 220 n.96
Walela, 78

Walker, Alan, 132

Waller, Fats, "Honeysuckle Rose," 97–99

Walton, William, *Façade*, 191, 194

Warrack, John, 237 n.24

Waters, Ethel, "You Brought a New Kind of Love to Me," 28

Watson, Derek, 110, 123

Weatherly, Frederic E., 171

Webb, Daniel, 56

Webber, Andrew Lloyd, 7
  Joseph and the Amazing Technicolor Dreamcoat, 168

Weber, Carl Maria von, 135
  Der Freischutz, 128–29
  Preciosa, 163

Weber, William, 45

Weill, Kurt, 180
  Die Dreigroschenoper, 190–93, 196
  Mahagonny Songspiel, 191

Weiss, Johann Baptist, 104

West, Mae, 19, 29–31
  "I Like a Guy What Takes His Time," 28
  I'm No Angel, 28
  SEX, 30

Westrup, J. A., 156

Whaples, Miriam K., 62

"When Day Is Done," 97–98

White, John D., 143–44

White, Maude Valérie, 213 n.100
  "King Charles," 51, 53–56

Whiteley, Sheila, 20

Whiteman, Paul, 183, 190

Wicke, Peter, 83, 203 n.3

Wilby, Philip, *Jazz*, 182

Wilde, David, 147–48

Wilkins, Dave, 82

Willet, John, 192

Williams, Hank, "Kaw-Liga," 72–73, 75, 77

Williams, Hugh, "Red Sails in the Sunset," 190 (*see also* Grosz, Wilhelm)

Williams, Raymond, 99

Williamson, John, 231 n.128

Wilson, Edmund, 240 n.1

Wilson, Olly, 184, 198

Windsor Castle, 38

Winklhofer, Sharon, 139

Wiora, Walter, 227 n.24

Wisconsin, 78

WithOut Rezervation, 78

Wittgenstein, Ludwig, 127

Wolf, Hugo, 122

Wolf Robe, 77

Wood, Elizabeth, 214 n.121

Woodforde-Finden, Amy, "Kashmiri Song," 168–70

Work, Henry Clay, "The Song of the Redman," 67

Wynette, Tammy, "Stand by Your Man," 18

Ye Olde English Swynge Band, 82

"Yes! Let Me Like a Soldier Fall," 51

"Yes Sir, That's My Baby," 96

Youman, Vincent, "Tea for Two," 196

Yradier, Sebastián, *El Arreglito*, 237 n.27

Zukunftsmusik ("music of the future"), 137

Zurich, Cabaret Voltaire, 194